VIRTUES *of* RENEWAL

✳

Wendell Berry's Sustainable Forms

Jeffrey Bilbro

UNIVERSITY PRESS OF KENTUCKY

Copyright © 2019 by The University Press of Kentucky
Paperback edition 2020

Scholarly publisher for the Commonwealth,
serving Bellarmine University, Berea College, Centre
College of Kentucky, Eastern Kentucky University,
The Filson Historical Society, Georgetown College,
Kentucky Historical Society, Kentucky State University,
Morehead State University, Murray State University,
Northern Kentucky University, Transylvania University,
University of Kentucky, University of Louisville,
and Western Kentucky University.

Editorial and Sales Offices: The University Press of Kentucky
663 South Limestone Street, Lexington, Kentucky 40508-4008
www.kentuckypress.com

Library of Congress Cataloging-in-Publication Data
Names: Bilbro, Jeffrey, author.
Title: Virtues of renewal : Wendell Berry's sustainable forms / Jeffrey
  Bilbro.
Description: Lexington, Kentucky : University Press of Kentucky, [2019] |
  Series: Culture of the land | Includes bibliographical references and
  index.
Identifiers: LCCN 2018027851| ISBN 9780813176406 (alk. paper) | ISBN
  9780813176420 | ISBN 9780813176413
Subjects: LCSH: Berry, Wendell, 1934—Criticism and interpretation. | Virtue
  in literature. | Environmental protection in literature.
Classification: LCC PS3552.E75 Z595 2019 | DDC 818/.5409—dc23
ISBN 978-0-8131-7640-6 (hardcover : alk. paper)
ISBN 978-0-8131-7641-3 (epub)
ISBN 978-0-8131-7642-0 (pdf)

ISBN 978-0-8131-7942-1 (pbk. : alk. paper)

This book is printed on acid-free paper meeting
the requirements of the American National Standard
for Permanence in Paper for Printed Library Materials.

∞

Manufactured in the United States of America.

Member of the Association
of University Presses

VIRTUES OF RENEWAL

*To Tom and Sharon Bilbro
and Mark and Monica Courtney,
couples who model virtues of renewal
and practice resurrection*

Contents

Preface

The chief criterion of thought . . . must be propriety—fittingness to our place in the world, in the order of things, and to our relations of dependence and responsibility with other creatures—which would enable humility, restoration, the practice of the virtues.

Wendell Berry, "Notes: Unspecializing Poetry"

Does poetry make anything happen? When confronted with our proliferation of environmental crises, even asking such a question may seem irresponsible. The usual approach to problems such as soil loss, species extinction, toxic waste, and rising seas is to devote all our resources and energy to STEM (Science, Technology, Engineering, and Math) research so that we can develop the innovative technological solutions we need to save the planet. Yet perhaps poetry can be a more radical source for ecological restoration.

Over the past fifty years, Wendell Berry has been arguing that our most pressing ecological and cultural need is a renewed formal intelligence. As the epigraph above indicates, such an intelligence does not look for big, one-size-fits-all solutions. Nor does it look to the latest political movement or activist campaign. Rather, it discerns and fosters patterns of health. When W. H. Auden famously declared that "poetry makes nothing happen," he was correct that poetry, like the other arts, doesn't coerce matter in the way that a tractor or an oil rig or a bomb does.[1] Yet Auden went on to write that poetry is "a way of happening," its beauty shaping readers' imaginations to better perceive and understand formal patterns. Such formative work is not dramatic or quick, but it can foster the deep, lasting change needed to cultivate a more sustainable culture and economy. As Vandana Shiva writes, "We need to change our mind before we can change the world."[2]

Perhaps literature might help accomplish this necessary mental and imaginative shift. The work of understanding literary forms can train us to discern healthy forms in other areas, such as agriculture, urban development, and public health. So though our first impulse when faced with a problem may be to call in technological experts and have them develop a big solution, more sustainable answers can be found by learning to see and foster health in our own lives and places. Studying the literary forms of Berry's poetry, essays, and fiction can hone our formal intelligence and train us to approach other problems with an attention to their underlying connections and interdependencies.

In particular, Berry's literary forms model and cultivate virtues of renewal. Our contemporary culture fears and shuns death, but natural ecosystems follow forms in which death feeds new life, and healthy human communities follow a parallel order. Cultures maintain such a sustainable order by practicing virtues of renewal, virtues that stand in sharp contrast to the techniques of control that our industrial culture encourages. As we will see, Berry's sustainable economy depends on attention rather than distraction or surveillance, on gratitude rather than busyness, on humility rather than moral codes, on hope rather than optimism, on memory rather than innovation, on fidelity rather than mobility, on convocation rather than independence. These are the sustaining virtues that Berry's literature models for readers.

Berry has become a popular spokesman for the local food movement, but if you know his work just from quotations you've seen printed on the menu of a hipster restaurant or chalked on the wall of a farmer's market, you don't really know his work. Berry's writings cannot be reduced to slogans because, like all literature, not only do they convey ideas, but they also model a posture toward the world. It is this posture that is the most important thing we can learn from Berry. To appropriate Marshall McLuhan's adage "the medium is the message," we could say that to understand Berry's "message" about sustainable living, we'll have to attend to—and then work to embody in our own lives and communities—the forms in which he writes.[3]

But maybe you have read Berry more thoroughly and have been challenged and inspired by his vision—you just aren't sure how to respond to it. If you don't want to be (or can't be) a small-scale organic farmer, are Berry's books just nostalgic elegies for a lost way of life? My claim is that Berry's writings offer an invaluable primer in the virtues—the habits, traits, or disciplines—that characterize people who foster sustainable cultures. More than any technological or political solution, it is these virtues that we desperately need. So even if you don't want to be a farmer—in fact, *especially* if you don't want to be a farmer—the writings of this Kentucky agrarian have much to offer.[4] My hope is that understanding the virtues that make Berry's poetry, fiction, and essays beautiful and compelling to so many people can lead us to embody these virtues in our own communities. Beneath this overarching purpose, I have three further goals: to clarify the distinct yet symbiotic features of the three primary genres in which Berry writes; to demonstrate the importance of the humanities and literature in cultivating sustainable economies; and to recover a more robust language for talking about sustainability, ecology, and death.

An Ecology of Genres

Berry writes prolifically in three genres: essays, fiction, and poetry. His work in these different forms leads some to ask what his best genre is. And because Berry is perhaps most famous for his uncompromising public stands, many assume that his most authentic form is the argumentative essay; thus, they tend to view his fiction and poetry as ideologically driven, or as some sort of direct transposition of his ideas into different forms.[5] I want to suggest, however, that both lines of thought are misguided. Berry writes exceptionally well—although to different ends—in all three genres, and his fiction and poetry are not translations of his essays. Rather, like disparate species interacting in a diverse ecosystem, each genre fulfills a particular niche. Writing in multiple genres allows Berry to imitate nature's formal diversity and fill his imaginative ecosystem with greater complexity and fecundity.[6]

Berry's fiction, for instance, is not a simple, one-to-one translation of the ideas in his essays. Although one of Berry's most famous (or infamous) essays is titled "Why I Am Not Going to Buy a Computer," nowhere in his fiction does a character explain why he or she will not buy a computer. And although it may surprise some readers of Berry's essays, many of the "bad" farmers in his fiction work with horses and some of the "good" farmers use tractors. Rather than simply translating his ideas between different genres, Berry knits the pieces of his vision into a complex whole, one that can be understood fully only by reading all three of the genres in which he works.

In one of his sabbath poems, Berry writes about the different motivations that inspire his writing in various genres:

> I would not have been a poet
> except that I have been in love
> alive in this mortal world,
> or an essayist except that I
> have been bewildered and afraid,
> or a storyteller had I not heard
> stories passing to me through the air,
> or a writer at all except
> I have been wakeful at night
> and words have come to me
> out of their deep caves,
> needing to be remembered.[7]

Clearly these motivations aren't mutually exclusive, but Berry suggests that his work in different genres originates from different sources. My argument is that in each of these genres, Berry works to cultivate virtues in his readers that are particularly appropriate to these motivations: the wakeful love that inspires his poetry leads us to be attentive and grateful; the fear and confusion that inspires his essays should cause us to seek humbly and hopefully for the clarity we need to guide our actions; the stories he overhears and narrates in his fiction shape us to remember the voices of our own communities, to listen faithfully, and to find our places within this convocation.

Admittedly, this list of virtues is not exhaustive; I could have chosen to focus on others of equal importance to Berry's writing and to sustainable economies, virtues like temperance, patience, and courage. Likewise, by dividing out particular virtues and associating them with specific genres, I don't intend to suggest that these virtues are discrete and itemizable. Unlike Ben Franklin, I'm not suggesting we can create a spreadsheet, list virtues across the top, and then chart our way to self-improvement.[8] Rather, particular virtues—and Berry's individual genres—are like species in a healthy ecosystem; they interrelate in complex ways and depend on each other.

And as Berry's poem suggests, the telos of his work as a writer is to foster more sustainable, loving ways of inhabiting our places. The words that come to Berry "out of their deep caves" do not just ask to be written down; instead, they need "to be remembered." The membership they require is not satisfied by a black-and-white existence bound within the cover of a book; for these words to have any healing effect, they must be re-membered in the lives and places of Berry's readers. Hence, the ultimate embodiment of Berry's vision is not in the rich ecology of his oeuvre, but in the virtuous, loving lives of his readers.

Sustainable Forms

This discussion of how Berry's writings work to shape sustainable communities leads to my second goal, which is to suggest that sustainable economies depend as much—or more—on rightly shaped imaginations as they do on advanced technology. Much ink has been spilled documenting and critiquing America's unsustainable economy and culture. By some measures, individuals in America consume thirty-two times as much as people in developing countries.[9] Our agricultural methods cause dangerous topsoil erosion, and we eat meat from animals raised in unhealthy Concentrated Animal Feeding Operations (CAFOs).[10] Our rural and urban communities face deep, systemic challenges.[11] Such huge problems can be overwhelming and paralyzing. In our technological age, with its focus on productivity, immediate results, and global solutions, we often turn to STEM fields for solutions to these large-scale challenges. These disciplines are certainly vital, but our preference for them comes, at times, from dubious motives; we want to engineer our way out of these problems without having to change the ways we think or live. Yet technologies amplify or extend human desires, so if our desires are selfish, all the technology in the world won't lead to sustainable communities.[12]

Thus, while we certainly need new technologies and political, systemic solutions, our deepest needs are a desire to live more sustainably, the imagination to see how we might do this, and the discipline to begin. The humanities, at least in their most robust forms, turn our attention to these fundamental questions regarding which ways of thinking and living are proper for humans. Answering such questions is essential if we are to find more sustainable cultural and economic patterns of life.[13]

Unfortunately, the academic study of literature and other humanities has been infected by our culture's broader shifts toward technocracy and short-term gain. On the one hand, politicians and business leaders dismiss the humanities unless they contribute to the bottom line. Even President Obama, who spoke powerfully of the value of the humanities and honored Wendell Berry with a National Medal of Arts, fed this narrative when he suggested that an art history major was less valuable than training in skilled manufacturing.[14] On the other hand, the professionalization of the humanities reinforces this notion that literature and the other arts are merely another specialty that are valuable only for those who plan to pursue a career in these fields.[15]

My aim in this book, though, is to persuade readers that literature matters for all of us because it is an indispensable means for reimagining how humans might live with each other and with the rest of creation. If, as Berry argues, a poem's "formal integrity" is analogous to the formal integrity of healthy, sustainable cultures, then better understanding the wholeness of his literary forms should enable us to perceive and tend such wholeness in our lives, our cultures, and our places.[16]

Responsible Language

I am well aware that many of the terms I've used so far—virtue, integrity, health, nature—are looked down on in some academic circles.[17] Furthermore, I'll be following Berry in relying on Christian language as well, in particular the term *resurrection*. On the one hand, Berry believes resurrection is something we can "practice," which may surprise those Christians accustomed to understanding resurrection as simply a distant event or a spiritual metaphor. Yet he also understands it religiously, which may make non-Christian readers uncomfortable.[18] In writing to his friend Gary Snyder, a Buddhist, Berry explained the difficult line he tries to walk in using Christian language: "Biblical concepts such as 'sabbath,' 'incarnation,' and 'resurrection' seem to me just particular names for general principles. That's misleading. They do have their particular meanings. What I think the churches have done is to use the particular meanings to obscure general ones. Though the terms of my poems are pretty literally Biblical, I tried to use them so as to keep them from being too specially understood."[19] As Berry's hesitation in this letter indicates, he wrestles with the dangers of such language while ultimately finding it necessary because it brings together the particular and the general, the religious and the ecological, and so better accounts for multifaceted human experiences such as death, love, and community. My third goal, then, is to recover a more complex, interdisciplinary language with which to talk about sustainability and death. So while I'll draw on some theorists and philosophers, I'll also rely on the less trendy language that Berry himself uses.

Modern specialization has led to a fragmentation of conversations, as each academic specialty relies on its own set of jargon. The danger in using older words like *creation, virtue,* and *resurrection* is that such words are loaded with history and cultural baggage. Yet instead of jettisoning these words and coining sterile, narrow terms, perhaps we need to engage with the complex history of our culture and language.[20] This history may be unfashionable, but as Berry argues, it is the history that has "made us what we are," and it has much to teach us—through both positive and negative examples—about how to care for our places.[21]

Furthermore, as Charles Taylor and others have shown, religion remains a vibrant and important force in shaping how people inhabit their places; the secularization thesis that justified a purely rationalistic, materialist mode of environmental thinking has been increasingly questioned by the realization that we are living in a postsecular age.[22] The postsecular reminds us that we don't have the luxury of ignoring religion in working toward sustainable cultures and economies. In fact, religion may play a vital role in guiding us toward more sustainable ways of living.[23]

One of the ways that Berry manages to appeal to readers across political and religious divides is by reasoning from both moral, theological grounds and practical, ecological ones; those not convinced by moral or religious reasons to live more sustainably may be convinced by environmental or pragmatic reasons. Hence, Berry roots his call to live more sustainably in our love for the other members of our places and communities, but he also argues that such love has practical, economic benefits.[24] As Berry puts it, "Whether we consider it from a religious point of view or from the point of view of our merely practical wish to continue to live, . . . we cannot exempt use from care." When we imagine what a more care-full economy might look like, Berry argues that "we have reclaimed and revalidated the ground of our moral and religious tradition. We now can see that what we have traditionally called 'sins' are wrong not because they are forbidden but because they divide us from our neighbors, from the world, and ultimately from God. They deny care and are dangerous to creatures." Similarly, "what we have traditionally called 'virtues' . . . are good not because they have been highly recommended but because they are necessary; they make for unity and harmony."[25] Thus, both those who are sympathetic to Berry's theology and those who simply recognize the ways in which greed and envy and intemperance have damaged the world can find common ground in searching for more sustainable economies.[26] It is because of this kind of natural law reasoning that many who do not share Berry's theological convictions still find his vision of virtuous, sustainable communities compelling.

Outline

This book consists of an introduction, seven chapters, and an epilogue. The introduction, "Sustaining Virtuous Forms," lays out these connections between literary forms and virtuous forms of life and argues that the virtues we seek to embody come from the narratives or economies we imagine ourselves to inhabit. Berry's agrarian perspective provides a vital alternative to our industrial imagination and fosters more sustainable ways of living.

The book's body examines each of the three main genres in which Berry writes. The first two chapters, "Attention" and "Gratitude," consider his poetry. In addition to close readings of particular poems, the first chapter traces how Jean-Luc Marion's phenomenological account of iconic perception illuminates the attentive posture Berry's poetry encourages. The second chapter shows how Berry's understanding of the sabbath—as evidenced in his long-running sequence of sabbath poems—leads to the practice of receptive gratitude and to a view of work as a response to the good gifts of creation rather than a frantic scramble for worth and productivity.

The third and fourth chapters, "Humility" and "Hope," turn to his essays. The occasional nature of Berry's polemics, the wide-ranging connections they make, and—perhaps unexpectedly—the binary structure they often follow evince his efforts to walk along what he terms a "way of ignorance," a way of approaching problems in light of our inevitable ignorance as finite human beings. His essays also sharply distinguish between optimism—which is an industrial trait founded on the belief that technological progress will continue to make our lives better—and hope—which is a virtue founded on specific examples of good work and good lives.

The final three chapters, "Memory," "Fidelity," and "Convocation," examine what is perhaps Berry's strongest genre, fiction. Berry's stories are often narrated by older characters looking back over their lives and stitching together meaning from disparate events; though memory is devalued in a culture where information is always accessible, it remains crucial to discerning complex coherence. Fidelity is a similarly overlooked virtue in a transient culture, but Berry's practice of careful revision, particularly evident in his early novels, demonstrates a patient faithfulness to develop his imaginative vision. The last chapter shows how Berry's fiction teaches us to listen in on a communal conversation as we come to know characters through Port William's talk about them. The virtue of convocation that this community practices shapes individual identities in the context of their joint membership in their place and in each other.

In each of these chapters I argue that Berry's writings model these virtues and shape his readers to practice them in their own lives and places. Communities characterized by these seven virtues would inhabit their places in more sustainable, healthy ways than the fragmented, extractive mode characteristic of industrial cultures. Such virtuous communities would not immediately remedy the injustices and destruction of our present industrial economy, nor would they magically evade death and loss. Rather, their members would practice resurrection by holding death in sustaining patterns, preparing the way for life to come to them, if it will.

Introduction

Sustaining Virtuous Forms

The word *economy* calls up lists of statistics and numbers: the unemployment rate, the Gross Domestic Product, the Federal Reserve interest rate, the S&P 500 index. When we remember, however, that the word *economy* comes from the Greek word *oikos*, which means household, these numbers become less important than the formal structure or household order they attempt to quantify. It is this formal order that Wendell Berry refers to when he contrasts the industrial economy with an agrarian or sustainable economy. In this introduction I want to explore the different forms, values, and virtues that are embedded in these contrasting household orders. Comparing the formal patterns of these economies reveals the significance of the imaginative work that Berry's literary forms undertake.

Berry's writings across all three genres critique the industrial structure that underlies our contemporary way of life, shaping areas as disparate as agriculture, medicine, education, science, architecture, aesthetics, and energy. These fields typically operate according to an industrial logic of specialization, competition, and capital. Though such a logic has proven remarkably effective in some ways, particularly in its ability to solve isolated problems, Berry argues that these industrial forms of life contribute to disease, are vulnerable to disruption, and cause lasting damage to their environments. Piecemeal solutions, ones that fix one symptom and cause collateral damage elsewhere, are inadequate; as Berry writes in "Solving for Pattern," "The whole problem must be solved, not just some handily identifiable and simplifiable aspect of it."[1] In the context of farming, an industrial approach might buy a bigger tractor to solve the problem of soil compaction or find new poisons to kill pesticide-resistant superweeds, yet these solutions only increase soil compaction and encourage the development of new superweeds. In other contexts, this approach leads to LED lightbulbs, energy-efficient appliances, and low-flow toilets; sustainability becomes a label affixed to various commodities while the structure of our economy remains unchanged.[2]

Instead of these superficial fixes, Berry challenges us to imagine more harmonious, formally complex solutions to our problems: "The real problem of food production occurs within a complex, mutually influential relationship of soil, plants, animals, and people. A real solution to that problem will therefore be ecologically, agriculturally, and culturally healthful."[3] As this statement indicates, Berry's standard for lasting, sustainable solutions is health.

As we will see, health is defined by formal relationships rather than isolated quantities. Through its formal order, health accounts for the one fundamental reality that an industrial logic seeks to ignore or conquer: death. This failure to acknowledge and incorporate death leads to moral and religious problems, but it also contributes to practical problems of waste and obsolescence: from nursing homes to euthanasia, Concentrated Animal Feeding Operations (CAFOs) to toxic runoff, landfills to planned obsolescence, our economy tries to ignore decay and death rather than honestly accounting for them. Sustainable economies, though, practice virtues of renewal and return, accepting death so that it serves life in ways that are analogous to the organic fertility cycle. In this way, such economies enable their members to practice resurrection.

In this introduction, I contrast an industrial grammar with the more sustainable, agrarian grammar that structures Berry's writings. As my use of the term *grammar* indicates, an industrial economy is structurally opposed to an agrarian one; they are two different languages that make radically different kinds of sense from the world. Understanding the contrasting forms of these economies (1) situates this study within broader philosophical, political, aesthetic, and religious debates, (2) clarifies the practical significance of the literary analysis that follows in the rest of the book, and (3) defines the terms I will use in examining Berry's literary forms.

An Industrial Economy

Love the quick profit, the annual raise,
vacation with pay. Want more
of everything ready-made. Be afraid
to know your neighbors and to die.
And you will have a window in your head.
Not even your future will be a mystery
any more. Your mind will be punched in a card
and shut away in a little drawer.
When they want you to buy something
they will call you. When they want you
to die for profit they will let you know.[4]

For Berry, industrialism names not just an economy, but a grammar that underlies much of contemporary life, a grammar characterized by division and specialization, competition and quantity: by isolating variables, industrialism aims to master them, eliminating unwanted quantities and mass-producing desirable ones. It divides in order to conquer. Its ultimate goal, then, is control, and the industrial method is simply the most effective way to gain power. Because our imaginations are so deeply formed by an industrial way of life, we are conditioned to rely on an industrial approach to solve our problems.[5] While its grammar is inherently violent and unstable, this specialized, assembly-line approach characterizes many facets of modern life: schools divide children by age and subject matter to make instruction more efficient, which weakens intergenerational and interdisciplinary relationships; urban planning treats housing, shopping, manufacturing, and agriculture as separate functions and creates discrete zones for each, which necessities many miles of driving; the geographic mobility required by many career paths divides families, which provides opportunities for corporations to sell services families used to provide freely—child care, end-of-life care, emotional and mental support, recreation; medical doctors specialize in particular diseases and body parts, which leads to incredible breakthroughs in some areas while obesity, diabetes, and other chronic diseases become more prevalent; mountaintop-removal coal mining values only one commodity, and companies are willing to destroy whole ecosystems to extract coal more quickly; monoculture farming and CAFOs promise to produce food cheaply, but they depend on massive chemical inputs and externalizing environmental and moral costs. While we may think America is transitioning to a postindustrial society, our cultural imagination remains stamped by the industrial model of division, competition, and mass production.

Even our so-called information economy continues to operate according to this grammar of division and quantity. Berry notes ironically that while "information" etymologically "has to do with the idea of form: a pattern, structure, or ordering principle," the information economy thrives on "a random accumulation of facts, all having the one common characteristic of availability; they can, as we are too likely to say, be 'accessed.'. . . . [They] arrive unformed and unexperienced." Thus, in the information economy, education ceases to cultivate community members who will tend the health of their communities and instead delivers quanta of "information" to individuals who will live in their careers.[6] Separating "facts" from their context—the people and places where they are known and used—enables companies to profit by providing access to them, but such abstraction warps knowledge and renders it irresponsible. It's no accident that we continue to rely on industrial metaphors to talk about information: we "mine" data and use word "processors."[7] Uprooted facts can be used by anyone for any purpose, which is why a presidential aide can refer to "alternative facts."[8]

Given this chaotic free-for-all, Berry concludes, "there is nothing deader or of more questionable value than facts in isolation."[9]

The industrial belief that freedom and power come from isolation and competition also shapes the political and economic structures of modern liberalism. Patrick Deneen traces this competitive grammar to the work of Francis Bacon and Thomas Hobbes: "At the heart of this tradition is a belief in natural scarcity, of a recalcitrant nature that only grudgingly provides the basic necessities of human existence."[10] On this view, nature consists of mere matter in motion, and science's task is to give us humans greater control over matter so we can make it yield what we want. For Bacon, knowledge is ultimately a form of power. It makes sense, then, that, as Berry argues in *The Unsettling of America*, modern agriculture relies on the technology of modern warfare.[11] After World War II, the United States transitioned its war machine from fighting Nazis and fascists to fighting nature.[12]

Viewing nature as a set of scarce resources that must be forcefully extracted and then hoarded leads to two destructive tendencies that Berry identifies in the industrial economy: its replacement of virtues or skills with technology, and its treatment of energy not as a living form or cycle but as a reservoir. Berry articulates these connections in his essay "The Total Economy": "We have assumed increasingly over the last five hundred years that nature is merely a supply of 'raw materials,' and that we may safely possess those materials merely by taking them. This taking, as our technical means have increased, has involved always less reverence or respect, less gratitude, less local knowledge, and less skill."[13] Or, as he puts it in *The Unsettling of America*, "The balance between life and machinery was overthrown . . . when people began to desire long-term stores or supplies of energy—that is, when they began to think of energy as volume as well as force—and when machines ceased to enhance or elaborate skill and began to replace it."[14] Treating nature as a standing reserve, we make it a set of fungible commodities, and our use of them is limited not by any discipline or other cultural limits, but merely by our technical capabilities.

This industrial grammar generates the colonialism, racism, and ecological devastation that plague our Western economies and politics.[15] An economy founded on power and violence leads inevitably to oppression and abuse, and many political theorists turn to the idea of individual rights, as developed by philosophers such as John Locke, to limit exploitation of the weak. Liberalism hopes that by granting individuals—and later wilderness areas and animals—rights, it will free them from oppression and coercion.[16] Yet when my rights come into conflict with your rights, whoever has the loudest voice, the most money, or the best legal team prevails. A reliance on rights does not escape the industrial grammar of competition and violence; it simply inscribes that grammar more deeply into our legal system.[17]

The state (or multinational organizations) steps into this competitive fray to enforce order. So today the "creative destruction" of entrepreneurs is countered by state regulation. And yet rather than being in actual opposition, these forces rely on each other.[18] As capital—which is, in essence, stored energy—becomes more concentrated, it enables powerful individuals to accrue more power and further threaten the rights of others. Then the regulators must be given greater authority to maintain order. Thus, big business and big government, the chaotic energy of the free market and the regulatory order of the state, depend on each other in an ever-escalating cycle; both profit from the violent competition of deracinated individuals.

Friedrich Nietzsche transposes this industrial grammar into a literary key in his classic *Birth of Tragedy*, in which he describes Greek tragedy as composed of the tension between Dionysian chaos and Apollonian order.[19] Nietzsche's use of these two Greek gods provides a useful shorthand that I will rely on to name this tragic conflict that is at the heart of our industrial economy and politics. He relishes the vitality of the Dionysian fecundity that must be ordered by Apollonian structure. As Nietzsche argues, these two are mutually dependent: "Both of these artistic drives are compelled to develop their forces in strict proportion to one another, according to the law of eternal justice."[20] David Bentley Hart, summarizing John Milbank, argues that Nietzsche's logic, particularly in the hands of his postmodern heirs, leads to an understanding of "being as sheer brute event, a chaos of [Dionysian,] countervailing violences, against which must be deployed the various restraining and prudential violences of the [Apollonian] state, reason, law, warfare, retribution, civic order, and the vigilantly sentineled polis; it is, to employ the typology favored by the early Nietzsche, the story of Dionysus, over whose primordial, chthonic, and indiscriminate violences must be imposed the factitious, sacred, and precisely discriminating violences of Apollo."[21] If we subscribe to this ontology of primordial violence, we get a war of all against all, and the coercive power of the state or institutional religion or big technology comes as a welcome relief to impose some order. In the American political context, to paint with broad strokes, Republicans tend to support Apollonian moral structures and Dionysian economic freedom, while Democrats flip these allegiances. What these superficial disagreements obscure, however, is the underlying ontological agreement: moral, economic, social, and physical reality consists of free individuals in violent competition. The only disagreements are tactical ones regarding whether greater freedom or constraint is preferable in particular circumstances.

The internal combustion engine offers a vivid embodiment of this formal structure that characterizes the industrial imagination.[22] An engine converts stored energy into usable force through controlled explosions: chaotic, Dionysian energy is contained by Apollonian metal walls. Furthermore, designing and building engines requires the specialized network of mining, engineering, manufacturing, marketing, and capital that characterizes the modern economy.

As time goes on and engines become more complex, this network of specialist work expands in a way that parallels the increasingly specialized parts in an engine itself. Such specialized networks, Berry argues, become "more and more organized, but less and less orderly."[23] The many specialized people whose work leads to the manufacture of an engine may be very good at their narrow tasks, but they have an increasingly difficult time recognizing whether their work serves the good of their community. As Berry explains, "Specialization is thus seen to be a way of institutionalizing, justifying, and paying highly for a calamitous disintegration and scattering-out of the various functions of character: workmanship, care, conscience, responsibility."[24] By externalizing care, responsibility, and skill, engines introduce a new and more dangerous kind of power. The specialized, violent power they harness and make useable is truly incredible: engines collapse time and space, making the world feel smaller and multiplying the results of human labor. If more power is needed, one simply has to build a larger engine with more horsepower. In this way, engines transform energy into simple quanta—measured, ironically, in horsepower. Yet as Berry observes, an internal combustion engine does not represent a closed structure; engines run on finite supplies of fuel, and they produce not just force but also pollution.[25]

Perhaps even more dangerously, engines promise to make virtues and skills obsolete; if one has enough power, one can accomplish tasks that used to require much practice and knowledge—hence our fetish for technologies that turn chaotic forces into usable power, whether the horsepower that propels us along the road, the explosive power that renders our enemies tractable, the computing power we can hold in our hand, or the big data that can explain complex forces in our world. This is the aesthetic of the technological sublime; we are in awe of the ease with which modern technology tames chaotic violence and renders it useable, at least to those who can afford to pay.[26]

A Sustainable Economy

So, friends, every day do something
that won't compute. Love the Lord.
Love the world. Work for nothing.
Take all that you have and be poor.
Love someone who does not deserve it.
Denounce the government and embrace
the flag. Hope to live in that free

republic for which it stands.
Give your approval to all you cannot
understand. Praise ignorance, for what man
has not encountered he has not destroyed.
Ask the questions that have no answers.
Invest in the millennium. Plant sequoias.
Say that your main crop is the forest
that you did not plant,
that you will not live to harvest.[27]

An industrial logic, as Nietzsche recognized, results in a deeply tragic view of the world. Caught in an endless cycle of violence, our only defense is to cling to whatever technology or tactic or force can increase our individual power. Yet if creation is not fundamentally violent but is, rather, a gift from a loving Creator—one whose creative work continues in his incarnation, passion, and resurrection—then humans are invited to imitate this self-giving love in their relationships with their neighbors and the rest of creation.[28] On this view, when we die to our individual desires and commit to working toward the good of others, we participate in the Creator's ongoing redemption of the world. We practice resurrection.

Obviously, my *if* in that last paragraph may strike some readers as introducing an unlikely claim. Hasn't Christian theology helped justify environmental destruction? Berry disagrees with this thesis, advanced most famously by Lynn White Jr., and continues to turn to his Christian tradition for wisdom about how to care for our places.[29] While Berry acknowledges that his Christian perspective may unsettle some readers, he nonetheless confesses, "I believe that the world was created and approved by love, that it subsists, coheres, and endures by love, and that, insofar as it is redeemable, it can be redeemed only by love. I believe that divine love, incarnate and indwelling in the world, summons the world always toward wholeness, which ultimately is reconciliation and atonement with God."[30] This belief in the primacy of love is why Berry borrowed E. M. Forster's declaration "it all turns on affection" for the title of his NEH Jefferson Lecture.[31] If the industrial economy turns on explosive violence, Berry's sustainable economy turns on affection. An industrial grammar is marked by division and competition and is oriented toward control, but a sustainable grammar is marked by membership and formal patterns and is oriented toward love.

As I pointed out in the preface, Berry justifies this foundation of love on both religious and ecological grounds. Yet if religion seems an unlikely source on which to base sustainable forms of living, ecology may seem an even more improbable source. How can nature provide an alternative to the competitive, violent structure of the industrial economy when, as Tennyson famously wrote, nature is "red in tooth and claw"?[32] Yet perhaps this understanding of nature says more about the imaginative lens through which the nineteenth-century poet looked than it does about the natural economy itself. Darwin, a contemporary of Tennyson's, acknowledged that he developed his theories of natural selection and survival of the fittest after reading Thomas Malthus's economic treatise *An Essay on the Principle of Population* (1798).[33] Malthus derived his paradigm of scarcity and competition from an industrial, capitalist economy, and in many ways Darwin's version of evolution reads this logic back onto nature; he sees species as specialists in competition for scarce resources. This tendency to see the natural world through particular cultural lenses is evident in the medieval theological view of nature as a harmonious, hierarchical order—a great chain of being—and continues today as our information economy gives priority to DNA and genetic information.[34] We narrate the natural order according to our cultural predispositions.

Though it's impossible for humans to read the natural world objectively—we are, after all, part of nature—the lens provided by traditional agrarians offers an alternative to Darwin's industrial view of nature, an alternative corroborated both by indigenous traditions and by more recent studies of ecosystems that highlight the importance of cooperation and community.[35] This agrarian view invites us to set aside Darwin's industrial lens long enough to consider the ways in which nature operates as a sustainable economy. From F. H. King, Albert Howard, Liberty Hyde Bailey, indigenous farmers in Peru, and the Southern Agrarians, among others, Berry adopts a way of looking at the natural world that focuses on its organic, cyclical processes.[36]

Significantly, several of the writers whom Berry acknowledges as key influences on his understanding of ecological patterns were themselves influenced by traditional indigenous farmers. Albert Howard traveled to India to spread Western agricultural science, but he ended up adopting many of the methods used by Indian farmers.[37] Similarly, F. H. King found that traditional farmers in China, Korea, and Japan had maintained healthy topsoil over many generations of intensive farming, whereas the methods being promoted by the USDA leeched nutrients from the soil.[38] Today, activists like Vandana Shiva continue to speak for farming methods that honor what she calls the "inviolable law of return," whereby plant and animal waste feeds soil fertility.[39] Shiva works with traditional farmers in India, including many women, and ensures the survival of local seeds through a network of community seed banks. In his foreword to a collection of her essays, Berry explicitly praises the "formal intelligence" that Shiva's work exemplifies.[40]

So although agrarianism is often blamed for being racist and patriarchal, this critique applies more to the industrial, agribusiness model that has come to dominate American farming.[41] In seeking to extract resources with maximal efficiency, this model carries out the exploitative logic that has tragically marked American agriculture from its colonial beginnings. In this regard, the history of colonial America is the history of the commodification of people and land so that they could be converted into capital.[42] Berry wrestles with this history in several essays, and while he acknowledges his ancestors' complicity in these injustices, he seeks to articulate and practice an alternative agrarian tradition in which humans participate in natural cycles of renewal and so foster genuinely sustainable communities.[43]

In his lecture "It All Turns on Affection," Berry explains the relationship between the organic fertility cycle and analogous human economies:

> The problem of sustainability is simple enough to state. It requires that the fertility cycle of birth, growth, maturity, death, and decay—what Albert Howard called "the Wheel of Life"—should turn continuously in place, so that the law of return is kept and nothing is wasted. For this to happen in the stewardship of humans, there must be a cultural cycle, in harmony with the fertility cycle, also continuously turning in place. . . . This is what is meant, and is all that can be meant, by "sustainability." The fertility cycle turns by the law of nature. The cultural cycle turns on affection.[44]

Howard's sustainable "Wheel of Life" contrasts with the violent competition and mass-produced quantities of the industrial economy. Whereas the industrial economy divides winners from losers, products from pollution, a sustainable economy fosters patterns of mutual dependence and membership. For a small-scale farmer, these patterns are quite literal. As Howard explains in describing the characteristics of a natural ecosystem—and a healthy farm—"The mixed vegetable and animal wastes are converted into humus; there is no waste; the processes of growth and the processes of decay balance one another; ample provision is made to maintain large reserves of fertility; the greatest care is taken to store the rainfall; both plants and animals are left to protect themselves from disease."[45] Howard's concrete, ecological descriptions outline a household order in which the various members work together to maintain healthy processes.

These processes enable life to flourish over time and sustain energy in ecological cycles. The industrial economy seeks security and power through storing energy and life in massive quantities, but the consequence is often waste. As Berry points out, "This kind of use turns an asset into a liability."[46] In contrast, the natural fertility cycles break down animal and plant wastes and return them to the soil to provide nutrients. Thus, Berry concludes, we have a fundamental choice to make in the way we use energy: "We can preserve energy in cycles of use, passing it again and again through the same series of forms; or we can waste it by using it once in a way that makes it irrecoverable."[47] The crucial feature of these sustainable cycles is that they hold death and waste in patterns of return or renewal:

> It is the principle of return that complicates matters, for it requires responsibility, care, of a different and higher order than that required by production and consumption alone, and it calls for methods and economies of a different kind. In an energy economy appropriate to the use of biological energy, all bodies, plant and animal and human, are joined in a kind of energy community. They are not divided from each other by greedy, "individualistic" efforts to produce and consume large quantities of energy, much less to store large quantities. They are indissolubly linked in complex patterns of energy exchange. They die into each other's life, and live into each other's death. They do not consume in the sense of using up. They do not produce waste. What they take in they change, but they change it always into a form necessary for its use by a living body of another kind. And this exchange goes on and on, round and round, the Wheel of Life rising out of the soil, descending into it, through the bodies of creatures.[48]

As Berry's description makes clear, humans participate in these cycles only through faithful care; there is no technological shortcut that can fulfill our responsibility to keep this Wheel of Life turning in place.

Although life in ecosystems survives in cycles, not stores, the industrial economy seeks ways to stockpile and market energy. Oil has of course been the chief means of storing and capitalizing energy, but attempts to quantify and store life abound in our culture. One example of this fascination can be seen in various lifespan extension technologies, whether cryonics—which stores human bodies in liquid nitrogen in the hope that future technologies will find ways to resuscitate them—or parabiosis—which injects recipients with the blood of younger people in an effort to slow the aging process.[49] Efforts to quantify life can even be seen in the predominant view of time as *chronos*, an evenly divisible quantity, rather than *kairos*, a cyclical pattern: we speak of time as wasted, spent, and saved.[50] It's no accident that the railroad caused the United States to establish standard time zones: whereas an industrial economy runs by the regular shriek of the train or factory whistle, a sustainable economy follows diurnal and seasonal cycles.

Trusting one's life to cycles is scary; farmers can't guarantee that next year's crop will be abundant. Each year that it comes, new life is a gift, a gift that we hope for but can't guarantee. It's understandable, then, that we would be tempted to rely on technologies that promise to free us from these cycles by turning the natural world into a set of resources to extract and hoard. Sustainable human economies, however, resist this temptation and skillfully tend the health of natural processes. Their members don't seek to maximize individual, short-term gains but instead find ways to participate in the ongoing cycles of resurrection, the patterns by which deaths serve new lives.

Berry's name for these harmonious, sustainable patterns is health. Health cannot be quantified or mass-produced. Rather, health, like beauty, emerges from interconnected, complex connections and is marked by analogous relationships between the parts of a whole.[51] Berry emphasizes the far-reaching implications of such healthy patterns when he explains that the "concept of health is rooted in the concept of wholeness. To be healthy is to be whole. The word *health* belongs to a family of words, a listing of which will suggest how far the consideration of health must carry us: *heal, whole, wholesome, hale, hallow, holy.*"[52] Given its rich connotations, it's not surprising that for Howard, "health is the 'one great subject,'" and Berry follows Howard when he claims that "there is only one value: the life and health of the world."[53] It is this value—rather than any monetary currency—that sustainable economies cherish and preserve.

If an internal combustion engine is the emblem of an industrial economy, topsoil models the kind of healthy order that characterizes sustainable economies.[54] As Berry claims in an essay on the formal parallels between poetry and marriage, "Form, like topsoil (which is intricately formal), empowers time to do good."[55] He expands on this claim in "Two Economies," explaining that healthy topsoil is a microcosm of a sustainable economy—what he terms "the Kingdom of God."[56] Two contrasts between engines and topsoil clarify the distinctions between the economies they represent.

First, though engines run on finite resources, violently burning them up, soil's power comes from holding its members in relation with one another. Soil is a "neighborhood" that humans cannot make or control.[57] So while industrial farmers treat topsoil as a fund or fuel, seeing it as a scarce resource whose potency must be increased through chemical or mechanical inputs, a sustainable approach considers the soil's health and looks for ways to enrich its ongoing life. This is because topsoil's fertility depends ultimately not on inputs of power but on proper forms and patterns. Thus, soil "is not a mechanical device but, among other things, a graveyard, a place of resurrection, and a community of living creatures."[58] A gardener, then, has the incredible opportunity and responsibility to assist in the creation of new life, but a gardener can never turn life into a commodity to be stored and controlled.[59]

Second, an engine is made by specialists to accomplish specialized tasks, but topsoil naturally has complex functionality. For instance, healthy soil has the "double ability to drain and retain water." This paradoxical ability is a feature of its diversity, a diversity that runs counter to the industrial method of specialization: "Industrialists see retention and drainage as different and opposite functions, and they would promote one at the expense of the other, just as, diversity being inimical to industrial procedure, they would commit themselves to the forlorn expedient of enlarging capacity by increasing area."[60] As Berry writes, this formal complexity is a feature of all healthy ecosystems: "Diversity increases capacity—or, to put it another way, . . . complications of form or pattern can increase greatly within quantitative limits."[61] Mechanical specialization tends to treat problems in isolation, but topsoil and other healthy ecosystems invite us to consider how particular formal qualities lead to health; they invite us to "solve for pattern."

The sustainable ecological cycles that enable topsoil to "mak[e] life out of death" are vulnerable not only to natural disruptions, but also to cultural patterns that violate their basic grammar.[62] Industrial economies of division and competition break apart pieces that can be healthy only when together. Sustainable economies, on the other hand, look for ways to solve for pattern by putting these fragmented pieces back together. As Berry writes, "If we are to live well on and from our land, we must live by faith in the ceaselessness of these processes and by faith in our own willingness and ability to collaborate with them."[63] At the core of this collaboration between sustainable human economies and natural cycles is an acceptance and even embrace of death. This may seem shocking. In an industrial culture where "death is looked upon with almost universal enmity, it is hard to believe that the land we live on and the lives we live are the gifts of death. Yet that is so, and it is the topsoil that makes it so. In fact, in talking about topsoil, it is hard to avoid the language of religion."[64] As Berry bluntly professes in one poem, "Christmas / night and Easter morning are this soil's only laws."[65] For Christians who await the final resurrection, death is the portal to redemption. In the words of the Eastern Orthodox Pascha hymn, "Christ is risen from the dead, / Trampling down death by death."[66]

Death and Resurrection

Say that the leaves are harvested
when they have rotted into the mold.
Call that profit. Prophesy such returns.
Put your faith in the two inches of humus
that will build under the trees
every thousand years.
Listen to carrion—put your ear
close, and hear the faint chattering
of the songs that are to come.
Expect the end of the world. Laugh.
Laughter is immeasurable. Be joyful
though you have considered all the facts.[67]

Death is decidedly un-American. It strikes at our core belief that we are free to do what we want. Death is the great limit, the fundamental problem our technocracy still can't fix. Yet in our fear and avoidance of death, we deny our membership in creation and hinder our ability to relate to others. In "Manifesto: The Mad Farmer Liberation Front," the poem from which all the epigraphs in this chapter are taken, Berry links our cultural avoidance of death with our broken relationships: we are "afraid/to know [our] neighbors and to die." He goes on to provide guidance for how we might overcome these related fears, including the blunt command to "listen to carrion." Being willing to look death in the face is the first step to looking our neighbor in the face. Such vulnerability can be terrifying, and it certainly violates our fondly held belief that we are self-made, free from dependence on others. Yet if creation's fundamental grammar is one of giving, then we participate in its healing and redemption when we give of ourselves to others.

Confronting death has been one of Berry's central concerns.[68] The first poem in his *New Collected Poems* is "Elegy," and his early fiction ponders death and our often flawed responses to it. "The Brothers," the first story Berry published and which he later incorporated into *Nathan Coulter*, involves Nathan and Tom's cruel murder of a crow and then the untimely death of their mother from sickness. Because their father, Jarrat, is unable to cope with his wife's death—on the day she dies he violently destroys the rosebush she treasured—he alienates his sons and warps his own life.[69] Jarrat succumbs to what Gary Snyder, in summarizing one of Berry's essays, identifies as "the basic error" humans repeatedly make: we try "to escape death."[70] As Berry writes, "Love must confront death, and accept it, and learn from it. Only in confronting death can earthly love learn its true extent, its immortality. Any definition of health that is not silly must include death. The world of love includes death, suffers it, and triumphs over it. The world of efficiency is defeated by death; at death, all its instruments and procedures stop. The world of love continues, and of this grief is the proof."[71] It makes sense, then, that the starkest contrast between an industrial economy and a sustainable one lies in the way each deals with death.

The industrial economy views death as a loss, a null value, and so does all it can to avoid and exclude death. Yet this mindset leads, as Berry puts it in one of his poems, to the invention of "death as waste."[72] In fact, it may even be that some—although certainly not all—vegetarians refuse to eat meat out of a futile wish to avoid all death.[73] Such attempts to avoid death lead to intractable philosophical puzzles and reductive calculations about which course of action costs the least life, and this line of reasoning almost inevitably treats life as a quantity.[74] Yet we cannot escape death. All that is living survives by the deaths of others, whether the death of creatures whose bodies feed rich soil, the death of the plants that we eat, the death of the wild ecosystems we suppress in order to cultivate our food, the death of the organisms we kill when we breathe and drink, even the apoptosis of cells in our bodies—our lives are inextricably implicated in death. We cannot choose whether we will cause the deaths of others; we can choose only how we will do this.

A sustainable economy recognizes that death is not a binary value, where life equals one and death equals zero. A particular death derives its meaning from its context. Some deaths are good, others are bad, and most are bittersweet. This is why we can see the death of an old person who has lived well and is surrounded by her family as a beautiful thing, while the death of a child in a car accident is tragic. This is why there's a difference between the life and death of a hog raised by a family who gave it opportunities to forage and who killed it respectfully and gratefully, and the life and death of a hog raised and slaughtered in a CAFO.[75] Both people die, both animals die, and yet their deaths have very different meanings because they take place in very different formal contexts.

Sustainability, then, is fundamentally about including death in the patterns of our lives. In business terms, sustainability involves turning liabilities into assets: instead of externalizing costs, you include them and find creative ways to turn them to account. In biological terms, sustainability describes the ways that ecosystems metabolize death. And in theological terms, sustainability describes how the Creator turns death inside out, redeeming it, "trampling down death by death."

As we have already seen, Berry's understanding of sustainable, resurrecting cycles is both agrarian and Christian, biological and religious. These two influences converge in one of Jesus' sayings that Berry cites: "Except a corn of wheat fall into the ground and die, it abideth alone: but if it die, it bringeth forth much fruit."[76] Hence, Berry follows Allen Tate in affirming that "the agrarian mind is, at bottom, a religious mind," and he concurs with Liberty Hyde Bailey's use of the adjective *holy* to describe the earth.[77] In using such language, these agrarians move from the realm of physical observation to the realm of faith. Berry's injunction to practice resurrection is founded in the faith that the Creator remains present in creation, loving and redeeming it.[78] Because of this faith, Christians no longer try to escape death but, rather, seek to participate in Christ's life so that their individual deaths can be caught up in his death and resurrection. As the Catholic theologian Hans Urs von Balthasar puts it, "The world wants to live and rise again before it dies, while the love of Christ wants to die in order to rise again in the form of God on the other side of death, indeed *in* death."[79] Thus, much of Balthasar's work is concerned with articulating how, in Christian theology, the "faculty for procreation and giving birth is connected with the finitude and death of those beings."[80]

A similar theological perspective leads Berry to cast a proper view of death in sacramental terms: "To live, we must daily break the body and shed the blood of Creation. When we do this knowingly, lovingly, skillfully, reverently, it is a sacrament. When we do it ignorantly, greedily, clumsily, destructively, it is a desecration. In such desecration we condemn ourselves to spiritual and moral loneliness, and others to want."[81] In claiming that a sacramental economy transforms death's meaning, Berry draws on the formal qualities of sacraments. There is no chemical, biological difference between the digestive process of a Christian partaking in the Eucharist and someone scarfing down a hamburger at a fast-food joint. What matters here isn't the quantity of calories we consume, but the formal context in which we eat. Similarly, Christians insist that the same sexual act takes on vastly different meanings depending on whether it takes place within a marriage or outside it. Christian theology teaches that sacramental forms are means of grace in which God aligns our human lives with his redemptive work.

Norman Wirzba, in his book *Food and Faith*, expands on the way that sacramental forms of eating, in particular, enable deaths to be transformed into lives marked by self-giving: "To offer food to another expresses a profound insight into the gifted and interdependent character of the human condition. In this offering people acknowledge that as creatures they are beneficiaries of an incomprehensible and costly generosity and hospitality. The clearest sign of this acknowledgment is that people themselves become generous and hospitable with others, offering from themselves and their livelihood what they have already received."[82] When Berry concludes his beautiful poem "Prayer after Eating" with the line "May I be worthy of my meat," he is acknowledging the undeserved gift that all food is and praying that the life he receives from it would likewise be given for the good of others.[83] The rhythm of sacramental eating is one of grateful reception and generous giving.[84]

In addition to agriculture and eating, the other form of sacramental self-giving to which Berry often returns is marriage.[85] When two people commit to a marriage, they must die to themselves in ways that lead to new lives, both a newly flourishing life for the beloved, but also the new lives of their children.[86] As he does with eating, Berry describes the "deaths" that marriage requires in religious terms: "Lovers, then, 'die' into their union with one another as a soul 'dies' into its union with God. And so here, at the very heart of community life, we find not something to sell as in the public market but this momentous giving. If the community cannot protect this giving [through the communal forms of courtship, marriage, and household], it can protect nothing—and our time is proving that this is so."[87] Love, like energy, cannot be safely stored. It must be given away to survive. The industrial tendency is to control and store our affections to minimize risk. What we need, however, is an economy that, rather than "protect[ing] the 'right' of profit, . . . exists for the protection of gifts."[88] Faithful marriages provide the foundation of an economy in which persons can give themselves freely. This economy of self-giving is of course not exclusive to marriage—several of Berry's most articulate fictional defenders of marriage are themselves bachelors—and people who remain single can certainly practice such forms of faithful, fruitful love.[89]

What is crucial is that the mutual giving a marriage serves to protect can lead to new life. Like healthy topsoil that holds its inhabitants in place so that their deaths serve new life, a marriage holds two spouses together so that as they give themselves to one another, "other living souls come into being. . . . The marriage of two lovers joins them to one another, to forebears, to descendants, to the community, to Heaven and earth."[90] A marriage thus protects the self-giving of each spouse so as to form the conditions for the flourishing of new life. New life is not guaranteed, of course—life is always a gift—but the form of marriage sustains the conditions for resurrection.

Healthy cultural forms shape persons who honor and sustain this self-giving or dying to self. Wirzba articulates this dynamic when he writes: "To live well, which means to learn to receive gratefully the gifts of others, requires that we also learn to die well by turning our living into a gift for others. Why? Because it is the most fitting acknowledgment of the gifts of life sacrificially given, and our most faithful way of participating in God's own self-offering life as revealed in Christ."[91] When we live this way, we act not as individuals who are divided from and in competition with others—so that death, no matter how it comes to us, counts as a loss—but instead as members who offer our lives as "gift[s] that creat[e] communion"—we become not individual subjects, but grateful members.[92] One of the themes that recurs in later chapters, then, is the way that Berry's sustainable forms imagine the self as a convocated member rather than an autonomous agent—what Charles Taylor terms a "buffered" self.

Some might object that this sacramental view of death is redemptive only if one takes a systemic perspective. Generational and ecological cycles may enable an individual death to serve the life of another, but the individual still perishes.[93] As Berry notes, such cycles offer "little comfort to individual humans in their suffering of their own mortality and that of their loved ones." While admitting that this is a great mystery, he points to the conclusion of *The Faerie Queene*, where Edmund Spenser "invok[es] our so far undying hope for a 'time,' beyond Nature's world and all of its stories, 'when no more change shall be.' "[94] Thus, Spenser concludes, "But thence-forth all shall rest eternally / With Him that is the God of Sabaoth hight: / O! that great Sabaoth God, grant me that Sabaoths sight."[95] This eschatological hope that individual persons and creatures will one day dwell in God's eternal peaceable kingdom depends on the efficacy of Christ's miraculous resurrection. Those who have this hope are freed to live lives of radical self-giving, participating in this miracle now as they practice the difficult virtues of renewal.

Literary Forms and Sustaining Virtues

As soon as the generals and the politicos
can predict the motions of your mind,
lose it. Leave it as a sign
to mark the false trail, the way
you didn't go. Be like the fox
who makes more tracks than necessary,
some in the wrong direction.
Practice resurrection.[96]

In contrasting these different manifestations of an industrial economy with the manifestations of a sustainable economy, I have been attempting to follow Berry's analogical method of thinking. By identifying the contrasting grammars of division, conflict, and mass extraction on the one hand, and membership, love, and sustainable pattern on the other, we learn to perceive the ways in which a confinement feeding operation is like a modern city is like a research university is like an internal combustion engine. Furthermore, a healthy community is like a marriage is like a poem is like fertile topsoil. These sustainable forms resonate harmoniously with one another because they are built on the same grammar. Central to this structure is the way sustainable forms make space for resurrection by cultivating in their members virtues of renewal. The industrial economy trains its constituents in techniques of production and consumption, but sustainable economies train their members in virtues of renewal, virtues that enable these members to practice resurrection.

Berry's understanding of virtue is closely connected to healthy forms. In essence, virtues of renewal are the arts or excellences of sustaining health, of tending beauty. If health is not a quantity but a form, then we sustain it by formal perception and practices of care. To borrow from Berry's definition of *husbandry*, virtues are "the practices that sustain life by connecting us conservingly to our places and our world; [they are] the art[s] of keeping tied all the strands in the living network that sustains us."[97] As such, sustaining virtues depend first of all on an imaginative ability to perceive the patterns of this living network; we can't sustain an order that we don't recognize and understand. Thus, Berry emphasizes the need for a formal intelligence that can inform and guide virtuous living. He explains this connection between imagination and virtue in an essay on poetry when he writes, "The chief criterion of thought . . . must be propriety—fittingness to our place in the world, in the order of things, and to our relations of dependence and responsibility with other creatures—which would enable humility, restoration, the practice of the virtues."[98] A perception of "fittingness" or "propriety" relies on a formal, imaginative mode of intelligence, which is why honing this perceptive faculty through the study of literary forms can make us better able to apply it to our places and communities.

Propriety of thought and literary form, then, has much to teach us about how to fit into our place in the natural world. As Berry warns, "We cannot keep things from falling apart in our society if they do not cohere in our minds and in our lives."[99] He expands on this connection in the context of poetry, arguing that studying poetic form can strengthen the other forms by which we live: "By its formal integrity a poem reminds us of the formal integrity of other works, creatures, and structures of the world. The form of a good poem is, in a way perhaps not altogether explainable or demonstrable, an analogue of the forms of other things. By its form it alludes to other forms, evokes them, resonates with them, and so becomes a part of the system of analogies or harmonies by which we live. Thus the poet affirms and collaborates in the formality of Creation."[100] Beautiful poetic forms are analogous to other sustainable forms of life, whether embodied in a spouse's faithful love, an engineer's elegant solution, a doctor's perceptive diagnosis, or a teacher's attentive care. Berry, for instance, likens his work as a farmer to his work as a writer, explaining that "to farm it well is to solve structural problems of the same nature as a novelist encounters."[101] Our industrial culture has neglected "the issue of form," but a sustainable culture depends on farmers, lawyers, businesspeople, engineers, neighbors, parents, and spouses who have the formal intelligence to perceive the tattered remnants of healthy patterns and the virtues to mend them.[102]

In a culture obsessed with quantity and power, this focus on imagination and formal coherence may seem odd. We tend to think quantities of energy will free us from work and make our lives safer, so we invest in the STEM fields in the quest for new technologies of control. Yet it is the marginalized humanities that emphasize the importance of the imagination in perceiving formal beauty. And as Berry explains, sustainable economies run not by mastering quantities of power, but by following healthy cycles: "The energy that is made available to us by living things . . . is made available not as an inconceivable quantity, but as a conceivable pattern. . . . It is conceivable not so much to the analytic intelligence, to which it may always remain in part mysterious, as to the imagination, by which we perceive, value, and imitate order beyond our understanding."[103] Whereas the analytic intelligence prized by an industrial economy looks to solve any problem it faces with a technological solution, the imagination or formal intelligence for which Berry advocates moves from perceiving healthy forms to valuing and imitating them. In doing so, it moves from recognizing beauty to loving it to embodying it. This movement from imagination to affection to practice charts the way in which a formal intelligence should, ideally, lead to virtuous living.

Yet in contrast to virtues that tend patterns of health, the industrial economy prizes a technical, self-centered way of relating to the world. As we have seen, an industrial use of energy turns on production and consumption, fuel and waste. It thus makes sense that an industrial economy celebrates techniques of production—thinking entrepreneurially, being innovative, finding technological breakthroughs—and consumption—branding, manufacturing discontent, fulfilling individual pleasure. Such techniques feed on vicious habits of distraction, surveillance, busyness, code fetishism, optimism, pessimism, innovation, mobility, and autonomy. And they focus not on tending health, but on satisfying our immediate desires. In this way, technology becomes a substitute for virtue: tractors and nitrogen fertilizers make small-scale, diversified farming obsolete; cheap birth control renders sexual temperance unnecessary; computers pay attention to each student so that teachers don't have to; medical breakthroughs promise cures without the need for exercise or healthy food. C. S. Lewis explains this relationship between techniques and virtues when he writes: "For the wise men of old the cardinal problem had been how to conform the soul to reality, and the solution had been knowledge, self-discipline, and virtue. For . . . applied science . . . the problem is how to subdue reality to the wishes of men: the solution is a technique."[104] Our reliance on techniques is symptomatic of a human tendency to make the world conform to our desires rather than fit ourselves into a pattern to which we belong.

Technologies in and of themselves are not evil, but when we use them to more easily attain flawed, selfish desires and avoid the hard work of personal change, we become parasitic, destroying our places. As Berry argues, "From the beginning of the history of machine-developed energy, we have been able to harness more power than we could use responsibly. . . . The energy crises is not a crisis of technology but of morality. . . . If, like the strip-miners and the 'agribusinessmen,' we look on all the world as fuel or as extractable energy, we can do nothing but destroy it."[105] James Smith makes a related point by citing a Michelob Ultra commercial "in which the world obeys the touch commands of an iPhone screen. Don't like that car? *Swipe* for a different one. Wish the scenery was different? *Swipe* for an alternative. . . . A way of relating to a phone has now become a way of relating to the world." As Smith explains, the way of relating to the world that an iPhone cultivates is centered on me and my desires: "To become habituated to an iPhone is to implicitly treat the world as 'available' to *me* and at my disposal—to constitute the world as 'at-hand' for me, to be selected, scaled, scanned, tapped, and enjoyed."[106] The promise of the iPhone is that if we learn a few gestures, a few techniques for deploying its vast technological powers, we can get whatever we want.[107]

Yet the physical world proves to be not so malleable as we might wish, and, as our various environmental crises indicate, nature has a habit of punishing those who abuse it. There are practical consequences for moral failings, although these consequences may be delayed or suffered most acutely by those who are not directly responsible.[108] Berry points to soil erosion and superweeds, habitat loss and species extinction, polluted watersheds and dead zones in the oceans as evidence that "dame Nature," to use Edmund Spenser's term, oversees a stern moral ecology.[109] To be sustainable, a culture must recognize and respect this natural order; like good artists, members of such cultures accept formal limits as gifts and creatively work within them. If industrial techniques aim to change the world to fit our desires, sustainable virtues change us so we can better fit our places—these virtues tune or stretch us so that we harmonize with our place's music. As Berry puts it, "A virtue must lead to harmony between one creature and another."[110] So virtues are rooted in love; they are the habits and practices of those who love their neighbors. The sustainable "cultural cycle turns on affection."[111] Rather than developing techniques to make our places more easily meet our individual desires, members of sustainable economies learn to die to their own desires and develop the virtues needed to serve the needs of their beloved places.

Such virtues allow us to sustain and participate in healthy patterns. As we have seen, these patterns preserve cycles of "return," and the renewal they bring depends not so much on powerful technologies as on virtuous members who can imagine and practice such return. In the following chapters, I will consider how Berry's literary forms embody some of these virtues: attention, gratitude, humility, hope, memory, fidelity, and convocation. Though such virtues can prepare the way for renewal, they cannot manufacture life; resurrection always comes as a gift. Nevertheless, these virtues are ways of practicing resurrection.

These virtues enable people in many different spheres of life to tend healthy forms. But to be successful, virtuous community members will also need more specialized skills that are appropriate to their particular work. For instance, a farmer, a doctor, and a mother will all need attention, but the practices through which they enact their attention will differ. Berry refers to these practical skills as "virtuosities": "Work that is authentically placed and understood within the Great Economy moves virtue toward virtuosity—that is, toward skill or technical competence."[112] My focus on literary forms—and the verbal virtuosities Berry's writings model—is not meant to suggest that technical skills needed for particular vocations are unimportant. On the contrary, particular sets of virtuosities are vital to tending health, but they need to be oriented and shaped by more fundamental moral virtues. Reading Berry's writings to learn virtues of renewal, then, is a first step that must be followed by the development of specific virtuosities or skills needed to practice these underlying virtues in specific contexts.

Despite Berry's literary skill, however, there is no guarantee that reading about sustainable communities will lead us to imitate them. As Auden insists,

"Poetry makes nothing happen." This is particularly true in regard to virtuous living, which, as Alasdair MacIntyre argues, is best learned in virtuous communities.[113] Berry would certainly agree that healthy local communities are the ideal teachers of virtue.[114] Yet becoming participants in his literary community can refresh imaginations desiccated by an industrial lifestyle, especially if our reading leads to a renewed practice of these virtues. We are all members of communities—families, neighborhoods, churches, cities—that depend on these disciplines for their sustenance and renewal. Attending to Berry's literary forms, then, may teach us to cultivate those sustainable forms of community and civic life that still thrive along the margins of an industrial economy.

Such an approach to reading runs counter to the literary culture of an industrial economy, in which authors and readers use literature for personal gain rather than to serve their communities. Berry likens the specialist poet or writer to "an industrialist, . . . interested in the subjects of the world for the sake of what they can be made to produce."[115] Tell-all memoirs mine personal relationships and experiences for salacious stories with little thought to the consequences of betraying private trust.[116] Avant-garde poets and artists exhibit more concern with winning prizes and offending "complacent" readers than actually strengthening their communities.[117] Self-help books promise to provide the secrets to personal success, encouraging individuals to focus on personal gain regardless of community health. Much of our art, then, follows an industrial grammar of division, violence, and consumption.

Yet the real culprit for our malformed imaginations may not be bad books themselves, but the fact that many of us take an industrial approach to our consumption of literature and other art. We "use" beauty—in the mode that C. S. Lewis identifies as a lower kind of reading—rather than "receiv[ing]" it.[118] We turn to art to distract us from unpleasant or boring surroundings or to satisfy our fantasies. As a recent essay in the *Atlantic* observes, "We live in a bourgeois society, where works of art—those that attract a large audience, anyway—teach you how to consume, or else make the process of consumption more pleasurable."[119] Hence, art has been flattened to therapy.[120]

Nevertheless, good literature—and I will argue Berry's writings are paradigmatic in this regard—resists being merely used. As Lewis argues, while a good work of art "may be used in the wrong way, . . . it will seldom yield to this treatment so easily as a bad one. [A man looking for pornography] will gladly turn from Tintoretto to Kirchner or photographs."[121] So, though a good reader can glean virtue from a bad book, and a poor reader can consume even a good book, a good book is distinguished by the way it "permits, invites, or even compels good reading."[122]

In the industrial mode, both authors and readers treat literature as a technology by which they can modify the world to suit their desires; this is the approach of the propagandist, marketing sloganeer, tell-all memoirist, specialist poet, and escapist reader. Such an approach treats language as if it were an iPhone with which we can manipulate those parts of the world that resist our desires. Yet this is a debased use of language, which in its highest form is not a tool to make things happen but, as Auden wrote, "a way of happening."[123] The way of happening that characterizes Berry's poetry, essays, and fiction is one shaped by virtues of renewal, virtues iPhones and industrial technologies don't generally encourage. By reading Berry, then, we might begin to learn "a language precise and articulate and lively enough to tell the truth about the world as we know it."[124]

Auden's poem that I have referenced several times now, "In Memory of W. B. Yeats," wrestles with the question of whether Yeats's poems did any good: they could not prevent his own death, nor could they resolve Ireland's ongoing political struggles, the onset of World War II, or poverty.[125] The poem's first section vacillates between the hope that Yeats's life and words might live on after his death, inspiring and guiding his readers, and the apparent reality that poems don't change anything important. On the one hand, Auden imagines Yeats's readers chewing on his words, ruminating on them in the core of their beings: "The words of a dead man / Are modified in the guts of the living." On the other hand, this doesn't seem that significant

> in the importance and noise of to-morrow
> When the brokers are roaring like beasts on the floor of the Bourse,
> And the poor have the sufferings to which they are fairly accustomed,
> And each in the cell of himself is almost convinced of his freedom.[126]

Ultimately, there isn't much hope that Yeats's poems will accomplish any significant change: the stock exchange will go on humming, the poor will stay poor, we will remain isolated in our buffered selves, and World War II will proceed unimpeded.

The second section implies that Yeats wasn't an exceptionally special person; he was "silly like us." And his poems haven't changed Ireland; its madness and cloudy weather continue in spite of them. (That's definitely one thing poetry can't do—make Ireland have sunny weather.) This leads Auden to his famous statement of poetry's futility:

> For poetry makes nothing happen: it survives
> In the valley of its making where executives
> Would never want to tamper; it flows on south
> From ranches of isolation and the busy griefs,
> Raw towns that we believe and die in; it survives,
> A way of happening, a mouth.

Poetry can't force change, it can't coerce anyone to do anything, it doesn't work by industrialism's instrumental logic. Poetry doesn't manufacture anything or generate horsepower. Rather, it survives, it continues in places hidden away from business executives and politicians, places of solitude, sadness, and rawness. Yet these are the places where humans live, and thus Auden writes twice that poetry "survives"; it is "a way of happening, a mouth." This poetic mouth contrasts with the utilitarian mouth of the thermometer in the first stanza: "The mercury sank in the mouth of the dying day. / O all the instruments agree / The day of his death was a dark cold day."[127] Instead of an instrument that quantifies and controls, poetry's mouth unites communities through communication and relationships. Like topsoil, it holds members in relation to one another, a relation that can lead to understanding, love, and sustainable patterns of living. So though poetry doesn't make things happen, it is a way of happening, a way of talking and living and sustaining community that stands in opposition to the world of industry and force, of war and the stock exchange.

Poets like Auden remind us that words cannot provide an "at-hand" world to us, a world that we can manipulate to cater to our every desire. War, environmental crises, death—these are realities that cannot simply be swiped away by better technology. Poetry, in its blatant inability to make anything happen, reminds us that none of the technologies we rely on to make things happen can actually deliver on such a promise. Rather than better technologies, our deepest need is for better, more virtuous ways of being in the world.

The final section of Auden's poem reflects on what might characterize the way of happening that poetry invites us to inhabit. While the "dogs of Europe bark" and each nation is "sequestered in its hate," the poet offers a noncoercive, free alternative: "With your unconstraining voice / Still persuade us to rejoice." Auden particularly alludes to the way that poetry or verse is a kind of plowing: "With the farming of a verse / Make a vineyard of the curse." *Verse* literally means "to turn," and the lines of a poem, like the lines of a plow, go back and forth in an attempt to break up the fallow ground of our hearts. This verbal turning opens a "healing fountain" that teaches free men how to praise.[128] The purpose of such versifying, Auden suggests, is to cultivate in individuals and cultures a more fruitful way of being that forms an alternative to the power games of war and international finance, power games that industrial technologies like the iPhone invite us to play and win; if we can't swipe away war and death, we can at least swipe away uncomfortable news and distract ourselves with something more amusing.

A frustration with the inadequacy of words to control others can lead some people to resort to technologies that can make things happen. When circumstances don't work out the way we'd like, we use technology to change them. We want to make the world fit our desires, and when words fail to serve this purpose, we often grow frustrated with them. This is why Auden reminds his readers that poetry makes nothing happen; it operates not by force or coercion, but by sitting in our guts and reshaping our deep longings, our vision of the world and of the good. Poetry offers an alternative way of relating to the fellow members of our places: not as avatars on a screen we control, but as irreducible, mysterious beings we will always be seeking to understand, to live with, and to love rightly.

It is in this way that literature's formal beauty offers to rearrange readers' imaginations and habits, shaping our souls to conform with a complex reality. Berry invites readers to experience sustainable forms in the shape of his poetry, essays, and fiction, and this experience prepares us to recognize and tend analogous forms in our own lives and communities. As Lewis argues, reading for virtue may depend more on the reader than it does on the book itself. The seed falls on good and bad soil alike, but it is only in the good soil that it bears lasting fruit. My ultimate hope for this book, then, is to cultivate the soil of our hearts so that we are prepared to find—in Berry's writings first, but also in other literature and art—the virtues of renewal that will sustain our communities and our places. If literary beauty stretches our hearts to be more attuned to healthy forms and more virtuous to tend them, then literature can indeed be a locus of healing, a place where we learn to practice resurrection.

1

Attention

When we sit down at the dinner table, many of us now bring along our own utensil: a smartphone. If the food looks good, you can post a picture of it to Instagram; if the conversation lags, you can see what your friends are saying on Facebook; if someone asks a question, you can Google it. Even if you haven't eaten a meal mediated through your phone, you've almost certainly watched others do so. Although smartphones are incredibly powerful and can make many tasks much easier to accomplish, they also reinforce perennial human tendencies toward self-absorption. So though most American adults own smartphones, many remain somewhat unsettled by the mode of community they foster. We might hesitate to agree with Eric Schmidt and Jared Cohen, two executives at Google, when they confidently proclaim that "the best thing anyone can do to improve the quality of life around the world is to drive connectivity and technological opportunity."[1] The optimism behind this claim seems to assume that more "connectivity" is always better—if we have access to more information, more stimulus, more people, then we'll be more fulfilled. Yet maybe what we really need is not more connections, but more sustaining relationships with those to whom we are already connected.

In the movement of his poems, Wendell Berry models a mode of patient, grateful attention that can foster such relationships. His desire to attend to where he is testifies to his faith that he lives in a marvelous and grace-filled place. Thus, Berry imagines heaven not as somewhere up in the sky with the saints, but right here, "this world as I know it, but redeemed / of our abuse of it and one another."

> A painful Heaven this would be, for I would know
> by it how far I have fallen short. I have not
> paid enough attention, have not been grateful
> enough. And yet this pain would be the measure
> of my love. In eternity's once and now, pain would
> place me surely in the Heaven of my earthly love.[2]

Berry's poetic practice of returning again and again to the same subjects is part of his effort to see faithfully, to pay attention, and so to honor the goodness and beauty of his place.[3] Attention is a particularly fitting virtue with which to begin a study of sustainable cultural forms because these forms depend, first of all, on members who are attentive to perceive and participate in the ongoing patterns of their places. Berry's poetry reveals that attention can be a strange thing; as he attends to his place, he finds himself attended to. Attention, then, may be more complex and reciprocal than we tend to think. And it is certainly more difficult to practice in a digitally networked culture that undermines the reciprocal dynamics of sustaining attention by encouraging the techniques of distraction and surveillance.

Berry and his friend Wes Jackson argue that the health of our soil depends on a relatively low eyes-to-acres ratio, one that enables a "competent watchfulness."[4] The health of our communities likewise depends on our attention, and yet we often fall back on the easier habits of distraction and surveillance, which are technological substitutes for the hard but necessary work of attention. Our web of screens surrounds us with mirrors that reflect back to us our own desires and preferences, in the process cutting us off from the complex realities of our places. Berry's poems, in contrast, model forms of attention that remind readers they are not the organizing subjects of the world. They portray his place and its members as what the philosopher Jean-Luc Marion calls "saturated phenomena," beings who exist beyond his capacity to see, and so there is always more to which he is obligated to bear witness. Berry's attentive witness to the life of his place deepens his participation in its cycles of death and life, and as he participates more fully, he finds himself seen—not only by the creatures with whom he lives, but ultimately by the Creator who is still at work redeeming and healing creation. Being seen by the resurrecting Creator transforms Berry so that he is better able to know and care for his place, to practice resurrection.

Distraction and Surveillance

Many cultural critics have observed that attention is being reshaped by new digital technologies, particularly the Internet and smartphones. We are now embedded in an "ecosystem of interruption technologies" that fosters a state of "continuous partial attention."[5] When we are at work, attending deeply to an idea or person or task, a smartphone offers the lure of easy entertainment. An infinite banquet of amusing tidbits is only a swipe away. Staying in tension with a recalcitrant reality is hard, and we have always been prone to distractions that relieve this tension by feeding us empty pleasures.

What makes digital distraction technologies particularly damaging is the ease with which they reduce other people and objects to the limits of our own desires and intentions. These technologies constantly tempt us to curate our lives in ways that put ourselves at the center of the universe; we no longer have to encounter others in their embodied complexity. The digital ecosystem reinforces narcissism by providing "a kind of self-centered distraction that reminds us that we are living, present, seen, clicked on, liked."[6] I can go through my day feeling as if the world revolves around me: I see the news filtered through the eyes of my friends, I count how many likes or favorites my updates generate, I order whatever I want to be shipped to my front door. In looking for the next interesting distraction, we turn our attention away from others and toward ourselves; our screens can act like the reflective pool of water in which Narcissus drowned.

Berry mourns the damage these technologies can inflict on our communities, cautioning that they threaten our ability to love one another:

> Looking at screens,
> listening to voices
> in nonexistent distance,
> seeing, hearing nothing
> present, we pass into
> the age of disincarnation,
> the death love finally
> realized as we become
> our pictures adrift,
> homeless in deplaced
> space of the mind only.[7]

The poem's language focuses on the way communication technologies shift the locus of our attention away from an embodied person and toward the medium that promises to make that absent person present. And when we shift our attention, we don't attend to those who are actually present. Berry describes the resulting loss in the ambiguous phrase "the death love finally/ realized." This phrase can, I think, be parsed in at least two ways. One way would render it as "the death [that] love finally/ realized"; the loss of embodied relationship is a kind of death, one felt and mourned by love, which depends on the difficult give-and-take of incarnation. But this phrase could also be read as "the death [of] love finally/ realized"; love itself dies, or at least becomes more shallow, when people relate not to each other but to simulacra. These two complementary readings inform the final image of uprooted identity. When we collapse others to their projection on a screen, we find that we have likewise flattened our own selves. For although social media allow us to quantify our relationships—to know exactly how many friends and followers we have—they do so at the risk of eviscerating these relationships, rendering love into mere connection.[8]

Nevertheless, the lure of instant gratification, new entertainment, and convenience keeps drawing us back to the mirror the Internet holds up for us. While chasing amusement along the pathways of the digital network, it's easy to forget that we are exposing ourselves to surveillance. Surveillance is the flip side of distraction; as we succumb to the easy pleasures of distraction, we open ourselves up to and make ourselves more dependent on surveillance. The most commonly critiqued aspect of surveillance is the way in which governments, corporations, and hackers collect incredible amounts of personal data, viewing their subjects as potential terrorists, customers, or victims.[9] Such digital manifestations of "Big Brother" are updated iterations of Jeremy Bentham's panopticon or Tolkien's ring of power; they see without being seen, and they use the information they gather to gain power or profit.[10]

Yet perhaps a more insidious form of surveillance, because we think of it as voluntary, is the way in which many of us offload attention to technology; being constantly watched by various devices makes our lives easier. As Alan Jacobs provocatively proposes, our dependence on surveillance threatens to replace loving attention: "If Simone Weil is correct in claiming that 'Attention is the rarest and purest form of generosity,' then surveillance is the opposite of attention."[11] Rather than undertaking the difficult work of giving myself to others, it's more convenient to let technology keep tabs on them. The Internet of things offers to survey my surroundings for me: I don't have to know which groceries I need if my refrigerator keeps track for me; I don't have to decide which temperature to set my thermostat to if it automatically adjusts; I don't have to pay attention to my body if my Fitbit monitors it for me.[12]

These examples of digital surveillance may seem innocent enough, but others are more obviously worrisome: farmers don't have to look at their fields if their GPS-equipped tractor keeps track of where they are and how much seed or fertilizer is needed; teachers don't have to know their students if computer programs will figure out what they need; doctors don't need to listen to their patients if the computer will diagnose their illnesses. There can be great benefits to offloading parts of my brain to the cloud and automating rote tasks, but as we outsource more of our responsibilities to technology, we become less aware of and attentive to those around us. Nicholas Carr charts this process in *The Glass Cage: Automation and Us*, arguing that technologies of automation "pull us away from the world."[13] Relying on digital surveillance separates us from our places and communities. As we reduce our interactions with our place to data points, we become less responsive to those around us.

Trusting technology to watch over our places corrodes the bonds of mutual attention that maintain healthy communities. One increasingly common news story goes something like this: someone sees a child alone and, instead of talking to the child, calls the police. Child Protective Services then gets involved in arbitrating whether the parents were negligent or merely giving their child appropriate freedom.[14] As Gracy Olmstead writes about this troubling pattern, "Concerned parents jump first to the State to care for the situation, rather than exercising any sort of personal involvement."[15] The concerned observer who calls the police never makes himself known to the child or his or her parents; like the panoptic algorithms that invisibly watch us, we want to see without being seen. In a surveillance culture, we forget the arts of neighborliness because we no longer need to watch over one another; we outsource that responsibility to Big Brother and erode the reciprocal watching that sustains healthy communities.

In a poem titled "To the National Security Agency," Berry contrasts loving, personal attention with digital, state surveillance, articulating his commitment to forms of mutual attention:

> I am away in a quiet valley,
> am busy at my quiet work
> in this comely small cup of country
> exactly fitted to my mind,
> my mind to it exactly fitted.

Berry is content to live and work in his local place. He finds it "comely" and refuses to allow his attention to be drawn away, outside the "small cup of country" where he dwells. And as the chiasmus in the last two lines I've quoted indicates, there is a reciprocity between his place and his mind; both have changed to fit each other. Even the poem's understated iambic meter conveys the rhythmic delights of the seasonal "time and wear and weather" that shape both his place and himself. Berry's way of attending to and dwelling in his place differs sharply from the National Security Agency's mode of watching its citizens from afar. And Berry concludes his poem by warning them that he also has his eye on them: "There's not much left I want to shoot, / but I would like to shoot a drone."[16]

Distraction and surveillance, these twin substitutes for attention, are ways of disconnecting from the fabric of our places. If the habit of distraction assumes that our place is boring and so allows our thoughts to drift elsewhere, the habit of surveillance separates us from our place by promising to give us control over it, allowing us to survey it from on high and manipulate its pieces to suit our desires. Distraction lures us with the vitality of Dionysian flux—we can float on a random current of hyperlinks—while surveillance promises to reveal or impose an Apollonian order. Thus, both depend on the industrial grammar of division and both generally lead to violence, whether through careless negligence or willful selfishness. When we succumb to the lure of distraction and surveillance, we demand that others conform to our desires instead of conforming our souls to reality so as to better serve others;

we pass into
the age of disincarnation,
the death love finally
realized[17]

instead of practicing resurrection.

Saturated Phenomena and Iconic Mutuality

Attention, as its etymology implies, involves deep mutuality or reciprocity and is thus at the root of love; it makes responsible care possible. To attend to something means literally "to stretch toward" it. The English words *tension, tune,* and *tend* all come from the same Indo-European root meaning "to stretch." *Tend* itself carries a dual meaning that speaks to the nuances embedded in this notion of stretching; "to tend" means both to move toward something, a tendency, and to care for something, to tend a garden, say. So *attention* signifies a relation stretched between two different things. And embedded in the connotations of these related words—to tend to another or to be in tune with another—is the suggestion of propriety in this stretching. When attention is exercised properly, a certain harmonious resonance comes into existence; two different beings, like two different pegs holding a string tightly, relate to each other across the tension of this interval. And while attention maintains a difference between subject and object, we do tend to become more like that which we attend to: we become what we love. It is impossible, then, to attend deeply and not both change and be changed. Sustainable cultures depend on responsible, caring forms of attention rather than on parasitic forms like distraction or destructive ones like surveillance.

As my metaphor of retuning is meant to suggest, Berry's participatory attention to his place ultimately changes him. Throughout his poems, there are moments when, while observing something, he finds his gaze returned—he is seen—and this experience of being seen—of sight as participation—changes him. This redirection of sight is akin to Jean-Luc Marion's phenomenological account of the "saturated phenomena" and iconic modes of perception.[18]

Marion contrasts two modes of seeing, the idolatrous mode and the iconic mode. When we gaze at an idol, we see our own preconceived notion of the divine reflected back to us; an idol limits the infinite to that which we can see, grasp, and contain. So the kind of gaze that an idol invites is a gaze that "settles," that forecloses what might be beyond our expectations. In this way, Marion claims that the "idol thus acts as a mirror, not a portrait: a mirror that reflects the gaze's image, or more exactly, the image of its aim and of the scope of that aim."[19] In

other words, an idol tells us more about the preconceptions and desires of its wor-
shipers than it does about God.

On the other hand, the icon serves to remind the devotee that the invisible
cannot be rendered fully visible, that God always remains beyond our
comprehension:

> Even presented by the icon, the invisible always remains invisible; it is not
> invisible because it is omitted by the aim (*invisable*), but because it is a matter
> of rendering visible this invisible as such—the unenvisageable. . . . The icon
> . . . attempts to render visible the invisible as such, hence to allow that the
> visible not cease to appear to an other than itself, without, however, that
> other ever being reproduced in the visible. Thus the icon shows, strictly
> speaking, nothing. . . . It teaches the gaze. . . . In this sense, the icon makes
> visible only by giving rise to an infinite gaze.[20]

The crucial difference between an idol and an icon, then, is that an idol mirrors
the worshiper's gaze and desires, whereas the icon becomes a window through
which the infinite God sees the worshiper; the icon brings us into a reciprocal
relationship with another whom we cannot grasp. As Marion puts it, "The icon
regards us—it *concerns* us, in that it allows the intention of the invisible to occur
visibly."[21] The result, as Marion writes elsewhere, is that "the constituting subject
is succeeded by the constituted witness."[22] Rather than being the organizing subject who gives meaning to the phenomenon I see, I am the witness of a reality that
gives itself beyond my ability to receive.

Marion's phenomenological account of the givenness of reality corresponds
with the formal composition of Eastern Orthodox religious icons. Berry has
acknowledged his debt to Orthodox theology, and this artistic and theological
tradition may be the source of the iconic features in his poetry.[23] In the Eastern
tradition, icons eschew realism; rather than giving the viewer an illusion of seeing three-dimensional reality, the icon gives the viewer the impression of being
seen by divine reality. There is no light source in an icon (as there is in Western
realism) and thus no shadows either. Instead, the icon itself acts as a light source
that illuminates our world. In addition, icons reverse the lines of perspective.
This is particularly evident in the famous Russian icon of the Trinity, *Troitsa*,
where the chairs on which the two flanking figures sit converge toward us. The
vanishing point is not beyond the surface of the painting but in front of it, where
the viewer stands. The icon literally depicts the persons of the Trinity as seeing
us. The significance of this form is that the icon, because it represents the more
real world of the divine, doesn't allow the viewer to imagine himself as the organizing subject; rather, the lines of perspective are inverted, constituting the
viewer as a witness to a divine reality.

For Marion, and I want to argue for Berry also, it is not just religious icons that have these iconic properties; creation itself is a saturated phenomenon, its beauty and reality always given in a way that exceeds the limits of our gaze.[24] As one of Berry's poems puts it, "The Creator is divided in Creation / for the joys of recognition."[25] Properly attended to, creation acts not as a mirror for our desires but, rather, as a window through which we attend to the Creator and are seen by him.[26] It is this fundamental givenness of creation that calls for an iconic mode of perception. Rather than reducing other creatures to the limits of our conceptual framework or the scope of our desires, we should stand before this unforeseeable gift of others, attempting to receive their being in its fullness.

The techniques of distraction and surveillance that our digital technologies encourage are modes of an idolatrous gaze, modes that shield ourselves from being seen and flatten others so they are less likely to surprise or challenge us. In *The Unforeseen Wilderness,* Berry compares our civilization to a reflective shell that shields us from the creation itself: "The mollusk-shell of our civilization, in which we more and more completely enclose ourselves . . . works . . . as a reflecting surface upon which we cast the self-flattering outlines and the optimistic tints of our preconceptions of what the world is."[27] Berry's analogy is particularly prescient, as he wrote this passage before the proliferation of our reflective screens. So much of the Internet ecosystem is designed to mirror what we already want; we see the news our friends post, get recommendations from Amazon that are based on books we've purchased, and watch movies that Netflix's algorithm thinks we'll like. Social media and the algorithms designed by corporations enclose us in an echo chamber—to switch from a visual to an auditory metaphor—that compounds the perennial human tendency to confirmation bias and results in what some term "cyber-balkanization."[28] We are always tempted to relate to others as idols, to view them through the lens of our desires, and the digital environment in which we increasingly operate fosters such an idolatrous gaze; we are less likely to be surprised or challenged by the unforeseen givenness of another when we encounter that person only in the flat image of a screen that we control. An iconic mode of embodied attention, on the other hand, brings us into a more harmonious relationship with our place, its members, and its redeeming Creator. This is the mode Berry models in his poetry as he participates in the life and redemption of his place.[29]

Bearing Witness

Berry's confidence in the significance of his place and its members motivates him to watch attentively, seeking to bear witness to them even as he knows they will always exceed his understanding or expectations. Citing a scientist who wrote that one tree could reward a lifetime of study, Berry concurs, adding, "Life is a miracle and therefore infinitely of interest everywhere. We have perhaps sufficient testimony, from artists and scientists both, that if we watch, refine our intelligence and our attention, curb our greed and our pride, work with care, have faith, a single tree might be enough."[30] If we grow bored with our spouse, our family members, our neighborhoods, or our towns, the cause may not be their intrinsic boringness, but a failure on our part to attend to them. As Marion puts it, one's ability to perceive another is limited by "the measure of the welcome that each participant can or cannot offer."[31] In other words, our own limitations as witnesses prevent us from recognizing the miraculous life around us.

To be able to participate more fully in the life of his place, Berry roots himself as a kind of "perennial vegetation" and strives to "bear witness as faithfully as possible" to this life.[32] Berry writes in the introduction to *This Day* that his Sunday walks in the local woods shape him to be more welcoming and hospitable to the wonders around him: "I go free from the tasks and intentions of my workdays, and so my mind becomes hospitable to unintended thoughts: to what I am very willing to call inspiration."[33] This persistent practice of hospitality enables him to be open to receive and marvel at the unforeseen, unexpected moments of beauty that continually retune him to the life of his place.

One poetic result of this hospitable attention is Berry's use of litanies in many of his poems. Such lists function as "an inventory / Of wonders and of uncommercial goods."[34] In one poem, after acknowledging the far-off, ongoing "war to end war," he returns to focus on his ewes preparing to give birth, the trees opening their leaves, the river flowing steadily by, the spring flowers blooming once more, and he concludes this litany of the mundane by stating, "This then may be the prayer without ceasing, / this beauty and gratitude, this moment."[35] Instead of allowing himself to be distracted by distant news about which he can do nothing, Berry chooses to attend to the life of his place and to witness its variety and vitality by listing its newsworthy events.

A more extensive litany forms the entirety of "The Satisfactions of the Mad Farmer," which begins:

> Growing weather; enough rain;
> the cow's udder tight with milk;
> the peach tree bent with its yield;
> honey golden in the white comb.[36]

The poem continues listing those good things inherent in the farmer's place and work. Such simple litanies may not seem very significant, but they name and bear witness to the glories present in our place, glories we can participate in as we stretch toward them. He would concur with the British nature writer Robert

Macfarlane, who writes that "language deficit leads to attention deficit," which in turn reduces our ability to know and care for our fellow creatures.[37]

Such stretching is not a onetime achievement; rather, it is a continual process. In "To What Listens," Berry begins by emphasizing his repeated efforts to understand a wren's seemingly joyful yet gratuitous song:

> I come to it again
> and again, the thought of the wren
> opening his song here
> to no human ear.

While Berry enjoys the bird's song, he is troubled by the knowledge that he himself will die, and the future human inhabitants of the land may disregard this song. In spite of Berry's good work and the beauty of the bird's song, "The farm will sink then / from all we have done and said." Yet he, like the bird, still finds the place beautiful and lovely: "how well I like it / as it is!" And he testifies to his love by listing what he sees: the river, the trees, the house, the pasture—all these make up a beloved yet fragile place. This litany gives Berry the courage to respond in kind to the wren's song: "Its songs and loves throb / in my head till like the wren / I sing—to what listens—again."[38] The lives of this place will pass into death, and yet it is still proper to attend to and delight in them. The concluding couplet inverts the opening rhyme, and this chiastic frame acts as Berry's response to the wren's call. His poetry takes up the bird's song and responds in kind.[39]

Like the birds who sing their same songs over and over again, in pure delight, Berry endeavors to see again and again. G. K. Chesterton notes—in a passage that coincides with Marion's phenomenology—that though we get bored with repetition, this is a reflection of our limited capacity to perceive and delight: "Perhaps God is strong enough to exult in monotony. It is possible that God says every morning, 'Do it again' to the sun; and every evening, 'Do it again' to the moon. It may not be automatic necessity that makes all daisies alike; it may be that God makes every daisy separately, but has never got tired of making them."[40] Berry's repeated litanies are the fruit of his efforts to see and name the members of his place again and again, enjoying them with the Creator's unending delight.

Participating in the life of a place merely by attending to it may seem too passive, yet as Berry's poetry attests, such attention shapes and retunes his understanding of where he is. We may think that we are more likely to perceive the miraculous nature of life in new settings or spectacular and unique places, but for Berry, it is precisely in watching his familiar place that he is most often surprised. As he writes,

> To one who has watched here many years,
> all of this is familiar. And yet

none of it has ever happened
before as it is happening now.[41]

In an essay that also links Marion's understanding of the icon with Berry's perception of his place, Bryan Wallis argues that for Berry the local, familiar place
provides more opportunities for the distortions and inadequacies of an idolatrous gaze to be corrected: "this shift occurs on the scale of the local because it is
the intimacy with the local, one's immediate surrounding that one has come to
know well, that tends to reveal its saturation and mystery."[42] This is why Berry
finds his local place both necessary and endlessly interesting even after many
years of watching.[43]

Berry's poems often record moments of surprise or correction, times when
his expectations are overturned by what he sees. In one poem he begins by offering an interpretation of the mockingbird's repeated song: "At first I called him
silly / and egotistical." But the next stanza corrects what may have been a naive
understanding—"And then I said, 'He's right!' "—and provides an alternative
interpretation of the mockingbird's indiscriminating mimicry.[44] Listening over a
long period revises Berry's initial impressions and deepens his sympathy for the
bird. In another poem Berry sees a hummingbird scratch its cheek while flying in
midair, and he exclaims, "Wonderful!":

> I never dreamed
> of such a thing before, and now
> after seventy-seven years
> of watching, I have seen it![45]

Such noticing invites readers to share in the poet's wonder and gratitude at such
unexpected moments of beauty.

Faithfully watching his place, and not turning away in boredom or seeking
to manipulate his fellow creatures, doesn't just cause Berry to better understand
them, it also enables him to witness the Creator's redemptive work in the midst
of death and loss. When faced with loss, our tendency is often to turn away, to
distract ourselves, particularly if we are somehow complicit in this loss. If we do
manage to stay engaged, we may seek to fix the problem quickly, looking for a
painless solution. These are the twin temptations of distraction and surveillance
rearing their heads again. Berry models a third way, patiently facing loss and
death. And as he remains attentive even to painful realities, he sees the Creator's
hand at work redeeming what Berry himself cannot.

"The Slip" exemplifies the way patient attention allows Berry to perceive
redemption in the midst of loss. The poem's title refers to an acre of land that
slipped into the river and was washed away. A place that once supported the life

of trees and grass and cattle is now simply gone. As Berry reflects on this loss, he confesses that human use contributed to the damage:

> Human wrong is in the cause, human
> ruin in the effect—but no matter;
> all will be lost, no matter the reason.
> Nothing, having arrived, will stay.[46]

Berry's "no matter" may seem callous, but it balances a difficult truth; human misuse and abuse are complicit in this loss, but loss and destruction are inherent in natural cycles, and even good human work cannot prevent them.

Even as the poem articulates this stark acceptance of loss, however, its language begins to point toward divine redemption. The nothingness left by the slip is like the nothingness "before the beginning" when the Creator spoke. Thus, "this nothing / is the seed of all—the clear eye / of Heaven." What we see as death is, from heaven's perspective, an opportunity for re-creation:

> The maker moves
> in the unmade, stirring the water until
> it clouds, dark beneath the surface,
> stirring and darkening the soul until pain
> perceives new possibility.[47]

This image seems to combine two biblical scenes: the original creation, when "darkness was upon the face of the deep. And the Spirit of God moved upon the face of the waters," and the Pool of Bethesda, where "an angel went down at a certain time into the pool and stirred up the water; then whoever stepped in first, after the stirring of the water, was made well of whatever disease he had."[48] As Berry watches the river flow through what used to be healthy farmland, he mourns the loss, but he also "perceives new possibility," possibility that depends on the God who created the world and who continues to redeem and heal it.

Our human responsibility, then, is to participate in this redemption, first by attending to it and only then by fitting our work to its pattern:

> There is nothing
> to do but learn and wait, return to work
> on what remains. Seed will sprout in the scar.
> Though death is in the healing, it will heal.[49]

Rather than swiping away the unpleasantness of death or seeking technological means to gain control over it, attention brings us face to face with death. Berry gains the courage to confront loss as he witnesses the Maker still moving in the unmade, and this perception gives him the deep joy of recognizing the Creator in creation.

Being Witnessed

Berry's patient attention, even to painful sources of loss, leads to the joyful opportunity to see the redeeming Creator at work. But it's not just that he witnesses the Creator healing a broken creation. As he watches God at work around him, he finds himself likewise attended to and healed by the Creator. In other words, as Berry resists an idolatrous view of the world, the reality he attends to becomes an iconic window through which the Creator sees him. And when he is seen by the Creator, Berry himself is transformed and healed.[50]

There are many poems in which this shift from watching to being watched occurs, but I'll look at just three. One of Berry's longer sabbath poems, "The Book of Camp Branch," explores the analogies between a flowing stream and language itself.[51] Near the end of the poem, the poet's efforts to use language to describe the stream falter as he reflects on what is lost in the translation from the stream to his words about the stream:

> "Make sense," I told myself,
> the song of the tumbling waters
> in my ears. The sense you make
> may make its way along the stream,
> but it will not be the stream's sense
> you make, nor yet your own
> quite, for the flux of language
> will make its claim too
> upon the sense you make.[52]

> The words fall at last
> onto the page, the turning leaf
> in the Book of Camp Branch
> in time's stream. As the eye,
> as the mind, moves from
> moving water to turning page,
> what is lost? What, worse,
> is lost if the words falsify
> the stream in your walk beside it?
> To be carried or to resist
> you must be a stone
> in the way. You must be
> a stone rolled away.[53]

This final image indicates that while words can falsify the stream they describe, the poet's ongoing efforts to shape words to fit reality change the poet himself.

The stone that alters the flow of the stream or the flow of language is itself rolled away. What seems to happen is that as the poet speaks and carefully tries to make sense—like a person walking down a stream along its boulders—he is transformed from "a stone in the way" to "a stone rolled away." In attentively listening to the music of Camp Branch, the poet has relinquished total control over his own song—he has died to his individual desires—and been resurrected into a communal harmony, one he learns as he steps along the boulders. He goes from the one speaking and seeing and trying to make sense, to the one spoken to and seen and made sense of. To put this in the terms of the etymological roots of attention—tension or musical tuning—there comes a point when the poet does not just attend to the world, but finds himself held in a line of tension between self and world. The poet is attended to as much as the poet attends to. He goes from the one attending to the one being tuned.

The allusion here to the stone rolled away from Christ's grave is reinforced in the final line of the poem, where the water that flows ever downward "by the sun is raised / again into the air."[54] While this literally describes the process by which water evaporates, it also alludes to the spiritual power that effects this shift: the water goes from being the shaping, active power to being the object of the sun's resurrecting power. Similarly, the poet goes from being the wielder of language, the one making meaning, to being the one seen and acted on. To practice resurrection, to tend the health of his place, Berry must first be resurrected himself. Attention changes us, bringing us in tune with the conditions and needs of our places, so that we can see them more accurately.

In two additional poems in which a similar shift occurs, Berry draws directly on the features of Orthodox iconography to convey his sense of being seen and the personal transformation this effects. The first of these poems reflects on how the incarnation has forever changed our relationship to the mundane, physical world in which we dwell. Even the simple act of walking out to the barn is now imbued with eternal significance:

> Remembering that it happened once,
> We cannot turn away the thought,
> As we go out, cold, to our barns
> Toward the long night's end, that we
> Ourselves are living in the world
> It happened in when it first happened.[55]

Because God was once born in a humble barn, all barns remain open to the possibility of the divine presence. Berry goes on to describe a vision of the holy family in his barn, concluding that they stand "in light / That lights them from no source we see." This description parallels the lighting in religious icons, where there is no definitive light source. Rather, the icon itself acts as a source of light that illuminates the viewer from a divine perspective.

Seeing the quotidian world illuminated by this divine radiance changes everything. The poet finds himself "Looking into another world / That is this world"; the cattle are still there, and he still has his work to do, yet his relation to his place has been transformed:

> we are here
> As we have never been before,
> Sighted as not before, our place
> Holy, although we knew it not.[56]

Caught in the light of this religious vision, the poet finds himself "sighted"; he is the object of a divine gaze. Participating in this mutual attention leads the poet to revise his understanding of his place. Where before he may have seen just an ordinary barn with its allotment of animals, he now knows that he inhabits a holy place. The sustained attention Berry gives his place, an attention that tunes him to its cycles and deepens his understanding of its inhabitants, culminates in a religious experience whereby he is constituted as a witness to its divine reality.

A similar epiphany occurs in one of Berry's more unusual sabbath poems, an ekphrastic poem written in response to Piero's fresco *The Resurrection*. What's particularly notable is the way in which the poet's close attention to the painting itself suddenly results in an awareness that the poet is incredibly *seen*:

> *"Why seek ye the living among the dead?"*
>
> Early in the year by my friend's gift
> I saw at Sansepolcro Piero's vision:
> The soldiers who guard the dead from the living
> themselves become as dead men, one
> tumbling dazedly backward. Awake, his wounds
> bleeding still, his foot upon the tomb, Christ
> who bore our life to its most wretched end,
> having thrust off like a blanket the heavy lid,
> stands. But for his face and countenance
> I have found no words: powerful beyond life
> and death, seeing beyond sight or light,
> beyond all triumph serene. All this Piero saw.
> And we who were sleeping, seeking the dead
> among the dead, dare to be awake. We who see
> see we are forever seen, by sight have been

forever changed. The morning at last
has come. The trees, once bare, are green.[57]

As Berry describes the painting, he discovers that Christ's face is literally unsayable; Marion's term "unenvisageable" is particularly apt here. Berry experiences a Dantean failure of language at the sight of the resurrected Christ. All he knows is that this face sees beyond sight or light, and this awareness of being caught in this seeing beyond sight wakes us up: "we who were sleeping . . . dare to be awake." The experience of being seen intensifies our attention. In fact, one of its effects is to broaden the poet's "I" to include "we"; in the gaze of the risen Christ, the poet becomes aware of himself as a member of a community composed of those who see that they are seen.

The syntax is intentionally ambiguous regarding the "sight" that is the agent of these changes: is it the sight by which we see or the sight by which we are seen? *Both,* the poem suggests. At this moment of heightened attention, when our gaze is returned from the icon, sight ceases to be a one-way act and becomes a mutual participation. Subject and object are both subject and object. Each is tuned toward the other, and the harmony produced by this attention transforms both the participants and their surroundings. For not only have we been forever changed, but the "trees, once bare, are green." As in Piero's painting, where the bare branches on the left are transformed into the new green of spring on the right, Berry's poem emphasizes that all creation participates in Christ's resurrection. Resurrection is at once theological and ecological. And through such iconic attention, we can take part in this resurrection that is healing a broken creation.

Practicing Attention

In one of his most well-known poems, "How to Be a Poet (to remind myself)," Berry offers a set of guidelines to cultivate this iconic attention. The poem begins with three short sentences that cover only two lines: "Make a place to sit down. / Sit down. Be quiet." These short sentences resist quick reading. They slow readers down, inviting them to pause at the end of each period. Such a deliberate, patient mode of being, Berry suggests, requires that we look away from our screens:

> Communicate slowly. Live
> a three-dimensioned life;
> stay away from screens.
> Stay away from anything
> that obscures the place it is in.

His efforts to slow down are motivated by his desire to attend more faithfully to his place. And Berry finds that often when he quiets himself and looks around him, he receives the gift of inspiration. The Muse, the Creator, speaks into the hospitable space the poet's attention holds open:

> Accept what comes from silence.
> Make the best you can of it.
> Of the little words that come
> out of the silence, like prayers
> prayed back to the one who prays,
> make a poem that does not disturb
> the silence from which it came.[58]

Again, Berry's making—*poem* comes from a Greek word that means, literally, "a made thing"—is the result of attending patiently and then receiving and shaping what comes from his place. His attention makes room for inspiration: he does not just attend, he is attended to; he does not just pray, he receives "prayers / prayed back to the one who prays."

Berry's poetic forms provide practical guidance for fostering such hospitable attention. Get away from screens. Name and list the creatures who share your place. Be willing to revise your initial impressions, particularly of the people and places you think you already know. Cultivate a craft that requires you to attend to the physicality of your material. For Berry, one such craft is poetry—he shapes his poems out of the "flux of language"—but for others this mutual attention might be found in the way a carpenter works with the grain of the wood, or a cook adjusts the thickness of a roux, or a teacher modifies instruction to fit the interests of a particular child. We can all attend to the people and creatures with whom we live and work. And as we do so, Berry's poems suggest that these others may become icons through whom we will receive gifts of life and redemption. As we receive these gifts, we will be more richly constituted ourselves, healed of the thinness brought about through distraction and surveillance. When we lose ourselves in attending to others, we receive a richer self in return.

The attention that Berry's poetry models forms the indispensable basis for a sustainable culture, one in which human inhabitants cultivate hospitable, reciprocal relationships with the other members of their places. Such attentive relationships constitute us as witnesses who are able to tend our neighbors. When we relate to the world as organizing subjects, surrounding ourselves with two-dimensional screens that mirror our own desires, we become increasingly flat ourselves and less able to know and love others. Many have argued that our digital habits of distraction and surveillance develop what Edward Mendelson calls a "permeable, and transient sense of self."[59] Perhaps the best phrase is from Bilbo Baggins, who said that carrying the ring of power—a technology of surveillance par excellence—made him "feel all thin, sort of *stretched*, . . . like butter that has been scraped over too much bread."[60] Bilbo is describing the flat, two-dimensioned sense of self fostered by an idolatrous way of seeing—a self that is stretched out aimlessly rather than stretched toward others. Alternatively, encountering others in their embodied givenness, as icons, constitutes a more communal, loving self.[61] When we are addressed by members we don't evade or survey or fully understand, we develop a deeper sense of self, one that is better able to care for others in their real complexity.

Some of the technologies I've criticized in this chapter may indeed help us reduce our energy consumption and find more healthy ways of living. If, however, we rely on these digital technologies to care for our places so that we don't have to, we will neglect the more important and difficult work of developing more attentive, caring selves. To tend others, we must first be given selves who can tend. The sustained attention that Berry's poetry cultivates addresses this root problem because it makes us visible to those around us. Seen by our fellow creatures, we find ourselves revealed more fundamentally than when we merely gaze at our own desires reflected back from the screens around us. As C. S. Lewis writes in the context of friendship, "In each of my friends there is something that only some other friend can fully bring out."[62] Every deep relationship changes and stretches us, revealing aspects of our selves that would otherwise not be developed. By attending to others, by stretching toward those around us, we find ourselves transformed: "We who see / see we are forever seen, by sight have been / forever changed." Attention thus changes not only our way of relating to others, but also our very selves, tuning us so that we can better tend the health of our places.

2

Gratitude

In the summer of 2014, many individuals across the developed world began see-ing videos of their friends dumping ice water on themselves. If a friend called you out by name, or tagged you on social media, you then had twenty-four hours to either pour ice water on yourself or make a donation toward research to treat ALS. The "ALS Ice Bucket Challenge" may have raised some money, but any last-ing benefits it had remain unclear, and it's symptomatic of our culture's self-centered approach to complex problems.[1]

Because our digital environments so often reflect our own desires and selves back to us, because they tell us that we are at the center of the world, they can fos-ter the perception that solving global problems depends on our own efforts. When faced with major problems—hunger, species loss, topsoil erosion, intrac-table diseases—we can feel a vague pressure to do something. Maybe we donate money to a nonprofit or post a story on social media or take part in the ice bucket challenge, but all the while we remain removed or buffered from the actual prob-lem. We want the good feelings that come from being involved in the solution without the vulnerability of being involved in the problem.[2] Central to the good feelings we get from helping others is the idea of *credit*; we want credit for the good that we do—whether in the form of recognition, honor, or self-satisfaction. This desire for credit may provoke us to take action, but it places an overwhelm-ing burden on individuals. Knowing that we are finite and that our lives and efforts will end in death, we may be tempted to work frantically, trying to accom-plish as much as possible before our end. Alternatively, we may simply throw up our hands and become apathetic, resigning ourselves to inevitable failure. Nei-ther of these tendencies serves a sustainable culture, and we most often vacillate between them.

Berry's posture of restful gratitude embodies the third way of sustainable cul-tures. Rather than merely questioning our motives for helping others or critiqu-ing our tendency to aggrandize ourselves, Berry's poetry proposes an even more radical shift. Instead of seeking credit, Berry's poems acknowledge his unpayable debts. As his attention ushers him into a wondrous, unexpectedly *given* world, he comes to rest in the presence of his fellow creatures and their Creator. If who we are is ultimately dependent on a life we have been given, then serving others is not a choice that redounds to my credit—it's an obligation that defines my very self. In one of his first sabbath poems, Berry describes how recognizing the world as given beyond his capacity to receive it redefines his mind and self:

> The mind that comes to rest is tended
> In ways that it cannot intend:
> Is borne, preserved, and comprehended
> By what it cannot comprehend.
>
> Your Sabbath, Lord, thus keeps us by
> Your will, not ours. And it is fit
> Our only choice should be to die
> Into that rest, or out of it.[3]

Berry comes to rest as he finds that his life is tended and cared for beyond his understanding. Receiving the gifts of life enables him to receive death as a gift also. As Berry writes, we cannot escape death. Our only choice in the matter is how we will die: we can try to forestall it and work harder and faster to get as much accomplished before our end, or we can rest in the grace of the one who gives life and death. If life is a gift, one we cannot earn or manufacture or control, then we sustain it by participating in this economy of giving. Despite the industrial economy's pressures to work harder and accrue more credit to one's name, Berry practices the sabbath as a means of dwelling gratefully in a gift economy.

Earlier in the poem Berry describes this gift economy in terms of the natural cycles of death, decay, and rebirth:

> Past life
> Lives in the living. Resurrection
> Is in the way each maple leaf
> Commemorates its kind, by connection
>
> Outreaching understanding. What rises
> Rises into comprehension
> And beyond. Even falling raises
> In praise of light. What is begun
>
> Is unfinished. And so the mind
> That comes to rest among the bluebells
> Comes to rest in motion, refined
> By alteration. The bud swells,

Opens, makes seed, falls, is well,
Being becoming what it is:
Miracle and parable
Exceeding thought.[4]

Though this natural economy of giving remains beyond Berry's ability to articulate—it "outreach[es] understanding" and "exceed[s] thought"—he describes its form in terms of resurrection. In "the standing Sabbath/Of the woods," tree leaves open, flourish, and fall to enrich the soil. Similarly, bluebell seeds fall, sprout, and open into beautiful flowers. Praise and thanks characterize the members of these cycles as "even falling raises/In praise of light." Inspired by these resurrecting patterns, Berry "comes to rest in motion." In this place, he realizes that he is not the source or manufacturer of life, but its grateful recipient and participant. Thus, the motion or pattern of this sabbath life is one not of frenzied activity, but of cyclical participation in the natural patterns by which the redeeming Creator sustains his world.

As this poem suggests, Berry's sabbath poems, a project he began in 1979, form part of his attempt to join in this "praise of light." As such, they counter our industrial culture's obsession with busyness and productivity, an obsession that not only leads to our frantic pace of life, but also contributes to a false view of the self as the source of life. In contrast to this, Berry understands the Christian sabbath to signify both the Creator's rest at the conclusion of his work of creation—it is very good—and Christ's resurrection on the first day of the week, the day most Christians now celebrate as the sabbath. As the poem I cited above indicates, Berry's model for how to participate in this gift economy is the woods. The trees form a "timbered choir" whose praise takes the shape of leaves that receive the light, flourish, and then die to enrich the next generation.[5] Given this underlying faith in the Creator's good, redemptive work, Berry offers his own agricultural and poetic work as a way of joining with the Creator's sustaining work. His efforts don't manufacture life or control it; they participate in creation's ongoing life.

Organizing Subject or Grateful Recipient

In the last chapter, I relied on Jean-Luc Marion's distinction between two forms of seeing: an idolatrous gaze that projects our own desires and expectations on those around us, and an iconic mode of sight that recognizes our neighbors and fellow creatures as more complex than we can understand and so endeavors to receive them ever more fully. These two different modes of seeing help illuminate the significance of Berry's poetic forms of attention, forms through which he endeavors to witness others faithfully and, ultimately, to be witnessed by them so that he can enter into deep, sustaining relationships with them. In this chapter, to elucidate the grateful rest that Berry's poems embody, I want to turn to a related contrast that Marion makes between the self as subject and the self as recipient. In brief, an idolatrous gaze comes from and reinforces an understanding of the self as the organizing subject of the world, whereas an iconic mode of sight comes from and reinforces an understanding of the self as the recipient of a given world.

Marion critiques the metaphysical subject posited most famously by Descartes's "I think, therefore I am." As a grammatical subject, "I" survey and act on a world of objects whose value and meaning I ascribe. Thus, Marion points out that the subject claims to "possess or produce phenomenon"; as a subject, I can own and manufacture others.[6] This is the kind of self reinforced by a smartphone that allows us to swipe and tap our way to whatever world we desire. Charles Taylor develops a related description of the modern subject that he terms a "buffered self."[7] The buffered self is autonomous, atomized, and disconnected from the world. This grants the self a sense of freedom, safety, and power, but it also renders the world "disenchanted" and forces individuals to choose for themselves what to see as meaningful and significant.[8]

Rather than this buffered self, the self as determining subject, Berry's poems model a grateful self, which is akin to Marion's "recipient" or "gifted."[9] If the subject comes before the object and sees it, the "receiver comes after the phenomenon" that gives itself, and the recipient is thereby constituted by the gift.[10] This notion of being constituted as a self by the phenomena that give themselves to us may seem absurd to those of us accustomed to think of ourselves as "buffered," autonomous agents. Our culture has become adept at masking our inevitable, ongoing dependence on others. Marion points to the origin of the self as paradigmatic: "My birth, which fixes my most singular identity even more than my existence, nevertheless happens without and before me—without my having to know about it or say a word, without my knowing or foreseeing anything."[11] Not only did our parents give us life, they also cared for us when we were utterly dependent, and they gave us the language by which we make sense of the world. Moreover, we all depend daily on clean air and water, on fertile topsoil and bright sun. A farmer like Berry, dependent as he is on the vagaries of weather and the obstinate individuality of livestock, has a hard time pretending he is an autonomous subject who can impose his will on the objects around him.[12]

We receive our selves not only in this physical sense, but also in the ways that we perceive and understand our world. We make sense of others only in response to the ways they first give themselves to us through our senses and intuitions. And others always give themselves beyond our capacity to understand; this is why Berry writes that a single tree can reward a lifetime of study. It is this priority of givenness that Berry articulates in "The Book of Camp Branch" when he tells himself to "make sense" while acknowledging that the sense he makes will be shaped both by the stream along which he walks and the language in which he shapes his thoughts: these phenomena are prior to Berry and give themselves to him beyond his ability to comprehend.[13] So instead of trying to assert some impossible autonomy, Berry freely acknowledges his indebtedness to others and comes to rest in the grace of a given world; he allows himself to be "borne, preserved, and comprehended / By what [he] cannot comprehend."[14] To receive the given self, one must first die to the autonomous self. This is why Berry chooses to die into sabbath rest. Practicing the sabbath, then, forms Berry to be a more grateful recipient of the given world.

What are the gifts, precisely, that are so difficult for the subject or buffered self to receive? Berry's sabbath poems suggest the two fundamental gifts we struggle to accept are creation and redemption. We want to think we deserve some credit for life, both our own and the lives we tend and benefit from, and we want credit for the good that results from our work. If we imagine ourselves as subjects, we can take credit for seeing, manufacturing, and owning others as commodities, but if we understand ourselves as recipients of a given life, then we have to acknowledge our indebtedness and dependence. This is incredibly difficult to do. As Marion writes, "There is actually nothing easy even about deciding to receive. First, because receiving might imply receiving what one did not expect or what one did not want, even what one feared the most. . . . Next, in order to decide to receive, one must have more than the desire to possess or the search for one's own interest, but one must clearly renounce the independence that permits oneself to be convinced that 'I owe no one anything.'" So being a recipient not only means that I might receive gifts I do not want—pain, loss, even death— it also calls into question the buffered self's perception of an autonomous identity—I can no longer define who I am. The "gratuity places in question nothing less than the autarky of the self and its pretensions to auto-sufficiency. To decide to receive the gift amounts to deciding to become obligated by the gift."[15]

A subject, however, strives to reject this obligation because it undermines the self-sufficiency that grounds the subject. One consequence, then, of viewing the self as subject is the commodification of relationships; human relationships that should be defined by deep self-giving are too often conducted by means of quid pro quo negotiations in an attempt to preserve one's individual rights and autonomy. For the subject, marriages begin not with vows of self-giving but with prenuptial contracts, children become means by which we can achieve our thwarted dreams (just watch the parents at your local Little League game), and friendships are leveraged via LinkedIn to advance one's career. As Marion explains, the subject strives (impossibly) to owe no one anything. Hence, when subjects are involved, givenness collapses into exchange. Marion follows Derrida, then, when he explains that "as long as the ego remains, givenness ceases. It only appears when the ego is bracketed."[16] The subject's ego imagines that he deserves life and redemption, and hence he refuses to accept them as gifts: "The ungrateful person . . . does not refuse this or that gift with this or that objective support; he refuses the debt, or rather, the self-avowal of being indebted."[17] How do we escape this "economic horizon of exchange" and recover the possibility of giving and receiving? According to Marion, we must first "recogniz[e] that the principle 'I owe no one anything' . . . admit[s] at least one exception."[18] We have to acknowledge that our lives and identities are not self-created but are dependent on the gifts we receive from others. When we hold a newborn infant or tend an aging parent, we are reminded that any pretensions we have to autonomy and self-reliance are fragile and temporary.

This distinction in understanding myself as a grateful recipient instead of an organizing subject is not mere quibbling over semantics. How we understand ourselves has far-reaching consequences. Viewing the self as a subject is damaging in that it authorizes me to treat other people and creatures as mere objects to be manipulated for my benefit.[19] Furthermore, rather than receiving life as a gift, an industrial culture encourages its subjects to try to hoard life in order to insulate themselves from its unpredictability. Buffered selves work frantically to manufacture and store wealth so that, like the rich man in Jesus' parable who built more barns, they can then "eat, drink, and be merry."[20] Of course, like the rich man, they find that all their efforts cannot prevent their own deaths.

If you are reading this book, however, you probably don't need to be convinced that commodifying and hoarding creation for individual gain is destructive. There are more subtle ways, though, in which the buffered self impairs sustainable cultures. In particular, efforts to live a healthy life can be co-opted by the frenzied busyness that characterizes mass movements. If we imagine that life and meaning depend on our own efforts, we are driven to try to accomplish more. Thomas Merton, citing Douglas Steere, laments that many nonviolent activists succumb to this temptation: "The rush and pressure of modern life are a form, perhaps the most common form, of its innate violence. To allow oneself to be carried away by a multitude of conflicting concerns, to surrender to too many demands, to commit oneself to too many projects, to want to help everyone in everything is to succumb to violence."[21] Even when trying to do good and improve the world, we often do so from the position of a subject, which leads to a flurry of activity without effecting real change. In fact, the main result of such activity is to further enshrine a false sense of the self as subject. In critiquing this damaging busyness, Walter Brueggemann writes that "multitasking is the drive to be more than we are, to control more than we do, to extend our power and our effectiveness. Such practice yields a divided self, with full attention given to nothing."[22]

Such frenzied activity perpetuates a flawed view of the self and inhibits fundamental change.

Viewing the self as a subject also hinders the formation of sustainable cultures because it encourages me to join movements based on how they will affect my personal identity. Our expressivist culture is obsessed with identity and authenticity, and constant efforts to shape my image isolate and exhaust me while corroding the bonds that form interdependent communities.[23] It's easy to want to accomplish more not so that I can better serve others or participate more deeply in the abundant life of my place, but, rather, so that I can be recognized as a good, important person. Subjects choose to participate in various movements, then, as a kind of virtue signaling: I'm the type of subject who supports environmental causes or ALS research. Writing in the 1970s, Berry worries that these dynamics will doom the environmental movement to achieve only the limited success of other popular movements: "It seems to me that the Civil Rights Movement and the Peace Movement, as popular causes in the electronic age, have partaken far too much of the nature of fads."[24] Of course, social media have only exacerbated the tendency for movements to become mere opportunities to burnish one's self-image. Berry goes on to explain that popular causes rarely achieve lasting change because their supporters remain personally disconnected from their activism. If individuals voluntarily choose to support a cause as an expression of their identity, they will back up this choice with various public gestures, but their support will probably fade away when they become burned out or when another issue becomes the cause célèbre. In fact, such expressions may actually reduce more genuine support because of what psychologists term "moral self-licensing"; when I perform some gesture that makes me feel good about myself, I'm more likely to give myself permission to slack off in the future.[25]

If we understand ourselves as subjects, we may justify busy activism by claiming that our work is necessary and that it does good things for others. Yet such efforts will inevitably fall short because sustainability isn't a commodity that one can produce or manufacture; it's a process that we receive and participate in. Berry's poetry practices a sabbath gratitude that counters the subject's frenzied efforts. This mode of grateful reception reminds us that all our efforts can't manufacture life. Our work does not produce meaning but, at best, enables us to participate in an abundantly given world. This realization frees me to rest, knowing that the world doesn't depend on my efforts and that my work merely participates in the gifts of life and meaning I receive from others. In the remainder of this chapter, I consider Berry's sabbath poems through the lens of two potential objections to his mode of grateful rest. To those who might see gratitude as a sentimental tactic to avoid the painful aspects of life, Berry offers a rich notion of sabbath as a day when even death is redeemed, and to those who see gratitude as passive or constricting, Berry's poetry offers the image of trees whose lives participate in the sustenance of their place.

Receiving Sabbath Rest and Redemption

If the organizing subject's core error is to try to commodify and control life, practicing the sabbath can act as an antidote. As Brueggemann writes, "Sabbath is a big no . . . to the worship of commodity; it is no to the pursuit of commodity. But it is more than no. Sabbath is the regular, disciplined, visible, concrete yes to the neighborly reality of the community beloved by God."[26] Berry's sabbath poems record his ongoing, concrete yes to this divinely sustained community. In the introduction to *This Day: Collected and New Sabbath Poems*, Berry labels himself a "bad-weather churchgoer," explaining that Sundays when the weather is good, or even "only tolerable," he doesn't attend church and instead walks the woods and stream banks near his farm. If the inspiration comes, he writes a poem, and if not, that is good also, for to "be quiet, wordless, in a good place is a better gift than poetry."[27]

Berry's poetic rest is modeled after and participates in the Creator's rest. As he describes it, "The sabbath is the day, and the successive days honoring the day, when God rested after finishing the work of creation. This work was not finished, I think, in the sense of once and for all. It was finished by being given the power to exist and to continue, even to repair itself as it is now doing on the reforested hillsides of my home country."[28] By resting on the sabbath, and walking through places whose health and flourishing don't depend on any human effort, Berry reminds himself that all his work depends on Nature's ongoing, sustaining cycles: "We are to rest on the sabbath also, I have supposed, in order to understand that the providence or the productivity of the living world, the most essential work, continues while we rest. This work is entirely independent of our work, and is far more complex and wonderful than any work we have ever done or will ever do."[29] This "standing Sabbath / of the woods" reminds Berry that, unlike Marion's subject, he does not "possess or produce" life; he stands as its grateful recipient.[30]

Berry's understanding of the sabbath includes the sense not only of rest but also of redemption; he can rest because he knows that nature renews and sustains life. Even in the Old Testament, the sabbath did not honor just God's rest after creation, but also his redemption of the Israelites from Egypt. When God gave Moses the Ten Commandments, which included the injunction to keep the sabbath, he began by reminding the Israelites that he had delivered them from Egypt, and when Moses recounted these commandments in Deuteronomy, this link between the sabbath and redemption became explicit: "Remember that thou wast a servant in the land of Egypt, and that the Lord thy God brought thee out thence through a mighty hand and by a stretched out arm: therefore the Lord thy God commanded thee to keep the sabbath day."[31] Israel can rest because its redemption comes from God rather than its own toil.

This redemptive significance becomes more central for Christians who now celebrate the sabbath not on the seventh day of the week, the day on which God rested after creation, but on the first day of the week, the day Christ rose from the grave. And it is this resurrection that promises the Creator's continuing, redemptive presence. Berry imagines each sabbath, then, as "the morning / also of the resurrection of Jesus."[32] Berry experiences this resurrecting power on his quiet Sunday morning walks through the woods. As he explains, "The idea of the sabbath gains in meaning as it is brought out-of-doors and into a place where nature's principles of self-sustaining wholeness and health are still evident." These ecological principles parallel the religious significance of the sabbath; the "fundamental miracle" through which death and decay serve life and beauty is both "natural and . . . supernatural."[33] His sabbath walks remind Berry that the order he cultivates on his farm ultimately depends not on his own efforts, but on the miraculous gift of life, on the "hard travail" of the God who "rests in rising."[34] His primary responsibility is to receive this creative, redemptive, sustaining gift.

This emphasis on redemption and wholeness may strike some as sentimental, as if it glosses over the painful aspects of life, most notably death. The Buddhist poet Gary Snyder, when reading early drafts of Berry's first sabbath poems, was put off by Berry's reliance on overt Christian theology and warned Berry to "beware of hymnal language-tone." In one of the poems he sent to Snyder, Berry celebrates the sustaining cycles of death, decay, and rebirth and concludes with an image that echoes the end of "Manifesto: The Mad Farmer's Liberation Front." That poem instructs readers to

> Be like the fox
> who makes more tracks than necessary,
> some in the wrong direction.
> Practice resurrection.[35]

In this early sabbath poem, Berry describes a fox whose mysterious yet purposeful path is an analogue to the mysterious, redemptive cycles of nature:

> Ruin is in place here:
> The dead leaves rotting on the ground,
> The live leaves in the air
> Are gathered in a single dance
> That turns them round and round.
> The fox cub trots his almost pathless path
> As silent as his absence.

> These passings resurrect
> A joy without defect,
> The life that steps and sings in ways of death.[36]

Though Snyder liked the line "The fox cub trots his almost pathless path" as well as the poem's final line, he wrote, "But 'a joy without defect' rings false—like a goopy line from a hymn—against the solidness."[37] Yet Berry left that penultimate line in the poem. His perception of what Snyder calls "the solidness" includes the restoration of defects and deaths into a joyous whole.

Despite Snyder's legitimate concerns, Berry's sabbath poems are not goopy Hallmark ditties. Berry insists on ultimate redemption, on a joy that will be without defect, but he doesn't shy away from our experience of death and pain. He grapples with the difficult gifts in order to make his gratitude more faithful and complete. As Marion notes, deciding to receive is difficult because we often receive what we don't want. Berry acknowledges this in the introduction to his collection of sabbath poems: "Nature of course includes damage as part of her wholeness. Her creatures live only by the deaths of other creatures. Wind, flood, and fire are as much her means of world-making as birth, growth, maturity, death, and decay."[38] Some might want to airbrush death and choose a sentimental celebration of life, and others might want to minimize nature's wholeness and beauty in order to see a hard-bitten view of death and destruction—nature "red in tooth and claw"—but Berry insists on keeping death and life together. So in reflecting on the sabbath as a celebration of God's redemptive power, Berry repeatedly turns to the biblical scene in which this paradoxical pair are most strongly contrasted and linked: Christ's death and resurrection.

In a poem written in his seventy-eighth year, Berry describes how his own mortality becomes more real as one by one his friends die, leaving him to live "from the loss / of one beloved companion / to the loss of yet another." Though it is hard to be grateful in the face of death, this is Berry's prayer:

> the old man prays to find,
> at the end of his own leash,
> his love for the world at hand,
> his heart at rest in gratitude.

While he desires to be grateful, even in his own death, his "nightmares / return" as he worries his beloved place will also be destroyed:

> He dreams of permanent
> destruction, his country broken,
> its woodlands felled, its streams
> poisoned. The future deviling

in his mind, his life shattered
and strewn in the public way,
his dreams recall the night
of Gethsemane, the fear
that the end of the way taken
is not to die merely,
but to die forsaken, the heart
finally broken.

    From this
despair he asks to be
remade, set free, let go
if only into the sanity of grief,
if only to suffer the suffering
of old companions he has loved
and loves. Sometimes his love
returns, finds him in his dream,
and leads him home.[39]

What Berry most fears is that death and destruction are ultimate. These fears take him to the night when Christ prayed to forgo his impending crucifixion. Yet Christ's prayer here includes both "remove this cup from me" *and* "not my will, but thine, be done."[40] His prayer thus enacts the difficult acceptance of an undesired gift.[41] Berry's poem follows this model, breaking in the middle of a line before he summons the courage to pray not that he might escape death or avoid its sufferings, but that he might love and be made whole in "the sanity of grief." His heart comes to rest in gratitude for those "he has loved and / loves." Through this gratitude, through giving thanks even in painful loss, Berry holds ruin in place so that, at least on occasion, his love returns and leads him home.

We sometimes do not recognize this redemptive love when it appears, however, because we demand that it come according to our expectations. We may think that love should simply abolish death. Berry articulates how these false expectations can blind us in a poem that turns to a scene after Christ's resurrection: his appearance to Mary Magdalene in the garden.[42] Mary was in a place of utter despair; all her hopes had perished with Christ on the cross. Our world can seem similarly hopeless, and yet Berry writes that Christ enters into this darkness:

    This is the Hell, this
the nightmare into which Christ descended
from the cross, from which also he woke
and rose, striding godly forth, so free

that He appeared to Mary Magdalene
to be only the gardener walking about
in the new day, among the flowers.[43]

Like Mary Magdalene, we can fail to recognize the risen Christ in our belief that death is the ultimate end. Yet the living Christ shows up in the midst of death and loss. Rather than removing death, he descends into it, and rather than appearing in spectacular victory, he appears as a humble gardener, quietly tending life in the midst of decay.

While Berry's gratitude for redemption may seem an easy answer to the pain of death and loss, Berry suggests that, in fact, those who deny redemption are taking the easy way out. As he writes in one celebratory sabbath poem,

> The little stream sings
> in the crease of the hill.
> It is the water of life. It knows
> nothing of death, nothing.
> And this is the morning
> of Christ's resurrection.
> The tomb is empty. There is
> no death. Death is our delusion,
> our wish to belong only
> to ourselves, which is our freedom
> to kill one another.
> From this sleep may we too
> rise, as out of the dark grave.[44]

Berry's opening image of the stream as the "water of life" suggests both that the stream provides life to others and that the stream's ongoing flow depends on the water cycle. This cycle, through which our streams and rivers are perpetually renewed, is analogous to the fertility cycle of death, decay, and rebirth. And of course Christ refers to himself as the source of living water, so this allusion links the poem's two halves.[45] Berry suggests that our motives for denying the resurrection, and the ongoing redemption present in creation, may stem from our "wish to belong only / to ourselves." The individual who insists that death is ultimate is, to use Marion's phrase, clinging to the "independence that permits oneself to be convinced that 'I owe no one anything.'" As Berry puts it in "Manifesto: The Mad Farmer Liberation Front," we are "afraid / to know [our] neighbors and to die."[46] These are the paired fears of the buffered self or organizing subject who does not want to acknowledge his dependence on others. And as Berry notes, this belief in death's ultimate power paradoxically frees us to kill others. If we imagine ourselves as autonomous subjects, we can simply eradicate our enemies, whether human or biological. Death becomes, as Hitler thought it was, "the final solution." We now use a more pleasant euphemism, "creative destruction," but as Fritz Oehlschlaeger argues, this belief in the simple efficacy of death justifies all manner of negations: "Mountaintops are removed, our countryside becomes 'deserted,' rural peoples are 'cleared,' workers become obsolescent, disposable, displaced (to God knows where), or replaced by machinery."[47] Our attempts to erase those persons and creatures we find inconvenient inevitably backfire, as we realize that we do not, in fact, "belong only / to ourselves." As the flowing stream and empty tomb testify, death is not a simple negation, and life remains at work even in loss. Thus, Berry concludes with a prayer: "from this sleep"—this illusion, this veil of false subjectivity, this belief that we are not dependent on the gift of life—"may we too / rise, as out of the dark grave."

Some readers may agree with Snyder that, at times, Berry's insistence on the reality of religious and ecological redemption "rings false." It is certainly true that Berry's gratitude depends on his belief in the Creator's redemptive presence, both in natural processes and in a religious, eschatological sense. But part of our reluctance to be grateful even in death may be that we do not want to receive life on the terms it is offered to us. Our sorrow over death can lead to an ingratitude that prevents us, like Mary Magdalene in the garden, from recognizing or receiving life when it comes to us. Berry's sabbath practice tunes him to receive both death and life, to be open to the mysterious ways of God's creative, redemptive grace, and to participate in resurrection.

Participating in Our Given Life

This mode of receptive gratitude might seem too quietist given the powerful violence that is destroying much of the world. Yet, rather than rendering him passive, gratitude frees Berry to participate in the creative, redemptive life of his place. According to one of his favorite metaphors in these sabbath poems, he becomes a tree whose fruit and leaves are the result of grateful rest. In one of the prefatory poems to *This Day*, Berry alludes to Psalm 1 when he compares the poet whose work will follow to a tree:

> He is a tree of a sort, rooted
> in the dark, aspiring to the light,
> dependent on both. His poems
> are leavings, sheddings, gathered
> from the light, as it has come,
> and offered to the dark, which he believes

must shine with sight,
with light, dark only to him.[48]

To put this metaphor in the cadences of the Psalmist, the blessed poet is like a tree planted by the Kentucky River, which brings forth its fruit in season; his poems do not wither, and whatsoever he imagines prospers. Interestingly, Berry inverts the Psalmist's image: whereas the *beatus vir* is rooted in the law of God and draws sustenance and fruit from this source to give to his community, Berry's poet gathers the gifts of a divine light and offers them to a dark place, where "trash" and "poisons" have gathered.[49] In both cases, however, the poet acts as a mediator between divine gifts and a diseased place. Berry returns to this set of arboreal analogies repeatedly—as an indication of its centrality, he titled earlier collections of his sabbath poems *A Timbered Choir* and *Leavings*—and this metaphor provides a response to those readers who see Berry's gratitude as passive or constricting.[50]

Being a recipient rather than a subject does not entail passive acceptance. We remain responsible for how we receive and care for the gifts we've been given. Berry's Mad Farmer poems make abundantly clear that when others misappropriate and abuse these gifts, righteous anger is called for.[51] But such anger is not Berry's habitual disposition. In imagining himself as a rooted tree, Berry is modeling a way of receiving the gifts of life and participating in their sustenance. In spring, deciduous trees spread out their leaves to receive the daily light of the sun. At the end of the summer, they release their leaves to die—in beautiful, vibrant colors—into the forest floor, enriching the soil through their deaths. In one poem Berry calls topsoil "old light held in soil and leaf." Leaves, then, are an elixir of life that through their miraculous alchemy convert light into soil. By holding light in time, Berry's poems enable the gifts of illumination and inspiration he has received to be passed down and enrich the soil of our culture. Through such grateful participation, we can "join our work to Heaven's gift."[52]

Trees are exemplary in that through their grateful acceptance of the gift of light, they enrich their communities, "making in the ground the only / real material wealth."[53] In one poem Berry imagines the woods returning to an abandoned clearing, resettling and restoring it through their patient labor.

Slowly, slowly, they return
To the small woodland let alone:
Great trees, outspreading and upright,
Apostles of the living light.

Patient as stars, they build in air
Tier after tier the timbered choir,

> Stout beams upholding weightless grace
> Of song, a blessing on this place.[54]

These trees are apostles, the sent ones of the living light. And by participating in this gift, they bless their neighbors: "Their life's a benefaction made."[55] These trees model a genuine Sabbath attitude; they receive grace gratefully, and they give their lives to unfolding it in forms that will bless those who live with them.

Trees bless their communities in many ways—for birds and other animals they provide shelter and food, and to their human neighbors their "gifts [include] a few fence posts and boards, / firewood for winter, some stillness / in which to know and wait."[56] For Berry, however, the paradigmatic way in which trees serve is through enriching the soil, so he writes in the hope that his poetic leaves will enrich our culture's abused language. In "The Book of Camp Branch" he compares language to the stream along which he walks, mourning its polluted flow:

> The language too
> descends through time, subserving
> false economy, heedless power,
> blown with the gas of salesmanship,
> rattled with the sale of needless war,
>
> worn by the mere unhearing
> babble of thoughtlessness.[57]

Berry's injunction to himself to "Make sense" is a response to this pollution, and he imagines his words falling into this damaged stream as "onto the page, the turning leaf / in the Book of Camp Branch."[58] By releasing his words into an abused and exploited language, he hopes to enrich it. Berry's view of poetry contrasts with Harold Bloom's reductive theory of influence, in which each generation of poets kills off its predecessors to make room for the most recent poets' work. It is worth noting that Bloom's "strong poet" bears a striking resemblance to Taylor's buffered self and Marion's subject; he exists in the industrial, Nietzschean world of competition.[59] Berry dismisses Bloom's "anxiety of influence," calling it "an adolescent critical theory."[60] For Berry, good poetry fertilizes a culture's language and imagination, enriching it even if the poet himself is forgotten. We may not remember which phrases came from Shakespeare, but his words have given us a more vital tongue. We may not know minor poets or authors, but their faithful efforts to speak well, to find "a language precise and articulate and lively enough to tell the truth about the world as we know it," have passed down a more vibrant language.[61] Berry is clearly not concerned with getting credit for himself; rather, he hopes his work responsibly cares for the gifts he has been given.

Good work, then, becomes a form of gratitude; through work we care for and sustain the good gifts we have received. In understanding "gratitude as *right use* of the gift rather than gratitude as *return*" or exchange, Berry escapes the economic horizon of exchange.[62] In its stead, he articulates this economy of gratitude—gratitude as stewardship or usufruct. In essays such as "The Gift of Good Land," he considers how God's gift of land to Israel can guide our understanding of "an ecological discipline."[63] As Berry states in the introduction to *This Day*, the Bible teaches that "the earth and our earthly livelihood are conditional gifts. We may possess the land given to us, that we are given to, only by remembering our intimate kinship with it." And Berry argues this understanding remains valid even for those outside the Christian tradition: "For some, the context of this thinking has shifted from religion to science, but the understanding of the land as a conditional gift has not changed."[64] Berry's willingness to receive the givenness of life enables him to work, not in an effort to earn or manufacture life, but from a desire to cultivate and participate in it.[65]

Many of his sabbath poems develop the proper relationship between gratefully receiving grace and responsibly participating in it.[66] In a poem titled "Amish Economy," Berry describes such good work as our only "fit reply" to the grace of life:

> We live by mercy if we live.
> To that we have no fit reply
> But working well and giving thanks,
> Loving God, loving one another,
> To keep Creation's neighborhood.[67]

The proper expression of gratitude for freely given grace is working well and in a way that honors the dignity of the gifts we've been given.

Thus Berry works not in desperation, thinking life depends on his own efforts, but in delight, knowing his work can participate in the redemptive work of the Creator. He doesn't think his work will accomplish anything on its own—as he says in one poem, "By grace we live." Yet receiving this grace obliges us to care for it:

> Having known the grace
> that for so long has kept this world,
> haggard as it is, as we have made it,
> we cannot rest, we must be stirring
> to keep this gift dwelling among us,
> eternally alive in time. This
> is the great work, no other, none harder,
> none nearer rest or more beautiful.[68]

This is sabbath work, work that understands it partakes of a deep rest and yet must be vigilant to maintain this rest. Sabbath work includes chores that don't fit under any category on a résumé or CV. Yet washing dishes, weeding our gardens, or taking a meal to a neighbor who has just given birth are the mundane ways in which we can tend life. If life is a gift, the proper response is to receive it gratefully through such tasks. When we participate in this work, we may not be adding to the GDP, but we are practicing resurrection and sustaining the health of our communities.

Paradoxically, then, gratitude frees Berry to work without the burden of being the source of life. In one poem he describes a farmer who each spring takes the seeds from their sack and plants them in his fields. This labor embodies a faith that these particular seeds will grow into a flourishing crop. By undertaking this work, the farmer

> has prepared a way
> for his life to come to him, if it will.
> Like a tree, he has given roots
> to the earth, and stands free.[69]

His life remains a gift, but the farmer's work prepares him to receive it. And the farmer's participatory work leads Berry to liken him to a tree. This farmer may not seem very free. After all, he is rooted to his place and is not free to leave it—if he does, his crops will probably wither and die. But by accepting the obligations the gift of life lays on him, the farmer becomes free to join in an abundant community.[70]

Some see gratitude as improperly limiting one's freedom, and indeed some cultures understand gratitude in oppressive ways.[71] Yet in disavowing all debts to others, the organizing subject pursues an isolating freedom. To be free is not to be a radical subject untethered by any obligations. Supreme Court Justice Anthony Kennedy famously voiced this warped view of freedom when he wrote in a decision, "At the heart of liberty is the right to define one's own concept of existence, of meaning, of the universe, and of the mystery of human life."[72] This is an absurd definition of liberty; if I try to define my own concept of meaning, I will merely isolate myself in my own little universe. Hence, as we have seen, the autonomous freedom that the buffered self desires is actually incredibly burdening; it's exhausting to wake up every morning with the impossible responsibility to define your concept of existence, meaning, and the universe.

Genuine freedom entails the ability to receive and to give of ourselves. *Friend* and *free* come from the same root word, which originally meant simply love.[73] This connection also resides in the word *liberal*, which means both free and generous. To love another, we must be free to give of ourselves and receive from the other, but the buffered self clings to its autonomy rather than making itself vulnerable. Hence, Marion's *Being Given* ends with the suggestion that love may be possible only when we understand ourselves as recipients rather than subjects.[74] When we accept the gift of selfhood, and the gifts of our place and its members, we are free to be generous and to love, we are free to dwell in community and participate in its flourishing.

Practicing Gratitude

Death and the buffered self are our delusions, ways of denying our indebtedness to others. We may be tempted to follow Melville's Captain Ahab, who shakes his fist at this condition and strives futilely to assert his subjectivity. Ahab curses his inability to be independent near the end of *Moby-Dick* when waiting for the carpenter to fashion a new peg leg for him: "Oh, Life! Here I am, proud as a Greek god, and yet standing debtor to this blockhead for a bone to stand on! Cursed be that mortal inter-indebtedness which will not do away with ledgers. I would be free as air; and I'm down in the whole world's books."[75] Like Ahab, no matter how hard we work we are always down in the world's books. But rather than endlessly striving to discharge his debts through his own efforts, Berry rests in the grace of a given world. If we owe our entire lives, then giving to others is not a choice we make that accrues to our credit; it is the means by which we sustain and care for the precious gifts we have received.

As the set of analogies Berry draws from the "timbered choir" of the woods suggests, we are more likely to work well if we are working from a position of dependence and mutual involvement rather than from a place that is buffered or insulated. The farmer knows he must work hard to prepare the soil, plant the seeds, and tend the crop, but he also knows that he is utterly dependent on the seeds' germinating, on the sun's light, and on the cooperation of the weather. The tree's work of enriching the soil and serving its community depends on gifts of light and water. So as we work toward sustainable cultures in our local places, we should do so in ways that acknowledge health is not some product our hard work can manufacture; it is a gift we must receive and participate in. There is no technique, no ice bucket challenge, by which subjects can magically fix death and disease. Maybe instead of posting videos on social media, we should sit with those who are suffering and receive their pain and fear. This is the difficult, slow work to which Berry's poems call us, the work of receiving both life and death as gifts.

We can begin this process by practicing the sabbath, resting from our efforts as a way of reminding ourselves that our work cannot create or restore life. And perhaps this practice will teach us what Jayber Crow, one of Berry's fictional characters, learned about prayer. Jayber had stopped praying and abandoned his seminary training when he realized that in spite of Christ's agonized prayer in Gethsemane, he still had to drink the cup of his crucifixion. At this point in his life, Jayber seems to view prayer as a technique that should enable the organizing subject to effect change in God's mind. When, many years later, Jayber begins again to pray, he takes up where he left off, praying, "Thy will be done." As he continues, he prays that his community would be blessed with grace and forgiveness, and, realizing how much he loved his community, he "prayed [his] gratitude." Jayber finds that his prayer does not change his circumstances as much as it transforms his self. It was "as though I had been in a house and a storm had blown off the roof; I was more in the light than I had thought. And also, at night, of course, more in the dark."[76] When he relinquishes his efforts to maintain a buffered self, he finds himself exposed and vulnerable, receptive to both light and dark, life and death. This can be a scary place to be; Jayber realizes he can't fix his community or stop its members from destroying their topsoil and woods. But this posture of gratitude and receptivity also opens Jayber to participate in the redemption and healing of his place. Berry's sabbath poems suggest, then, that the most radical change we can make to foster a sustainable culture is to stop imagining ourselves as buffered subjects and begin living as grateful recipients.

3

Humility

Codes, checklists, and bureaucracies are defining features of contemporary American life. While some of these rules are certainly necessary, our reliance on them can become rather absurd. Probing the ironies of what Charles Taylor terms our "code fetishism" may reveal how an arrogant fear of not being in control, of not being the organizing subjects of our world, can lead us to take refuge in the false moral clarity that codes promise.

In 2015 the Intercultural Affairs Committee at Yale University cautioned students to avoid culturally insensitive Halloween costumes.[1] Erika Christakis, a master at one of the residential colleges, wrote an e-mail to students questioning this "institutional (which is to say: bureaucratic and administrative) exercise of implied control over college students." Maybe, she suggested, students should "talk to each other" if they are offended by a particular costume. Apparently, however, questioning whether college administrators should really be making rules about student costumes was more offensive than the rules themselves. Student protests over her e-mail—some of which were quite vitriolic—drew national attention and sparked a discussion about trigger warnings and safe spaces.[2] As a story in the *Atlantic* concludes, "These students were offended by one person's words, and were free to offer their own words in turn. That wasn't enough for them, so they spat on different people who listened to those words and called one minority student a traitor to his race. In their muddled ideology, the Yale activists had to destroy the safe space to save it."[3] The irony seems lost on the protestors. The point is not that students shouldn't be offended by any costumes—some costumes may be genuinely offensive—the point is that institutions tend to deal with disagreement by imposing a set of bureaucratic guidelines rather than fostering the difficult and messy work of dialogue.

It's not just students who want the easy assurance of following a code. Like many other universities and government agencies, Yale enthusiastically embraces the Leadership in Energy and Environmental Design (LEED) certification program for sustainable buildings; since 2009 all new buildings at Yale have been required to be LEED Gold certified.[4] Making buildings more energy efficient is certainly a laudable and important goal, but the LEED program exemplifies how a reliance on codes can turn sustainability efforts into marketing gimmicks. Universities and businesses tout their new LEED buildings, but studies of such "green" buildings have found little if any actual energy savings.[5] Indeed, one Las Vegas casino received LEED certification—and $27 million in tax breaks—in spite of features that seem anything but "green," including "an indoor waterfall, a smoke-filled gaming area, seven decorative fountains, and guest suites with three TVs and power-controlled curtains." Though LEED guidelines reward some important design choices, they are structured to perpetuate a bureaucratic system: "The most popular LEED option—earned in 99.7% of [LEED-certified] buildings—has no direct environmental benefit but generates millions of dollars for the building council by giving one point if a design team has a LEED expert. People become experts by passing a LEED course and paying $550 to $800 to a non-profit that the building council created in 2007."[6] Given the perverse incentives of marketing and tax breaks, checking off boxes becomes more important than actually using less energy.

Berry has little patience for these kinds of codes because they inevitably foreclose a complex reality. As I argued in the previous chapter, he strives to gratefully receive the wonder and welter of a given world, a world whose mysteries transcend human understanding. So while a fear of losing control, a fear of complexity, can lead us to take refuge in codes or systems that impose an intelligible order, Berry's essays come from a different fear, the "fear of foreclosing [reality] or of reducing it to some merely human estimate."[7] In keeping with this fear, Berry's essays are decidedly nonsystematic. He calls them "ad hoc" and "amateur"; they are "trials" and "attempts" aimed at breaking out of the codes that keep us buffered in a false sense of security.[8]

Berry's essays begin from the conviction that humans are finite, ignorant creatures; we can never know all that we want or need to know. Some people respond to these limits by looking for codes that can guide their actions, and others respond by relishing an antinomian freedom. These are the Apollonian and Dionysian tendencies that characterize the conflicts of an industrial culture. Berry, however, working in the vein of Ivan Illich and Charles Taylor, proposes a way of humble love, one that seeks to tend the formal coherence we can sometimes sense but not exhaustively describe. His essays, then, are occasional and incomplete, often relying on lists or questions to sketch out possibilities. Yet Berry does not allow his readers to rest in uncertainty; he also employs morally charged binaries that can guide concrete action in the midst of uncertainty. Through these formal features, his essays model a way of humbly loving our places and communities in all their wonderful and terrifying complexity.

Code Fetishism, Antinomianism, and the Way of Love

Berry writes from the conviction that humans are irremediably ignorant. This may seem overly pessimistic given our "information age" and the explosion of new knowledge, but Berry argues that no matter how much we learn, we cannot appreciably shrink the domain of the unknown: "What we have come to know so far is demonstrably incomplete, since we keep on learning more, and there seems little reason to think that our knowledge will become significantly more complete. The mystery surrounding our life probably is not significantly reducible."[9] This state of ignorance would be bad enough, but, as embodied, time-bound creatures, we also have to act in spite of our incomplete knowledge: "One of our problems is that we humans cannot live without acting; we *have* to act. Moreover, we *have* to act on the basis of what we know, and what we know is incomplete."[10] Being ignorant and yet having to make final, irreversible acts is a scary place to be, and it is this fear that motivates Berry's efforts as an essayist. In his essays, then, Berry seeks an appropriate way of living with our ignorance: "Because ignorance is . . . a part of our creaturely definition, we need an appropriate way: a way of ignorance, which is the way of neighborly love, kindness, caution, care, appropriate scale, thrift, good work, right livelihood. . . . The way of ignorance, therefore, is to be careful, to know the limits and the efficacy of our knowledge. It is to be humble and to work on an appropriate scale."[11] Yet if his fear sends Berry along this way of ignorance, it sends others toward either an Apollonian code fetishism or a Dionysian antinomianism.

What Berry sees as an inevitable and irremediable state of ignorance, the industrial mind sees as a problem in need of a solution. As Berry puts it, "Some scientists and their gullible followers think that human ignorance is merely an agenda for research."[12] This belief that we can overcome our ignorance through increasing the quantity of our knowledge is hubristic, and it fails to cultivate "the cultural means [needed] to keep incomplete knowledge from becoming the basis of arrogant and dangerous behavior."[13] He critiques such dangerous arrogance in his essay titled "The Way of Ignorance," which begins, "Our purpose here is to worry about the predominance of the supposition, in a time of great technological power, that humans either know enough already, or can learn enough soon enough, to foresee and forestall any bad consequences of their use of that power. This supposition is typified by Richard Dawkins's assertion, in an open letter to the Prince of Wales, that 'our brains . . . are big enough to see into the future and plot long-term consequences.'"[14] Berry calls this assertion "a superstition of the most primitive sort. We recognize it also as our old friend hubris, ungodly ignorance disguised as godly arrogance. Ignorance plus arrogance plus greed sponsors 'better living with chemistry,' and produces the ozone hole and the dead zone in the Gulf of Mexico." It also produces Halloween costume guidelines, green building codes, organic labeling and inspection requirements, and the host of other codes and bureaucracies by which we try to impose order on a complex world.[15] Commodifying sustainability may be easy and profitable, but it forgoes the difficult, adaptive work of loving our places and communities.[16]

Such code fetishism looks for big, one-size-fits-all rules that can make sense of our world. Berry calls this a corporate or professional way of thinking, one that "aspires to *big* answers that will make headlines, money, and promotions. It longs, moreover, for answers that are uniform and universal—the same styles, explanations, routines, tools, methods, models, beliefs, amusements, etc., for everybody everywhere."[17] This search for a universal set of codes stems from an arrogant denial of the human condition. The fundamental error underlying this code fixation is an anthropological one. Code fixation stems from a dualism that assumes humans are fundamentally mental processors that just need the right intellectual or moral system to be made whole. All these processors need is the right training and education, the right set of rules to guide their actions. But the human person isn't a computer that just needs updated software. Humans are finite, fallible creatures called to follow "the way of neighborly love."

Charles Taylor outlines the "code-fixation" of modernity, and he critiques its reductive logic. On Taylor's account, our reliance on codes is so much a part of our lives that we no longer even question it: "It is taken for granted that the way to achieve certain important collective goods, like tolerance and mutual respect, lies in a code of behaviour, like the 'speech codes' which some campuses have put in place. The contours of disrespect are codified, so that they can be forbidden, and if necessary sanctioned."[18] In spite of their ubiquity, Taylor argues that codes are inadequate, for two primary reasons. First, codes fail to account for the particularity of complex situations: "Events are unforeseeably various; no set of formulae will ever capture all of them." What is needed is *phronesis*, the ability to discern the good in particular situations, not some universal code. The second shortcoming is that "there is more than one good," and codes are terrible at balancing different goods in complex, contingent situations.[19]

If we think we can escape the contingency and mystery of our world by developing a foolproof moral code, we will only perpetuate the very violence we are trying to cure. We will become enmeshed in absurdities like "the Yale activists [who] had to destroy the safe space to save it."[20] Berry alludes to the same infamous description of a Vietnam offensive—to justify the bombing of civilians, a military commander claimed, "It became necessary to destroy the town to save it"—in his condemnation of code fixation, or what he terms the "corporate approach."[21] Such an approach inevitably leads to "absurdity: We destroy a village in order to save it; we destroy freedom in order to save it; we destroy the world in order to live in it." As Taylor writes, "Codes, even the best codes, can become idolatrous traps that tempt us to complicity in violence. [Ivan] Illich reminds us not to become totally invested in the code—even the best code of a peace-loving, egalitarian variety—of liberalism."[22] This code fixation results in the head-scratching craziness of luxury Las Vegas casinos—parasitic businesses that shouldn't be built anywhere, much less in a desert—being certified as "green" buildings.

Given these limitations, many want to throw off all codes and pursue a libertarian freedom. This is the Romantic "principle of rebellion," and it motivates not only nineteenth-century nature poets, but also business executives seeking to evade regulations and college students impatient with any restraint on their speech or actions.[23] In his reflections on speech codes and our culture's apparent inability to sustain healthy disagreement, Alan Jacobs describes how our reliance on codes leads to interminable conflict: "Modernity, at least since Kant, is characterized by constant tensions and frequent eruptions of hostility between two great opponents, the *antinomians* and the *code fetishists*. Most of the fights that afflict social media today are versions of this conflict: just think of the recent skirmishes between the self-described free-speech advocates on Reddit and the opponents whom they refer to as SJWs (Social Justice Warriors)." Though these two groups may think they are fundamentally opposed, Jacobs, quoting Taylor, sees both as improperly fixated on codes themselves: "But what if this is a false dichotomy? What if the code fetishists and antinomians are *both* wrong, and wrong for the same reason: because they have unwittingly accepted the false idea that 'the entire spiritual dimension of human life is captured in a moral code'? What if rule-following doesn't produce justice, and the antinomians have an inadequate conception of freedom?"[24] Some try to find a better code and enforce it more strictly, and others rebel against all codes. Lost in this opposition are the virtues needed to sustain communities, particularly the virtue of humility, which underlies constructive disagreement and dialogue. As Jacobs writes about how this conflict plays out on college campuses, "the cultivation of virtues is replaced by ever-increasing *surveillance* of students."[25] Speech codes substitute reductive rules for the give-and-take of honest conversation in the same way that LEED guidelines substitute a checklist for the hard work of creative building design and virtuous use.

Both code fetishists and antinomians imagine public conversation to be like an engine, whereby explosive individuals are forcibly constrained by rigid, codified walls. Yet this image leaves out what Taylor calls the "vertical dimension," the possibility that persons might be called by love for another, inspiring them to cultivate the internal disciplines and virtues needed to take the way of neighborly affection. Both Taylor and Berry turn to the same source to describe what this "vertical dimension" looks like: Ivan Illich's reading of the parable of the Good Samaritan.[26] Berry's collection of essays titled *The Way of Ignorance* begins with an epigraph from the introduction to Illich's *The Rivers North of the Future*. This epigraph makes the crucial distinction between the "good," which is formal and personal and beloved, and "values," which are codified and abstract and coercive: "The good, as [Illich] came to understand it, is what is uniquely and incomparably appropriate to a given setting. It observes a certain scale, displays a certain proportion. It fits, and the senses can recognize this fit. . . . Values, on the other hand, are a universal coin without a proper place or an inherent limit. . . . Values undermine the sense of due proportion and substitute an economic calculus. What is good is what is always good; a value prevails only when it outranks a competing value."[27] Illich's critique of "values" is directed at an arrogant code fetishism: by rigidly adhering to a set of values, we neglect the importance of love for particular goods.

In keeping with this distinction, Illich reads the parable of the Good Samaritan not as inaugurating a new, more universal ethic, but as upending all attempts to institutionalize or codify love.[28] "Most preachers," Illich claims, interpret this parable as being "about how one *ought* to behave towards one's neighbor, that it proposed a rule of conduct, or an exemplification of ethical duty. I believe that this is, in fact, precisely the opposite of what Jesus wanted to point out."[29] Illich argues that though "it has become almost impossible for people who today deal with ethics or morality to think in terms of relationships rather than rules," we must resist the "institutionalization of neighbourliness."[30] The priest and the Levite—tightly buffered within their religious and political codes—pass by the wounded man. The thieves who beat the traveler reject this code with antinomian, Dionysian violence. But the Samaritan models a third way, the way of neighborly love that enables him to participate in the abundant life of God.[31] In holding the Samaritan up as an example, Jesus is not offering a better code; he is telling the inquiring lawyer that the way of neighborly love supersedes all codes.[32]

Taylor and Berry both trace a desire to find the "right" system of rules to a fear of reality's messiness. Like the lawyer, we often seek to justify ourselves by making categories that delimit who is and who is not our neighbor. As Taylor explains, "These shuttings out, those of atheists and those of believers, can be strongly motivated. 'Human kind cannot bear much reality' ([T. S.] Eliot). . . . Too much reality is not only destabilizing; it can be dangerous. It will be so to the extent that we try to overcome our disorientation by the false certainty of closure, and then try to shore up this certainty by projecting the chaos and evil we feel in ourselves onto some enemy. . . . We assure ourselves of our integral goodness by aggressive action against evil. I fight pollution, therefore I am pure."[33] To avoid this arrogant reduction of a complex reality, this "false certainty of closure,"

Berry flatly declares, "Our ignorance finally is irremediable." He makes this confession in an essay titled "The Burden of the Gospels," which is included near the end of *The Way of Ignorance*. Berry quotes from John's gospel: "And there are also many other things which Jesus did, the which, if they should be written every one, I suppose that even the world itself could not contain the books that should be written." If there is more to say about Jesus than the world can contain, there is certainly more to say than our finite human minds can comprehend. Such a realization should prevent us from thinking that we could ever have Jesus' message figured out and codified. And so Berry rejects all who claim to have a complete grasp on reality, whether religious leaders, politicians, or scientists: "Reductive religion is just as objectionable as reductive science, and for the same reason: Reality is large, and our minds are small." The religion that Jesus' parable calls us to practice, then, is one that subverts all reductive codes: "As inhabitants of the modern world, we are religious now perhaps to the extent of our desire to crack open the coffin of materialism, and to give to reality a larger, freer definition than is allowed by the militant materialists of the corporate economy and their political servants, or by the mechanical paradigm of reductive science."[34] In calling us to imitate the Samaritan who helped the injured man, Jesus calls us to practice a love that cannot be institutionalized or codified. He calls us to take the "way of ignorance, which is the way of neighborly love."[35]

This doesn't mean we can just get rid of rules, but it does mean that even our best rules are only an approximation, a rough guide, toward the higher calling to love particular others in particular circumstances. As Taylor puts it in his foreword to Illich's book,

> the network of agape puts first the gut-driven response to a particular person. This response cannot be reduced to a general rule. Because we cannot live up to this—"Because of the hardness of your hearts"—we need rules. It is not that we could just abolish them, but modern liberal civilization fetishizes them. We think we have to find the right system of rules, of norms, and then follow them through unfailingly. . . . By contrast, contingency is an essential feature of the story of the Good Samaritan as an answer to the question that prompted it. Who is my neighbour? The one you happen across, stumble across, who is wounded there in the road. . . . But in order to hear this, we have to escape from the monomaniacal perspective in which contingency can only be an adversary requiring control.[36]

Rather then looking for the perfect system of rules, Taylor follows Illich in claiming that we need to "find the centre of our spiritual lives beyond the code, deeper than the code, in networks of living concern, which are not to be sacrificed to the code, which must even from time to time subvert it."[37] This is what Taylor elsewhere calls "the vertical dimension," the way of love that leads us out of the perpetual conflicts between antinomians and code fetishists.[38]

Amateur Attempts

If the Good Samaritan helps the neighbor he "happen[s] across, stumble[s] across, who is wounded there in the road," Berry's essays respond to the questions and concerns that he happens across. They are his loving attempts to bind up the wounds around him. This does not mean his essays address only a narrow range of issues, but it does mean that they are ad hoc and locally rooted. Many of them, in fact, were originally written as speeches to be given to particular audiences.[39] So Berry never offers a panoptic, systematic vision in his essays; rather, he begins with particular subjects or problems and tries to fit them into a harmonious pattern. His essays always remain limited, bottom-up attempts to respond to his own bewilderment rather than comprehensive, top-down assertions of some reductive order. In the preface to his collection *Home Economics,* Berry turns to the etymology of the word *essay* to explain this method, stating that each of his essays is "a trial or an attempt" to make sense.[40] Or, as he says elsewhere, "An essayist is, literally, a writer who attempts to tell the truth."[41] Thus, Berry works in the hope that each attempt to make sense of problematic particulars contributes to a greater understanding of their coherence, of their relationships to one another.

Yet because of our finite human condition, our attempts to make sense remain fragmentary. Berry insists time and again that there are no large solutions to our large problems, so he doesn't try to solve our social ills in one grand, comprehensive work; rather, he makes ad hoc, occasional attempts to clear the ground. To borrow a phrase from T. S. Eliot, his essays are "raid[s] upon the inarticulate."[42] As he writes in the preface to *The Way of Ignorance,* "I hope my readers will recognize what an ad hoc affair my essay writing has been. . . . My work is no more professional than it is official. . . . The work that I feel best about I have done as an amateur: for love. But in my essays especially I have been motivated also by fear of our violence to one another and to the world, and by hope that we might do better."[43] In responding to this fear, his essays compose an inventory of love. They are written from a place of bewilderment and fear; Berry lists out the pieces that he does see, the parts he does understand, in an effort to lay them out and try to fit them together. By not imposing an arbitrary coherence, his fragmentary essays embody his humility before the endless complexity of a beloved creation.

One of the ways that Berry formally acknowledges the ad hoc nature of his investigations is by using lists and other disjunctive structures. For instance, "Thoughts in the Presence of Fear" consists entirely of twenty-seven paragraph-length sections, each demarcated with a Roman numeral and set apart with white space. These are Berry's rough thoughts in the wake of September 11; he doesn't have a solution to propose that would ensure peace; instead, he questions the assumptions and values that September 11 revealed to be flawed, the "unquestioning technological and economic optimism that ended on that day."[44] Other essays follow a similar format, and many of them declare their fragmentary structure in their titles: "Out of Your Car, Off Your Horse: Twenty-seven Propositions about Global Thinking and the Sustainability of Cities," "Peaceableness toward Enemies: Some Notes on the Gulf War," "Notes: Unspecializing Poetry," "Twelve Paragraphs on Biotechnology," "Six Agricultural Fallacies," "Paragraphs from a Notebook."[45] Such essays offer a series of discrete claims or observations on a particular subject. The added white space between each section calls attention to the nonlinear, fragmented nature of these attempts to make sense of a complex and mysterious world. Like the stepping-stones Berry describes in "The Book of Camp Branch," these inventories list the boulders that mark his path through a flowing, opaque world.

Even in more unified essays, he often employs lists or other ways of formally acknowledging the fragmentary nature of his subjects: "The Total Economy" provides fourteen false assumptions on which an industrial economy rests; "Conservation and Local Economy" begins with a list of seven principles regarding land use; "Solving for Pattern" gives fourteen standards by which to judge whether a solution is solving for pattern or is just an isolated quick fix; "Why I Am Not Going to Buy a Computer" concludes with nine "standards for technological innovation"; "Our Deserted Country" ends with "an inventory of the resources we have at hand that will support us in our effort to do better," and he is careful to clarify that "this is *an* inventory, not *the* inventory."[46] I could give many more examples.[47] In some essays, these lists take the form of questions, as in "Major in Homecoming," where he provides a "curriculum of questions" that could guide a rooted education.[48]

Other essays don't employ numbered lists, but many of them lay out disparate sides of a particular issue in an effort to see how these pieces form a more coherent whole. For instance, in "Imagination in Place" he attempts to describe the mutually informing relationship between his fiction and his life on a Kentucky farm, but the complexity and irreducibility of this relationship lead him to write, "When I am asked how all this fits together, I have to say, 'Awkwardly.' "[49] His essay responds formally to this awkward coherence by employing discrete sections, each of which addresses a facet of his place or his fiction without providing a too simplistic transition between them; the connections between these sections are as awkward as the connections between these facets of his life.

In spite of these fragmentary structures, Berry writes that the subject of his essays is "the fact, and ultimately the faith, that things connect—that we are wholly dependent on a pattern, an all inclusive form, that we partly understand." Yet the search for this pattern, this all-inclusive form, must remain, as Berry explains, tentative and incomplete: "I am never completely happy with this project, and sometimes I am not happy with it at all. I dislike its necessary incompleteness, and I am embarrassed by ceaseless insinuation that it is a job for somebody better qualified. I keep returning to it, I think, because the study of connections is an endless fascination, and because the understanding of connections seems to me an indispensable part of humanity's self-defense."[50] As Berry's description implies, his essays strive to make wide-ranging, often surprising connections. He terms one essay a "wandering excursion," which is apt given the broad range its fifteen pages cover: topsoil, mud daubers, the Amish, marriage, violins, multigenerational communities, the moral law, good work, discipline, harmony, tractors, Tennyson, Homer, and the Ogallala Aquifer.[51]

Thus, while Berry's essays are local and proceed in fragmentary attempts, they are by no means narrow in scope. For a Kentucky agrarian, Berry writes about a remarkable range of subjects. To provide only a partial catalogue, his essays address national topics such as Clarence Thomas's Supreme Court nomination hearings, foreign policy, capital punishment, terrorism, the Boston Marathon bombings, and Guantanamo. They consider cultural and social issues such as race, abortion, gay marriage, theology, the medical industry, and education. They cite many literary figures from Shakespeare and Spenser to Kathleen Raine, William Carlos Williams, Wallace Stegner, and Ernest Gaines. And of course they include agrarian and environmental concerns such as sheep breeds, draft horses, forestry, strip-mining, and nuclear power.

By bringing together these diverse topics, Berry endeavors to expand the context of his locally rooted work. As he writes, "Amateur standards, the standards of love, are always straining upward toward the humble and the best. They enlarge the ground of judgment. The context of love is the world."[52] Or, as he states elsewhere, "The context of everything is everything else."[53] For while love must begin with the wounded one at our feet, "the commandment to 'Love your enemies' suggests that charity must be without limit; it must include everything."[54] His essays move, then, from literary criticism to agricultural policy to sexual politics in order to bring together aspects of our culture and economy that we normally treat as separate. If arrogance can lead us to exclude or marginalize things that don't fit neatly into our systematic codes, humility strives to understand the connections between things even when these connections can't be fully pinned down.

One corollary of his effort to trace connections is Berry's refusal to consider hot-button topics—such as abortion, tobacco, or racism—in isolation. In a postscript to his essay "The Conservation of Nature and the Preservation of Humanity" he explains: "The issue of abortion is now so volatile that it is difficult to contain satisfactorily in an essay about something else—as I have shown here. I have more that I need to say. And yet it may be that one should write of abortion *only* in an essay about something else. It is not a subject unto itself; treating it as such leads to further trouble. It is a subject, on the contrary, that appears to call always for greater complexity and consistency of thought." Thorny problems cannot be understood, much less solved, in isolation. But the remedy isn't to apply some code of values to square the circle; rather, we should begin from the properly humble recognition that "we humans must think about our evils from the inside," and then strive to put our failings in their broader context.[55]

Hence, in an essay on tobacco, Berry imagines a dialogue in which he tries to convince a skeptic that tobacco is a morally complex issue. It's easy to label tobacco as an evil and then ignore the other addictions—oil, war, shopping, drugs—that are just as damaging.[56] So while Berry doesn't defend tobacco as a drug, he argues that as a crop it sustained his community's economy.

Questions surrounding race are even more fraught, particularly for Berry, who is a descendent of slave owners. Berry admits in the afterword of his book on racism that "*The Hidden Wound* is in some ways the least satisfying essay that I have written. Such an essay, to begin with, can hope to be only a tiny part of a conversation; this particular conversation was old when I entered it, and will be much older before it is concluded. The passages in which I attempted to think about the problem of racism are, therefore, necessarily inconclusive."[57] Though Berry's reflections on racism must remain inconclusive, the structure of his book is indicative of his approach; he begins by recounting his family's history with slavery, then recalls his own relationship with a black couple who lived on his grandfather's farm. From this personal, local experience, he works outward to expand its context. In his efforts to articulate the dualism that contributed to violence against Native Americans, African Americans, and the land itself, he draws on literary works as diverse as *Tess of the d'Urbervilles, The Autobiography of Malcolm X, The Odyssey, Huckleberry Finn, Anna Karenina,* and *War and Peace.* And rather than arguing for some political "solution," he follows Confucius in striving to articulate the "profound metamorphoses that occur when men 'rectify their hearts,'" for these are the deep changes required to begin healing the painful wounds of racism.[58] His refusal to settle for a neat political solution may make this his "least satisfying essay," but no less a writer than bell hooks calls this book an "important testimony," praising its honesty and citing it as a formative work in her own life and thinking.[59]

Industrial Codes versus Loving Forms

In following love's requirement to expand the context of his work, Berry runs the risk of writing his way into antinomian ambiguity. Racism and tobacco and abortion—like energy efficiency and healthy dialogue on college campuses—are complex issues, and Berry is right to insist on not foreclosing their bewildering complexity. His way of ignorance, however, could become a way of forestalling action, of thinking that we don't know enough to act. Yet indecisiveness does not represent a properly humble response to the mysteries of life but is rather an arrogant denial of our human condition; we will never know everything, and yet we have to act regardless of our incomplete knowledge. What then should guide our actions in an ambiguous and uncertain world? Berry's essays often contrast two answers to this question: the code fixation of the industrial economy and imaginatively perceived patterns. In fact, I employed this binary structure in the introduction to this book when contrasting the rigid order of an internal combustion engine with the complex order of fertile topsoil. Though such binaries run the risk of arrogant oversimplification, Berry uses them to draw stark moral contrasts and to provide forms that can guide the work of love. His binaries, then, are not totalizing systems that sort a complex world into two simplistic categories; they are prophetic pry bars wielded to loosen our calcified hearts.

Ambiguity can be a way of forestalling action, of fooling ourselves into thinking that we don't know enough to do what is right. Berry eviscerates those who would take refuge in ambiguity or relativism for failing to live responsibly:

> I do not believe that it is possible to act on the basis of a "tentative" or "provisional" conclusion. We may know that we are forming a conclusion on the basis of provisional or insufficient knowledge—that is a part of what we understand as the tragedy of our condition. But we must act, nevertheless, on the basis of *final* conclusions, because we know that actions, occurring in time, are irrevocable. That is another part of our tragedy. People who make a conventional agreement that all conclusions are provisional—a convention almost invariably implied by academic uses of the word "objectivity"—characteristically talk but do not act. Or they do not act deliberately, though time and materiality carry them into action of a sort, willy-nilly.[60]

As Berry explains, our fundamental problem is not that we don't know enough; it's that we don't want to do those things that we do know to be right. We don't need more information so that we can think more accurately about something as much as we need to practice what we already know.[61] Knowledge should be a means of better loving others, and Berry's way of ignorance reminds us that our primary obligation is to love others rather than to think about them. Paradoxically perhaps, indecisiveness does not represent a properly humble response to the mysteries of life but is, rather, an arrogant denial of our human condition.

Thus, the way of ignorance is not tentative or deferential or nonthreatening. Indeed, readers of Berry's essays know that they can be demanding, assertive, contrarian, and bold. They often follow binary structures that chart stark contrasts between two opposing ways of guiding our decisions in a bewilderingly diverse reality. Essays such as "Two Economies," "Two Minds," and "Quantity vs. Form" contrast the industrial economy with the Kingdom of God, the rational mind with the sympathetic mind, the standard of "limitless quantity" with the standard of "formal completeness."[62] Such binary structures seem to leave little room for gray in their black-and-white articulation of the world, and this moral certainty seems far from humble. Yet because it is impossible to refuse to make moral decisions, Berry contrasts two opposing standards for guiding our actions, arguing that imaginatively perceived formal patterns can orient loving action better than reductive codes can.

So although Berry's stern moral dichotomies may seem anything but humble, they are his way of getting us to recognize the high stakes of our daily choices and actions. Because of our technological power and our interconnected lives, seemingly innocent acts have lasting consequences. Berry explains that "past a certain scale, as C. S. Lewis wrote, the person who makes a technological choice does not choose for himself alone, but for others; past a certain scale, he chooses for *all* others."[63] It is this sense of the magnitude of our choices that lies behind his infamous essay "Why I Am Not Going to Buy a Computer." Berry doesn't frame all technology in binary terms—he uses plenty of modern-day technology—but he does understand that some technological choices are Adam and Eve–type choices: once you choose them, it's almost impossible to unchoose. This is true not just of nuclear weapons or GMO seeds; even buying a computer or a smartphone or a car changes our lives, families, and communities in ways that we cannot predict. Because no amount of information can render the consequences of these choices clear, properly humble action should be guided by communal forms or standards. With the stakes this high, true arrogance is dithering about in ambiguities or forging ahead according to a reductive code. Berry's formal standards limit heedless, destructive choices and so hold open the possibility of renewal and resurrection.

Some readers have taken offense at Berry's bold moral distinctions, arguing they are too simplistic. Alan Jacobs, for instance, critiques Berry's use of Wallace Stegner's contrast between boomers and stickers. In a paradigmatic passage, Berry writes:

> Stegner . . . thought rightly that we Americans, by inclination at least, have been divided into two kinds: "boomers" and "stickers." Boomers, he said, are "those who pillage and run," who want "to make a killing and end up on Easy Street," whereas stickers are "those who settle, and love the life they have made and the place they have made it in." "Boomer" names a kind of person and ambition that is the major theme, so far, of the history of the European races in our country. "Sticker" names a kind of person and desire

that is, so far, a minor theme of that history, but a theme persistent enough to remain significant and to offer, still, a significant hope.[64]

In responding to this passage, Jacobs asks, "Why does he insist on the validity of this binary code? It's useless—it's worse than useless, it's simplistic and uncharitable. There are many reasons why people stay home, and many why they leave; and probably no single person is driven by one reason only."[65] Jacobs offers two reasons for disagreeing with Berry; one is that some people have good reasons to leave home, and the second is that our motives are almost always mixed. Yet Berry, I think, would concur with both points. Boomers are not those who leave home because they are forced to or because they are following a higher calling. Rather, boomers "pillage and run"; they leave home because they imagine themselves as buffered individuals whose ultimate goal is to achieve individual profit. Second, Berry emphasizes that he is contrasting conflicting "desire[s]" or "motive[s]" that are present in each person. In another essay in which he uses Stegner's terms, he is even more clear that he is not labeling people as good or bad but is naming conflicting desires within each of us: "To lay out these pairs of opposites is . . . to define a historical and cultural split that characterizes us Americans. And by 'us' I mean all of us. . . . All of us, I think, are in some manner torn between caring and not caring, staying and going."[66] The binary pair of "boomer" and "sticker" contrasts the desire to escape the unpleasant consequences of our narrow, imposed orders with the desire to learn from these consequences and imagine how to make our places better.[67]

So why does Berry use binary contrasts when he also insists that reality is nuanced and messy? Because binaries are a rhetorical form that can prophetically pry open the too narrow codes in which we buffer ourselves from this complex reality. In contrasting them with stickers, Berry shows what the boomers' code leaves out, demonstrating how boomers seal themselves off from the consequences of their actions by moving on.[68] Yet while he pulls no punches in condemning this behavior, he also writes about the dangers of "condemnation by category," and he is certainly not making "a categorical refusal of kindness" to boomers or others with whom he disagrees.[69] Rather, his bold contrast is a kind of prophetic speech intended to break open readers' false categories and spur them to right action. Berry's binaries stand in the tradition of Moses—who set before the Israelites the mountain of blessing and the mountain of cursing—the biblical prophets, and Jesus, whose parables are full of binary contrasts: the good tree and the corrupt tree, the wise man and the foolish man, those who cared for the least of these and those who did not.[70] In "desperate situations," times when false assumptions have infected our reasoning, "the stark, harsh focus of prophetic indictment becomes necessary."[71]

The biblical edge to Berry's binaries is particularly evident in "Two Econo-mies," which sets up a contrast between the industrial economy and the King-dom of God. The industrial economy, like the boomer mentality, excludes what it doesn't understand; it "is . . . not comprehensive enough, [and], moreover, it tends to destroy what it does not comprehend." Berry goes on to describe an economy "that does not leave anything out": "The first principle of the Kingdom of God is that it includes everything; in it, the fall of every sparrow is a significant event. . . . Another principle, both ecological and traditional, is that everything in the Kingdom of God is joined both to it and to everything else that is in it; that is to say, the Kingdom of God is orderly. A third principle is that humans do not and can never know either all the creatures that the Kingdom of God contains or the whole pattern or order by which it contains them."[72] The order named by the Kingdom of God will always remain mysterious and beyond our ability to codify, yet as Berry sketches its features, he reveals what an industrial economy leaves out. His binary opposition between the industrial economy and the King-dom of God, then, helps readers see the ways in which their assumptions may warp reality.

The negative terms of Berry's binaries—the industrial economy, boomers, the rational mind, quantity—name our human tendency to codify and reduce a complex and mysterious reality to something that we can understand and con-trol. In a letter to his friend Wes Jackson, Berry refers to a soil scientist to illus-trate how this reliance on codes leads us to exclude or ignore those parts of the pattern that don't readily fit our systems. This scientist claims that rainwater passes through a forest's canopy and soil in "randomized fashion." Yet, Berry writes, no one can know enough to say whether the water is flowing randomly, for although "pattern is verifiable by limited information, . . . the information required to verify randomness is unlimited." Hence, a more accurate description would say "that rainwater moves from mystery though pattern back into mys-tery. . . . To call this mystery 'randomness' or 'chance' or a 'fluke' is to take charge of it on behalf of those who do not respect pattern. To call the unknown 'random' is to plant the flag by which to colonize and exploit the known." Labeling the rain's path "random" simply brackets whatever doesn't fit within one's system or code, and Berry worries that whatever we exclude in this way is liable to be harmed: "To call the unknown by its right name, 'mystery,' is to suggest that we had better respect the possibility of a larger, unseen pattern that can be damaged or destroyed." As an alternative to this dangerous arrogance, Berry turns to his way of ignorance: "If we are up against mystery, then knowledge is relatively small, and the ancient program is the right one: Act on the basis of ignorance. . . . Both the Greeks and the Hebrews told us to watch out for humans who assume that *they* make all the patterns."[73] Proper humility, then, seeks to perceive patterns rather than forcing a complex reality into a rigidly defined system and lopping off whatever bits of reality don't fit.

The positive terms of Berry's binaries—the Kingdom of God, stickers, the sympathetic mind, form—posit complex, formal standards for our lives and work. Paradoxically, too simple standards—more production, longer life, more explosive power, complete safety on campus or from terrorists, energy-efficient buildings—create overly complicated bureaucratic regulatory structures to compensate for their reductive standards.[74] In this regard, Berry's critique of reductive, colonizing systems parallels Charles Taylor's analysis of why codes are inadequate. As we have already seen, Taylor argues that codes fail both because "events are unforeseeably various" and because "there is more than one good."[75] As Berry would have it, codes are oriented toward simplistic, quantifiable goods rather than complex, formal patterns that sustain multiple goods in tension. Hence, Berry's essays unite disparate topics not through some systematic, inevitably falsifying order, but through an imaginatively perceived formal coherence. Our ability to imagine this formal coherence is vital because, as he defines it, "the imagination is our way in to the divine Imagination, permitting us to see wholly—as whole and holy—what we perceive as scattered, as order what we perceive as random."[76] This imaginative faculty that draws the fragments of our experience into a coherent whole is what Berry finds lacking in the reductive codes of many scientists, politicians, and religious leaders. The positive terms of his binaries propose more complex, formal standards—health, ripeness, community, love, the Kingdom of God—that can guide ad hoc, locally adapted attempts.

At the core of these complex standards is a sense of proportionality. We sense this proportionality through our bodies and imaginations, not with discursive reason, so we can desire such standards even without fully understanding them. And because of this, they orient our affections and actions in spite of our inevitable ignorance. If codes are mental and tend to reinforce a mind-body dualism, health and ripeness and harmony are physical and must be sensed. They name a formal order that resonates with our bodies.[77] Rather than answering all our questions, they tune our guts. In the paragraph from which Berry takes the epigraph to *The Way of Ignorance*, David Cayley articulates how Illich's standard of goodness, the standard he finds in the Good Samaritan's act of radical love, is sensible in a way that exceeds utilitarian explanations:

> The good . . . observes a certain scale, displays a certain proportion. It fits, and the senses can recognize this fit, just as they can recognize what is out of tune. Values, on the other hand, are a universal coin with a proper place or an inherent limit. They rank and compare all things according to their utility or their relative scarcity. The value of prayer can be measured by its calming

effect on brainwaves; the recreational amenity provided by a forest can be compared to the monetary worth of its biomass; death can be administered to a failing patient when the cost of further treatment would exceed the quality of life it would yield. Values undermine the sense of due proportion and substitute an economic calculus. What is good is what is always good; a value prevails only when it outranks a competing value. With this distinction in view, Illich pursued the history of the senses and studied the ways in which the senses had once been attuned to the good, and the ways in which this attunement had been lost.[78]

A code of abstract values forecloses the complexity of goods—such as prayer, trees, and life—that can be sensed but not explained.

The parable of the Good Samaritan, however, points to a good that is richer than any code of values. Codes are bloodless—they don't inspire our loves in the way that beautiful forms can, and so they don't invite us into the vertical dimension to which Taylor aspires. In summarizing Illich, Taylor emphasizes that the good is something we participate in physically rather than apprehending intellectually: "Jesus points to a new kind of fittingness, belonging together, between the Samaritan and the wounded man. They are fitted together in a proportionality which comes from God, which is that of agape, and which became possible because God became flesh. The enfleshment of God extends outward, through such new links as the Samaritan makes with the Jew, into a network which we call the Church."[79] The Samaritan doesn't help the wounded man because some intellectual or moral code tells him he should; rather, the Samaritan is "moved by compassion." The Greek word translated as *compassion* refers to one's guts; compassion happens in our guts, at a level that's underneath our rational efforts to explain the world. Illich's language of attunement recalls the mutual attention I described in my first chapter, and poetry and other art forms are particularly suited to this kind of bodily attunement or stretching.[80] As Auden writes, poetry is read and modified "in the guts of the living." In an interesting analogue, violin strings used to be made from the intestines of sheep or goats, so that the beautiful harmonies of a symphony would flow from properly stretched guts. Berry's formal, complex standards work to stretch our guts and our loves; they invite us to imagine certain formal relationships with those around us, relationships that foster compassion and affection. These formal standards tune us, they stretch our guts, rather than arranging our thoughts according to some prescribed formula.[81] And as we stretch toward those around us, we are better able to tend their wounds.

Because they are sensed imaginatively, Berry's formal standards can guide us even when we don't have all the facts. In his essay "Quantity vs. Form," for instance, he begins by considering a friend who died well after living a "ripe" life.

It may be impossible to fully articulate what constitutes "the form of a lived life," but it is nonetheless possible to live a ripe life because "one does not have to know everything in order to do well."[82] We know when a fruit is ripe by its color, texture, scent, and taste, not by running a battery of tests on it. Similarly, we don't judge a life by checking off boxes or measuring its length but by sensing its completeness, its fittingness. So Berry refuses reductive attempts to quantify ripeness or health because such simplistic standards authorize destruction: "The exclusive standard of productivity destroys the formal integrity of a farm just as the exclusive standard of longevity destroys the formal integrity of a life. . . . The desire for quantity replaces the desire for wholeness or holiness or health. The sense of right proportion and scale cannot survive the loss of the sense of relationship, of the parts to one another and to the whole. The result, inevitably, is ugliness, violence, and waste."[83] In discussing the importance of complex standards, Berry returns again and again to marriage as a form that can guide right action in the midst of ignorance.[84] While "marriage reveals the insufficiency of knowledge"—two people can never know enough to commit to spending their lives together—the form of marriage "suggests the possibility that decisions can be informed in another way that *is* sufficient, or approximately so." Romantic love can be guided by the cultural forms of marriage and community: "Our decisions can . . . be informed—our loves both limited and strengthened—by those patterns of value and restraint, principle and expectation, memory, familiarity, and understanding that, inwardly, add up to *character* and, outwardly, to *culture*. Because of these patterns, and only because of them, we are not alone in the bewilderments of the human condition and human love, but have the company and the comfort of the best of our kind, living and dead. These patterns constitute a knowledge . . . that includes information, but is never the same as information."[85] The shape of a ripe life, the form of a beautiful marriage, the inclusive, mysterious order of the Kingdom of God—these forms are gifts for finite creatures, orienting our affections and actions in a bewildering world.

Practicing Humility

Perhaps, then, we should "judge a person's intelligence, not by the ability to recite facts, but by the good order or harmoniousness of his or her surroundings."[86] Such a standard would prevent us from calling a luxury casino in the middle of the desert "sustainable," and it might provoke more thoughtful discussions about Halloween costumes and other kinds of community speech. The formal characteristics of Berry's essays that I have considered in this chapter—his ad hoc approach, his efforts to unite disparate topics, his use of binaries to replace reductive standards with more formally complex ones—suggest that rather than trying to come up with one universal, abstract code to guide sustainable living, we should undertake many local, occasional attempts to understand and love our neighbors. These attempts will be necessarily piecemeal and prone to error, but they can be part of the "way of ignorance, which is the way of neighborly love, kindness, caution, care, appropriate scale, thrift, good work, right livelihood." Berry's way of ignorance reminds us that sustainable thinking can't become fixated on finding big political solutions or implementing new policies; these will never be adequate to the complex dilemmas reality presents. Rather, we'll need to begin as stickers who are attentive to the problems in our communities and who seek to love and care for the wounded creatures among us. This care will be locally rooted, but it will inevitably involve us in far-flung interconnections—there's no knowing what knowledge or skills will be required to love our neighbor in the Kingdom of God.

4

Hope

Climate discourse trades in numbers and statistics: population growth, carbon dioxide concentrations, topsoil and species loss, barrels of oil, toxicity levels, climate refugees. In the face of such overwhelming global problems, Berry's humble, local approach to sustainability may seem woefully inadequate. When the problems are described in terms of quantities, the responses we can most easily imagine are variants of either pessimism or optimism. The pessimist figures there's nothing he can do in the face of such huge numbers, so he might as well distract himself or, at most, find some insignificant gesture—like installing energy-efficient lightbulbs—to make himself feel a bit better. The optimist agrees that there's nothing an individual can do, but then turns to big, institutional solutions, whether political or technological.

Framing the problems in terms of vast quantities encourages us to ground whatever hope we can muster in solutions large enough to put a dent in global problems. Some turn to political solutions: the next United Nations climate accord might produce a new breakthrough, the next Intergovernmental Panel on Climate Change report will provoke real change. Others turn to technological solutions and pin their hopes on geo-engineering or the next scientific breakthrough.[1] As a 2016 Pew survey found, 55 percent of Americans think that within fifty years "new technology will solve most problems from climate change."[2] Such technological optimism makes figures like Elon Musk its heroes. Musk hopes to revolutionize transportation through Tesla's electric cars, which would be charged by a solar-powered grid. If that fails and earth becomes uninhabitable, his SpaceX shuttles will take humans to colonies on Mars and elsewhere.[3] Those who aren't quite as wildly utopian as Musk settle for geo-engineering technologies that can sequester carbon dioxide or modify the planet's albedo, or reflectivity.[4] Some have even proposed using "balloons [or] artillery guns" to release sulfates into the stratosphere and reflect solar heat away from the earth.[5] Other technological approaches are more modest: the Ocean Cleanup is developing passive screens that, when placed across ocean currents, can begin collecting and recycling the five trillion pieces of floating plastic that currently contaminate our oceans.[6]

By all appearances, the Ocean Cleanup is an innovative, elegant approach, yet I worry that one of the reasons solutions like this are so popular is that they don't require us to change our behavior. If we develop technological solutions to fix the weather and clean polluted oceans, then our industrial economies can carry on with business as usual and trust that brilliant scientists will engineer our way out of whatever problems may arise. Big solutions absolve individuals from moral agency and responsibility; if the problems are so big I can't do anything about them, I don't have to change my life—the technocrats will take care of it. On this optimistic view, the millennial kingdom is just around the corner. And for those who don't have faith in Musk and his compatriots, then apocalyptic devastation seems unavoidable. The optimist and the pessimist are two sides of the same coin, and they represent yet another iteration of Apollo and Dionysus, of perfect order and perfect chaos. The quantified discourse of the planet's climate shuttles between Apollonian utopia and Dionysian apocalypse, but proponents of both agree that the scale is so vast that no individual action matters— our future is determined, and it's just a question of whether we're determined to live in a Silicon Valley paradise or to go up in smoke.[7]

As always, Berry seeks a third way, which in this case is the way of hope. For Berry, good work is worth doing regardless of whether it will fix our global problems. Because he grounds his ultimate hope in a *given* redemption, he is freed to do good work without having the impossible pressure of fixing global problems. So while some of these technological and political ideas are worth pursuing—if we can find a way to clean up the trash in the ocean, we should certainly do that— such solutions are a poor foundation for hope because they will inevitably disappoint us: no technology can make us live forever, and no political system can make us live in harmony with one another. If global efficacy is the standard of our work, then most of us have no good work to do. As Berry writes, "If we think the future damage of climate change to the environment is a big problem only solvable by a big solution, then thinking or doing something in particular becomes more difficult, perhaps impossible."[8] Good work practices the virtue of hope regardless of whether such work is scalable or efficacious because good work participates in the healing, sustaining forms of the Kingdom of God. We help the wounded who are beside us because their lives are worth loving and caring for right now, not because they are part of some quantity that can be saved.[9]

Berry's posture of hope rests on two pillars: an eschatological vision of wholeness, or shalom, and particular, practicable examples of redemptive living.[10] He repeatedly insists that both are necessary; we cannot embrace one without the other, and we cannot try to collapse them together. One of our great temptations is thinking that individual acts will realize the *eschaton,* but they won't. Nevertheless, individual practices of healing—of helping our wounded neighbor—participate in the abundant life of the Kingdom of God. Throughout his essays, then, he turns to exemplars who demonstrate the kind of good work that is possible. Berry finds hope in locally committed artists such as the painter Harlan Hubbard and the poet William Carlos Williams, in Amish communities that practice a loving economy, and in the moral conversions Shakespeare dramatizes in *King Lear*. These examples form constellations that orient Berry and guide him in the midst of a dark, bewildering world.

Eschatological Hope and Practicable Examples

Berry insists on maintaining a gap between the ideal and the real, the hoped for and the actual. In a culture that is obsessed with efficient, scalable solutions, it can seem quixotic to advocate practices that are blatantly inadequate to achieve the health and wholeness for which we hope. Yet that is precisely what Berry does. As he writes in "The Purpose of a Coherent Community," "We are going to need the hope and the purpose of a coherent community, clearly articulated and steadily borne in mind. And we are going to have to resign ourselves to patience and small steps."[11] It is this combination of eschatological hope and practicable examples that gives shape to Berry's hope. This seemingly odd pair parallels the formal coherence and the incomplete lists that I described in the previous chapter. On the one hand, Berry's essays aspire to an ideal wholeness, to the Kingdom of God, to a formally complex shalom that leaves nothing out. And on the other hand, they celebrate particular, local, partial efforts to do good work.

There are historical reasons why our industrial culture finds it difficult to maintain this gap between the ideal and the actual. In the last chapter I outlined Charles Taylor's argument that our culture's code fixation stems from an arrogant desire to master a heterogeneous, complex reality. Taylor traces this desire to the time of the Protestant Reformation, when reformers of various stripes sought to remake society so that the masses could actually attain the religious and political ideals espoused by their leaders. Taylor distinguishes between "small-r reformers" who looked for particular, local modes of improving the church or ameliorating social ills, and capital-R Reformers whose "'rage for order'" led them to smash the old distinctions between sacred and profane in an effort to make everything sacred.[12]

This Reformist "drive to make over the whole society to higher standards" is predicated on a deep optimism about the possibility of transforming the present world to realize our ideals.[13] The effect of this Reformist impulse is to unleash a radical freedom to "re-order things as seems best."[14] Such freedom brings a heady optimism: we can change the world to usher in the millennial kingdom. This profound optimism has particularly shaped America; in the nineteenth century it generated many utopian communities and animated various reform movements—temperance, women's suffrage, abolition, the eight-hour workday.[15] Techno-utopians like Musk are just the latest iteration of this American millenarianism.

When these reform efforts inevitably fall short of their lofty goals, however, despair can quickly follow. James Smith, in summarizing this portion of Taylor's narrative, describes how, as the "gap between the ideal and the real" shrinks, people choose one of two seemingly opposite routes: "If people aren't meeting the bar, you can either focus on helping people reach higher or you can lower the bar. This is why Reform unleashes both Puritanism *and* the '60s."[16] So capital-R Reform leads to both Apollonian optimism—some new technique, some new code, some new technology will fix our problems and realize the *eschaton*—and Dionysian pessimism—our problems are unsolvable, antinomian chaos abounds, Armageddon is upon us.

Near the end of his narrative, Taylor points to a third way that avoids both optimism and pessimism by reestablishing a necessary gap between the ideal and the actual. As he argues, Christian eschatology maintains such a gap by locating hope in a divinely inaugurated redemption at the end of history: "This is a transformation which cannot be completed in history. In the nature of things, Christianity offers no global solution, no general organization of things here and now which will fully resolve the [tension between the ideal and the real]. It can only show ways in which we can, as individuals, and as churches, hold open the path to the fullness of the kingdom." And we hold this path open by means of specific, practical examples. Christians "can't exhibit fully what it means, lay it out in a code or a fully-specified life form, but only point to the exemplary lives of certain trail-blazing people and communities."[17] Christian hope, then, is distinguished by its faith in a final redemption and its conviction that humble acts of love—like tending the wounded neighbor at our feet—can participate in this redemption.

Berry links these two Christian virtues—faith and hope—in describing the gap between the broken world he experiences and the ideal he nevertheless hopes for: "Paul's letter to the Romans is precise and unrelenting in his definition of hope: 'For we are saved by hope: but hope that is seen is not hope: for what a man seeth, why doth he yet hope for? But if we hope for that we see not, then do we with patience wait for it' (8:24–25). 'Faith,' at root, is related to 'bide' and 'abide.' It has certainly the sense of belief, but also the sense of difficult belief—of waiting, of patience, of enduring, of hanging on and holding together."[18] Because the redemption for which Berry hopes is a gift he awaits and not an achievement he merits, he doesn't worry that his efforts are laughably inadequate. In fact, the gap between the scale of his work and the size of our problems is a constant reminder of the need for hope: to return to Paul, "hope that is seen is not hope."

Accepting this gap between our limited practices and our eschatological ideal frees us to act, whereas a focus on quantities and scalable solutions is paralyzing. A utilitarian ethic that measures success in terms of the greatest good for the greatest number can make particular responses to global problems seem pointless. If there are seven billion people in the world, what difference does it make if I drive my car less or buy grass-fed beef? The book *Numbers and Nerves* provides a psychological description of this phenomenon. Social scientists have found that people are more likely to donate money to help one child if they aren't reminded of the millions of children who need food. Similarly, people are more likely to provide water for 4,500 people in a small refugee camp (one with 11,000 people in total) than they are if told these 4,500 are in a large camp (one with 250,000 people). It seems that expanding the scale of the problem imparts a sense of helplessness or "pseudoinefficacy": "compared with the large numbers of persons out of reach, the prospective aid created a sense of inefficacy, that is, a 'drop-in-the-bucket' feeling." The authors argue, however, that this pseudoinefficacy "is nonrational. We should not be deterred from helping one person, or forty-five hundred, just because there are others we cannot help."[19] Yet in a culture that values quantifiable, wide-scale change, it's no surprise that people feel that their individual actions are useless.

In other words, efficacy itself may be the wrong standard. It's the standard of both optimists and pessimists, it's the standard of an age that's obsessed with quantities, but it's a standard that erodes hope, good work, and sustaining communities because it forecloses the possibility of resurrection. According to the standard of efficacy, our actions are worthwhile only if they lead to quantifiable change. This is the standard of Taylor's Reform rather than of eschatological hope, it's the standard of the organizing subject rather than the given self, it's the standard of a universal code rather than contingent neighborly love. So creating locally adapted art or being part of a flourishing community or undergoing a moral conversion will probably not reverse climate change or make a quantifiable dent in the vast problems of our world—although it's certainly possible that these humble actions are just as efficacious as the grand schemes of the techno-utopians—but we shouldn't judge the rightness of our actions by their efficacy. We help a refugee not because this is a way of "doing our part" in some mass movement or because we can help everyone who needs food and shelter. Rather, we provide food and water because the one refugee we help is valuable and worthy of care. Our hope should not depend on our individual actions causing widespread change; more often than not one person's good actions don't snowball into a large-scale movement. So if we do good only because we think our actions will lead to systemic change, we will grow discouraged and succumb to pessimism. We can't pin our hopes on achieving 350 parts per million of carbon dioxide or closing down CAFOs or reversing soil erosion. Thus, although Christian eschatology is often accused of justifying the reckless use of environmental resources, it can also free us to do good work by lifting the paralyzing burden of efficacy.[20]

Indeed, Berry's Christian vision does not expect that the health for which he hopes will be achieved in time, and yet his hope remains practicable. Berry's hope lives in disciplines and practices that participate now in the health and redemption for which he longs. While his hope is oriented toward a vision of eschatological shalom, it lives in the present. As he writes, "A desirable end may perish forever in the wrong means. Hope lives in the means, not the ends."[21] He expands on this in an interview, contrasting hope with both optimism and pessimism: "Optimism and pessimism are based on the idea of how things are [going to] turn out. Hope is grounded in the present; it's not about the future. It's about the reality of possibilities, this sense of possibility that you can do better."[22] Thus, Berry advocates for practices that "are good now, according to present understanding of present needs. . . . Only the present good is good. It is the presence of goods—good work, good thoughts, good acts, good places—by which we know that the present does not have to be a nightmare of the future. 'The kingdom of heaven is at hand' because, if not at hand, it is nowhere."[23] Such hope leads to good, redemptive work regardless of whether it results in measurable benefits. It motivates the kind of faithful action that Hebrews 11 celebrates as "the substance of things hoped for"—action that embodies the redemption we hope for even while we know we will not experience its fullness.

In this way, Berry's focus on local examples parallels Michel de Certeau's celebration of everyday or "diversionary" practices.[24] In contrast to Foucault, whose focus on systemic injustice leads him to chart the ever-tightening grip of a disciplinary society, Certeau traces the "tricky and stubborn procedures that elude discipline without being outside the field in which it is exercised, and which should lead us to a theory of everyday practices, of lived space."[25] These practices are not motivated by an expectation that the systems within which we live will be transformed or redeemed. Instead, Certeau explains, "The actual order of things is precisely what 'popular' tactics turn to their own ends, without any illusion that it will change any time soon. Though elsewhere it is exploited by a dominant power or simply denied by an ideological discourse, here order is *tricked* by an art."[26] In other words, we don't have to change the system to practice good, hopeful lives; instead, we need a certain kind of artistic creativity to imagine how to live well within the constraints of a broken world.

Certeau argues that such subversive practices or "tactics" require both artistic skill and a kind of hopeful joy: "People have to make do with what they have. In these combatants' stratagems, there is a certain art of placing one's blows, a pleasure in getting around the rules of a constraining space. We see the tactical and joyful dexterity of the mastery of a technique."[27] These creative practices "introduce *artistic* tricks and competitions of *accomplices* into a system that reproduces and partitions through work or leisure. Sly as a fox and twice as quick: there are countless ways of 'making do.' "[28] Certeau's analogy here echoes, almost certainly unconsciously, the conclusion of Berry's "Manifesto: The Mad Farmer Liberation Front":

> Be like the fox
> who makes more tracks than necessary,
> some in the wrong direction.
> Practice resurrection.[29]

The wily fox tracing unexpected paths models an artistic, creative approach to life. Certeau's joyful "making do" is a way of practicing hope even in situations where the "metrics" would justify pessimism.

Berry never cites Certeau, but he uses the phrase "make do" in a similar sense when praising the courageous persistence and creativity of African Americans who made do in oppressive, seemingly hopeless circumstances. In spite of the unjust system in which they lived, African Americans in Berry's rural Kentucky community found creative ways to enact hope; they "were skilled in the arts of make-do and subsistence."[30] In her book recounting her return to Kentucky, bell hooks cites this passage approvingly and notes that her grandparents had a similar view of competent, self-sufficient work as "humanizing"; they found ways to cultivate health "on the margins."[31] This mode of subversive creativity embodies the kind of hopeful action that Berry thinks remains possible in the midst of unjust systems.

Throughout his essays, Berry points to particular people or communities that exhibit these kinds of creative, hope-supporting modes of life. Rather than advocating for abstract principles or systems, he points to a particular artist (*Harlan Hubbard: Life and Work*), a particular poet (*The Poetry of William Carlos Williams of Rutherford*), a particular wilderness (*The Unforeseen Wilderness: Kentucky's Red River Gorge*), a particular forester ("A Forest Conversation"), a particular agrarian community ("Seven Amish Farms"), a particular interracial friendship (*The Hidden Wound*).[32] Such examples act as signposts or cairns that can guide our own lives. To understand the characteristics of these hope-giving examples, I will focus on just three that Berry returns to repeatedly: the local artists William Carlos Williams and Harlan Hubbard; the coherent communities preserved by the Amish; and the moral conversions that Shakespeare dramatizes in *King Lear*. What Berry writes about *King Lear* applies more broadly to all these examples: "Human hope may always have resided in our ability, in time of need, to return to our cultural landmarks and reorient ourselves."[33] These examples of good work and good lives are not likely to transform society, but, freed from the impossible burden of fixing the world's problems, we can orient our own lives by these landmarks. As Berry writes in describing Williams's poetry, "Local work, well done, is applicable elsewhere, not as prescription but as example."[34] The examples, then, may not be scalable, but they can be imitated. There's only one Harlan Hubbard or William Carlos Williams, we can't all become Amish, and each person's conversion is utterly unique; nevertheless, learning from these examples can inspire creative, hopeful ways of practicing resurrection in our own lives. They can teach us how we might shape our art, our communities, and our lives in proportion to the redemption for which we hope. By following these examples, we can be Certeauian foxes who practice resurrection, delightedly living well in the midst of a broken system.

Local Artists

Berry often points to authors or artists who have influenced him, but he devotes an entire book to the painter Harlan Hubbard and another one to the poet William Carlos Williams. In many ways, these two could not be more different. Hubbard was an eccentric painter who spent several years living with his wife, Anna, on a houseboat before establishing a Thoreauvian, off-the-grid household at Payne Hollow on the bank of the Ohio River. Williams was a pediatrician in suburban New Jersey who became a prominent modernist poet. In his books about these two very different men, Berry highlights similar aspects of their work: they both committed themselves to particular, marginal places; they both refused the modern habit of specialization that would divide their art from their lives; and they both worked in the hope that inspiration or grace would breathe life into their humble efforts. Their examples guide Berry's own efforts to be a person and writer committed to his place, and though the work of such relatively obscure artists may seem insignificant in the context of global problems, they demonstrate how faithful individuals can practice a hope for the healing of their places.

Berry read through Williams's poetry the summer after he completed his master's degree, and this reading challenged his general ambition to "be a poet, to write poems that would be admired and published."[35] This literary ambition threatened to distance Berry from his place. Reading Williams, however, enabled him to imagine how he could be a poet who would not "inhabit a career" but would write in the service of his place.[36] A few years after reading Williams, Berry happened on Harlan and Anna Hubbard's homestead while taking a canoe trip on the Ohio River, and the following year he and his wife, Tanya, moved back to Port Royal, Kentucky.[37] Both these artists remained committed to out-of-the-way places in spite of the cosmopolitan condescension they encountered, and their lives demonstrated to Berry how his art might serve and be enriched by his own place.

In describing what he values in Williams's poetry, Berry explains how Williams taught him to use his writing to more fully inhabit his place. "Local adaptation," Berry writes, involves "discovering where one is in relation to one's place (native or chosen), to its natural and human neighborhood, to its mystery and sanctity, and with discovering right ways of living and working there. . . . From [Williams's] example I learned to put my own work under [the heading of local adaptation], to see it not as an end in itself but as part of the necessary, if never finished or finishable, effort to belong authentically where my life had put me."[38] As Berry sees it, this work of local adaption is an essential responsibility of human culture, and, by extension, art: "The effort to adapt the economic life of a human community to the nature of its place is an effort intricately cultural, involving the relation of all work, including poetry, to 'the ground underfoot,' and involving inevitably the quality of that relation."[39] This effort to adapt our lives and economies to the shape of our places requires that we value where we are. And as Williams worked to see the inherent value in suburban New Jersey, so the Hubbards worked to care for and renew a marginal, overlooked place: "The paramount historical significance of the Hubbards' life is that they lived and thrived in a place in which, by the conventional assumptions of our time, all human possibilities were exhausted."[40]

Because of their local commitments, both Williams and Hubbard advocated for particulars over abstractions. Williams's famous poetic dictum—"no ideas but in things"—declares this allegiance. Such a commitment opposes a bureaucratic preference for abstract quantities. As Berry explains, "To imagine, to speak of and for, the things, persons, and places by which we actually live is to break the carapace of official identity and general ideas."[41] This official preference for abstraction is an inheritance from the European settlers who came to a new place and saw not it but their vision of what they wanted it to be: "We have lived in and exploited our country largely by preconception and wishful thinking, imposing on each new place we have come to the assumption that it is like the old place we have left, refusing to recognize where we are and to live within the limits of natural circumstance." As Berry understands him, Williams is not rejecting ideas as such, but abstract ideas, ones "divorced from the natural world, the senses, experience, and human scale."[42] So Williams's poems return again and again to the people and images of his home in an effort to see them fully and bring the "mass of local details" into an imaginative coherence.[43] Given the difficulty of this task, Williams didn't write a few perfect poems; rather, his immense body of poetry records his lifelong struggle to come to terms with his place, to imaginatively discern the wholeness that would unify and give meaning to its particulars.[44]

Harlan Hubbard likewise understood that seeing and valuing the particular members of his place was a way of resisting the reductive abstractions of the industrial economy, abstractions that authorize thoughtless destruction. Berry summarizes the ethical implications of Hubbard's aesthetic: "If one is going to destroy a creature, the job is made easier if the creature is first reduced to an idea and a price. Reduction, that is, facilitates manipulation or use without affection, and use without affection is abuse."[45] Like Williams, Hubbard refused to reduce particulars to their abstract categories because such reduction, while necessary for large-scale analysis and technological efficiency, makes these particulars fungible and vulnerable. Practicing hope entails honoring the inherent value of the creatures and people who live with you; it entails loving your wounded neighbor rather than looking for solutions to statistical abstractions.

Hubbard's aesthetic insistence on the value of particulars informed not just his painting but also his economic mode of life. And in shaping his entire life according to his vision of the beautiful, he rejected "the specialist's divisions between work and life and between art and work." Instead, he understood "his life [to be] a greater work to which his art belonged, which informed his art and was informed by it."[46] He "was a painter intent not only upon the art of painting, but also upon the art of living."[47] Hence, Berry explains that the care and love with which Harlan painted his place also motivated the Hubbards' household economy: "He wanted to know the earth in its particulars, for that is the only way that it can be known with love. But in order to preserve the identity of the earth in one's consciousness, it is necessary—and this is the bent of Harlan's genius—to give the body a significant life in the world—a life at once economic and, in the broadest sense of the word, artistic. The body, that is, if it is to mean more than the statistics of its existence, must support itself in a way that is dignifying and pleasing to itself."[48] To "make a life 'in harmony with the landscape,'" Harlan and Anna had to be not just musicians and painters, but also gardeners, carpenters, boatwrights, canners, and beekeepers.[49] In learning these practical arts, the Hubbards became skilled at making do, at crafting a beautiful, "elegant" household on the margins of an ugly, destructive economy.[50] And thus their life together partook in the imaginative wholeness that Harlan's paintings envision.

While Williams didn't lead such a countercultural life, he united two professions that tend to demand extreme specialization. Williams wrote at a time when both poets and doctors were becoming increasingly credentialed and professional, yet his local commitment led him to reject these tendencies: "A doctor who ministers to his home community and his neighbors is not in the modern sense a specialist, because he is also, always and at the same time, a neighbor and a citizen. A poet who is a doctor who is a community member likewise is not, because he cannot be, in the modern sense a specialist."[51] And this local commitment inflected both his poetry and his medical practice. He understood poetry to be "a civic obligation, a kind of work relating to community membership and neighborhood."[52] Similarly, as a doctor he "treated his patients as individual persons, as neighbors, rather than as 'cases' or 'types.'"[53] Williams demonstrated this attitude by often accepting chickens or vegetables from his patients in exchange for his medical care.[54]

As a doctor who regularly welcomed new life into the world, it's not surprising that Williams emphasized the role inspiration played in his poetry. Both he and Hubbard worked in the hope of inspiration or grace. Without this gift, all their efforts would be in vain, and yet inspiration remains a mystery. After quoting some of the poems in which Williams gestures toward this gift, Berry writes: "Nobody can account for inspiration. Like all who have experienced it, Williams was grateful for it, knowing he needed all the help he could get."[55] Hence, his poetry embodies "a prayer-like reaching beyond that may be indigenous to all art worth the name."[56] Yet in reaching toward the source of his inspiration, Williams remained committed to his place: "The two poles of Williams' imagination were the eternal moment and the ground underfoot."[57] Inspiration is not opposed to quotidian particulars but, rather, comes through particular people and creatures.

Hubbard had a similar understanding of the local sources of inspiration. Berry surmises that this faith was shaped by the Hubbards' life drifting down the river: "In giving oneself to the currents, in thus subordinating one's intentions, one becomes eligible for unintended goods, unwished-for gifts—and often these goods and gifts surpass those that one has intended or wished for. And so a drifter subscribes necessarily to a kind of faith that is identical both to the absolute trust of migrating birds and to the scripture that bids us to lose our lives in order to find them."[58] Such reliance on the gifts of grace and inspiration is a way of practicing resurrection; by giving up control and placing his hope in unforeseeable goods, Hubbard looks to an eschatological, given redemption, one that we may yet glimpse and participate in here and now. In his paintings, then, he strove to express "the 'richness' that 'shines through' the world."[59] Despite his rejection of orthodox Christianity, he associated this richness with "the incarnate Christ— the Christ of this world."[60] One example of Hubbard's efforts to see transcendent beauty, the beauty of "Christ himself," as immanent or incarnate in the world around him is a painting commissioned by the Mount Byrd Christian church in Milton, Kentucky. The church asked for a "baptismal scene," and it apparently expected "the Jordan of the Sunday School pictures." Hubbard, however, painted the Ohio River with its patchwork of farmland and, above it all, the sunlight breaking through the clouds. As Berry concludes, "The message is unmistakable: There is no need to look in a far-off country for a sacred river. Here is a nearer one, your own."[61] This faith in an ever-present, indwelling redemption motivated the Hubbards' artistic, locally rooted way of life. As Harlan Hubbard resolutely declared, "I believe that whatever we need is at hand."[62]

Though such a humble hope may seem absurd in the face of our global problems, Berry recounts a story that suggests the deep significance and lasting effects of the Hubbards' faithful opposition to an industrial economy. Near the end of their lives, a nuclear power plant was built across the river from their home. Berry himself was active in public protests against the plant, and he was frustrated by the Hubbards' refusal to get involved. Yet he came to understand "that by the life they led Harlan and Anna had opposed the power plant longer than any of us, and not because they had been or ever would be its 'opponents.' . . . What could be more radically or effectively opposite to a power plant than to live abundantly with no need for electricity? As the power plant rose, demonstrating the wrong way to live in the Ohio Valley, the Hubbards' life at Payne Hollow quietly went on as before, demonstrating the right way, without bothering to think of itself as a demonstration." And the Hubbards' mode of life won out. The Marble Hill power plant was never completed; it "collapsed under the burden of technological folly and economic fantasy."[63]

In his afterword to *Harlan Hubbard,* Berry concludes that "the most desirable result" of studying Harlan's life and work "is not an idea or a set of ideas, but his return to our minds, more vividly than ever, as presence."[64] And his presence is, as Berry wrote about William Carlos Williams, "an encouragement and a consolation."[65] These two artists committed themselves to their places, to making their art serve "community membership and neighborhood." And their example suggests that while such a commitment necessarily involves sacrifices, it also prepares us to receive "goods and gifts [that] surpass" those we intend. Beyond any calculable expectation, they were graced with resurrection, and their witness becomes another landmark that can inspire and guide our own efforts to live in hope.

Local Communities

Individuals like Harlan Hubbard and William Carlos Williams demonstrate the possibility of locally committed artists, but they are lonely examples that their communities, for the most part, did not heed. So Berry is also drawn to multigenerational communities that find ways to sustain healthy, placed cultures. He has written about many such communities over the years, from the hill farms of Tuscany to traditional Irish agriculture to indigenous farmers in Peru.[66] But the Amish are the community to which Berry most often turns when looking for an example of a community that has resisted the siren song of the industrial economy and has maintained the health of its members and its land. Their example gives him hope that sustainable communities can indeed thrive on the margins of a destructive industrial economy.

What makes the Amish such a powerful, hope-giving example for Berry? It's not that all of them are perfect or that their communities represent some utopian vision. Nonetheless, they sustain a communal order that subordinates individual desires to communal goals. And this communal order is at once religious and economic; they seek to practice neighborly love by refusing to outsource their responsibilities to institutions or technologies. The Amish don't seek to realize some grand ideal. They don't strive to convert the "English" or make everyone farm the way they do. Rather, they strive to tend their place and community and to pass it on undiminished to their children. And because they align their lives according to this hope, they actually care for the present good.

While working on *The Unsettling of America*, Berry went looking for examples of good farming that he could point to as proof that the kind of small farming he was advocating remained viable. Maury Telleen, a farmer and longtime editor of the *Draft Horse Journal,* introduced Berry to several Amish farmers who farmed with horses. As he visited these farmers and talked with them, Berry began "to know something of Amish farming and to understand its value as an example, and a measure, [by which to judge] industrial or 'conventional' agriculture."[67] In his later writings about small family farmers, then, Berry repeatedly points to the Amish as evidence that such agricultural practices remain possible. As he writes in one essay, "I have not been talking from speculation but from proof. I have had in mind throughout this essay that one example known to me of an American community of small family farmers who have not only survived but thrived during some very difficult years: I mean the Amish." He goes on to clarify that the Amish aren't some idyllic, perfect community—"I do not recommend, of course, that all farmers should become Amish, nor do I want to suggest that the Amish are perfect people or that their way of life is perfect."[68] As he writes in a letter to Gary Snyder, "Their government is tolerable only as long as there is somewhere to escape to if you don't like it."[69] Nevertheless, they offer evidence that there are real alternatives to the industrial economy; in the face of a culture that worships inevitable technological progress, the Amish enact their hope in a different kind of redemption.

Amish communities have survived, Berry argues in *The Unsettling of America*, because their members sacrifice individual desires to serve a communal good. Berry focuses on three particular aspects of this shared commitment: their religious faith, "a religion unusually attentive to its effects and obligations in this world"; their mistrust of institutions, such as insurance, that would permit them to outsource their neighborly responsibilities; and their deliberate limitations on technologies, which they judge on the basis of whether they will serve "the wholeness or health of the community."[70] Instead of individuals asking whether they want a particular technology or how a technology might benefit them personally, the Amish work—sometimes relatively harmoniously, sometimes not—to decide together how a given technology would affect their ability to care for each other and their places.[71] Such an approach to technology—and to institutions, which are themselves a kind of technology—posits a communal good to which individuals are responsible. Rather than looking for the most efficient way of caring for the elderly (nursing homes) or the least costly way of coping with unexpected disasters (insurance), they look to participate in the work of loving membership. Rather than efficacy, their standard is love, and the irony is that their communities are, in many ways, more "efficient" than industrial economies.

Though the Amish way of farming is, Berry argues, "ecologically and economically" better, they are largely overlooked in discussions of sustainable farming. Berry suspects this is because their methods don't enrich corporations; it's hard to make a profit from a community that does its own work and relies on natural cycles rather than petroleum and new commodities. Individuals in competition are profitable; neighbors loving each other aren't. The industrial economy is structured to look for new technologies that can be sold to individuals rather than new virtues that need to be practiced by communities. So the Amish are "living disproof of some of the fundamental assumptions" of the bigger-is-better orthodoxy.[72] If you're trying to solve global problems, you'll overlook humble communities faithfully tending small farms.

The root of Berry's admiration for the Amish is perhaps best articulated in his sabbath poem "The Amish Economy." Referring to people and themes that Berry describes in various essays, this poem uses a quote from David Kline to articulate the key distinction between the Amish and the industrial culture:

> My friend David Kline told me,
> "It falls strangely on Amish ears,
> This talk of how you find yourself.
> We Amish, after all, don't try
> To find ourselves. We try to lose
> Ourselves"—and thus are lost within
> The found world of sunlight and rain.[73]

By losing themselves to the given world, the Amish heed Jesus' paradoxical teaching: "He that findeth his life shall lose it: and he that loseth his life for my sake shall find it."[74] This religious subordination of the individual leads to an economy guided by love. As Berry writes in an essay in which he reflects further on the Kline's Amish economy, the "Amish community [is] a loving economy, for it is based on the love of neighbors, of creatures, and of places."[75]

Instead of searching for some total Reform or trying to manufacture some big solution, the Amish practice a hope that is grounded in the good gifts of the world in which they find themselves. And so their hope doesn't depend on the latest innovation coming out of Silicon Valley. Even those of us who aren't Amish can learn from them that our hope lies not in Elon Musk's funding the right venture, but in families and communities that choose not to outsource love to technologies or institutions. And these choices are real. Families can choose to own fewer cars, smartphones, and TVs and can work to make their homes centers of production and recreation and hospitality. Such decisions are made locally, around our dinner tables, and they ripple out to our workplaces and churches, neighborhoods and towns.

Moral Conversion

The Amish may provide an inspiring example of what our communities could be, but most of us do not belong to coherent, intergenerational communities. If we are broken individuals in a broken world, is there hope that we too can change, that we can lead more loving, redemptive lives? The radical conversions dramatized in Shakespeare's *King Lear* suggest that, yes, even the most warped and broken among us can change. And on this hope—that individuals can undergo a moral conversion—rests any hope for the redemption of our cultures. Without such conversions, all the technologies and all the political institutions in the world will never bring fundamental change.[76]

At the beginning of *Life Is a Miracle,* Berry writes that *King Lear* has been one of the redemptive examples on which he has grounded his hope: "Human hope may always have resided in our ability, in time of need, to return to our cultural landmarks and reorient ourselves. One of the principal landmarks of the course of my own life is Shakespeare's tragedy of *King Lear.* Over the last forty-five years I have returned to *King Lear* many times."[77] This play supports hope by imagining a "redemptive force" that can transform even the most warped humans.[78] On Berry's reading, *King Lear* is essentially about redemption, about finding one's life only by losing it: "The tragic play broods constantly on the idea, in Matthew 10:39 and also in the other three gospels, of losing one's life in order to find it. This theme is stated plainly in [I], i, when the King of France says to Cordelia, 'Thou losest here, a better where to find,' and this strikes so nearly to the heart of the play as to be virtually its subject."[79] By willingly sacrificing their aspirations and pride, the faithful servants—"Kent, Edgar, Cordelia, even the Fool, and finally Albany"—practice resurrection and thereby participate in the redemptive action of the play.[80]

The great evils that lie behind the play's tragic events—the evils that these sacrificial servants work to remedy—stem from a hubristic belief that life can be fully understood and controlled. Lear and the Earl of Gloucester cause great pain by "treating life as knowable, predictable, and within [their] control," and when their plans finally shatter, they both fall into despair.[81] As these characters demonstrate, hubristic optimism and apocalyptic pessimism are two sides of the same coin; both view life as inevitable and, thus, once events spin beyond their control, both give up on life.

Yet to believe life is determined, Berry argues, is to "pass beyond the possibility of change or redemption." Writing against the technocratic tendencies of our age, he explains that "suicide is not the only way to give up on life. . . . We can give up on life also by reducing it to the terms of our understanding and by treating it as predictable or mechanical." So both Lear and Gloucester succumb to "the human wish, or the sin of wishing, that life might be, or might be made to be, predictable."[82] And this is the same sin that our data-obsessed culture falls prey to: "It is becoming clear that to reduce life to the scope of our understanding (whatever 'model' we use) is inevitably to enslave it, make property of it, and put it up for sale. This is to give up on life, to carry it beyond change and redemption, and to increase the proximity of despair."[83] Big data and sophisticated climate change models may be powerful, but they tempt us to believe that we can understand and control life itself, a belief that inevitably has tragic consequences.

When we treat life as a machine or computer that can be quantified, manipulated, and fixed, we give up on life—we give up hope in the given, miraculous processes by which death serves life, by which we find our lives only in losing them. For Berry, this deterministic view of individual lives as integers that can be isolated and controlled is both an ecological and a theological mistake: "No individual life is an end in itself. One can live fully only by participating fully in the succession of the generations, in death as well as in life. Some would say (and I am one of them) that we can live fully only by making ourselves as answerable to the claims of eternity as to those of time."[84] Gloucester rejects these claims, and so Berry understands his "attempted suicide [as] an attempt to recover control over his life."[85]

What, then, is the alternative? Rather than acquiescing to evil or escalating their technological force to try to defeat evil on its own terms, the heroes in *King Lear* respond with "good and faithful service"; those who have been unjustly exiled from court work to serve the good of the very leaders and friends who have wronged them—they love their enemies. Their service doesn't magically fix the ramifying evil of the play, but it practices hope: "Lear and Gloucester in their selfishness are too vulnerable, and the wickedness of their adversaries is too real, to permit to the good servants any considerable practical success. They can give no victory and achieve no restoration, as the world understands such things. Their virtues do not lead certainly or even probably to worldly success, as some bad teachers would have us believe. They stand by, suffering what they cannot help, as parents stand by a dying or disappointing child. This assures only the survival in this world of faithfulness, compassion, and love—which is no small thing."[86] Shakespeare does not offer some naive, sentimental redemption; the play remains a tragedy. Yet if faithful service cannot bring global transformation, it can yet change individuals. These servants "restore those defeated old men to their true nature as human beings. They can waken them to love and save them from despair."[87] So by the end of the play, the two foolish, hubristic men who set the tragedy in motion have been redeemed by faithful, sacrificial service.

Yet hope-giving service must stem from a desire to participate in the present good rather than from the expectation that it will effect some systemic, large-scale change. When the Earl of Kent is unjustly banished by Lear, he tells himself, "If thou canst serve where thou dost stand condemned, / So may it come thy master whom thou lov'st / Shall find thee full of labors."[88] Berry reads this both literally and allegorically: "This is a literal description of Kent's predicament in the play, if we read 'thy master' as King Lear, and 'condemned' as Kent's exile. But it is also, and just as literally, a description of the human predicament and consequent obligation, if we read 'thy master' as Christ, and 'where thou dost stand condemned' as the fallen world."[89] Our hope is not somehow to effect our own redemption or to save the world—that is beyond our control—rather, our hope should be that when the end comes, when Christ brings his eschatological redemption, our master whom we love "shall find [us] full of labors."

A parallel mode of hopeful service leads Edgar, banished by his father, Gloucester, to disguise himself and remain to help his father. When Gloucester is blinded by Lear's ungrateful children and thrown out to die, Edgar follows him. And thus he is present when Gloucester asks for help in committing suicide. Edgar agrees to lead Gloucester to a cliff, but he instead takes him to a flat field and weaves for the blind Gloucester an imaginative description of a vast precipice. Gloucester falls forward, thinking to kill himself, and when Edgar speaks to him again he does so in the guise of a poor man who saw him fall "many fathom down." Because Gloucester has survived this immense "fall," Edgar tells him, "Thy life's a miracle. Speak yet again."[90] Believing that he has been miraculously saved, Gloucester repents of his efforts to presumptuously take control of life: "You ever-gentle gods, take my breath from me; / Let not my worser spirit tempt me again / To die before you please."[91] Through the imaginative experience that his disguised son leads him through, Gloucester, Berry writes, undergoes "a rite of death and rebirth"; he "finds his life by losing it."[92] And the result of this experience is that "he renounces control over his life. He has given up his life as an understood possession, and has taken it back as miracle and mystery." He has learned that "to treat life as less than a miracle is to give up on it."[93] So when at the end of the play Gloucester dies, he does so not in presumptuous optimism or pessimistic despair but "twixt two extremes of passion, joy and grief."[94] This is the in-between state of human hope, a state that holds in tension the extremes of eschatological joy and of grief over our present brokenness. Gloucester learns to live and die between these extremes rather than arrogantly trying to collapse this gap.

King Lear remains a tragedy, but Berry still sees it as redemptive: by the end, every one of the villains is dead, the kingdom is ruled by just men, Cordelia and Edgar "freely forgive their erring fathers," and faithful service has transformed these two flawed old men.[95] Berry understands Lear's final redemption to parallel Gloucester's resurrection. Both of them have been blind—one figuratively and one literally—yet at the play's end, as Lear holds the dead body of his now beloved daughter, he "at last *sees* Cordelia: 'Do you see this? Look on her! Look, her lips, / Look there, look there.'" Lear is finally jolted out of his self-absorption and sees his daughter as the beautiful person she is: "Cordelia, the play's only wholly undisguised character, has been disguised to Lear until the end by his self-preoc-cupying pride, anger, outrage, guilt, grief, and despair; and . . . when his vision clears at last and he can see her as she was and is, he is entirely filled with love and wonder. And so the play may be said to show us at last a miracle: that Lear, dying, is more alive than he has ever been until this moment."[96] By finally dying to his pride, selfishness, and arrogance, Lear is resurrected into the life of love and community that his daughter has been inviting him into throughout the entire play. He is ushered into a given life. The play holds out hope, then, that even the most prideful, self-absorbed people can be resurrected into a miraculous and mysterious life.

Practicing Hope

In our age, it is not only political authorities whose power tempts them to hubris-tically give up on life. Vast technological power underwrites the techno-utopia-nism of Elon Musk and other Silicon Valley denizens. And anyone with an Internet connection has at his or her fingertips the power of big data, fast proces-sors, and sophisticated scientific models. Such power can be useful, but it also tempts us to put our hope in the ability of technology to quantify, predict, and shape the future. And when we place our hope in technology and technocrats, we too give up on life, forgoing the difficult work that authenticates hope. Political and technological solutions will be an important and necessary part of address-ing our global climate crises, but they should not be the grounds of our hope. Rather, Berry argues that we should place our hope in the possibility that persons and communities can adapt their economies and cultures to their places, and that even those who have made mistakes in the past can change. In other words, we should place our hope in the practice of good, loving work. Hope is not an expectation that things will get better—that's optimism—it's faithful work that serves the present incarnations of the final redemption for which we wait.

In response to an interviewer's question about whether he could "envision . . . worldwide cataclysmic effects of climate change and global warming," Berry answered with a sharp rebuke:

> Well, I think that's easy to envision, but totally useless, illegitimate. People are always having visions of the future, but I don't think that we're called upon to do that. It's so much more important to have a vision of what is right. You can't outfox all the variables that are weighing on the future. Nobody knew about 9/11, nobody foresaw that. Nobody foresaw that the election of 2000 would be decided by the Supreme Court. I think that's a very foolish game that people play, saying "the water will be 18 feet deep in Manhattan" or something like that. To hell with it. I'm not interested in that. I mean, I'm unwilling to commit interest to that sort of thing; I have children and grandchildren and I have the appropriate fears for them, but the important thing is for me to fulfill my obligation to them. Which is to try to do the right thing now: to pass my memories on to them, and to give them good advice, knowing that they're going to ignore it for a while. But I don't like this futurology stuff. It doesn't move me.[97]

What does move Berry is work that tends present goods. Berry's mode of hopeful work resists totalizing Reform and disavows any arc of history that supposedly bends inevitably toward progress. Rather, Berry thinks that we practice hope when our faith in an eschatological redemption leads us to do good work now, right where we are. This is the logic that lies behind Martin Luther's apocryphal statement: "If I knew the world would end tomorrow, I would plant a tree." In other words, if we believe that God is going to save the world, then we have time to salve our neighbors' wounds.[98] When he comes, may we be found "full of labors."

5

Memory

An industrial culture encloses its inhabitants in a particular kind of time, time as the sequential succession of undifferentiated quanta. This experience of time is pungently expressed in the early twentieth-century adage "Life is just one damn thing after another."[1] Yet as Charles Taylor points out, this understanding of time is a relatively recent phenomenon, one brought about, in part, by "the disciplines of our modern civilized order [that] have led us to measure and organize time as never before in human history. Time has become a precious resource, not to be 'wasted.' . . . We have constructed an environment in which we live a uniform, univocal secular time, which we try to measure and control in order to get things done. This 'time frame' deserves, perhaps more than any other facet of modernity, Weber's famous description of a 'stahlhartes Gehäuse' (iron cage)."[2] In contrast, Berry's fiction imagines characters who remain outside this iron cage. They inhabit their places redemptively by dwelling in a different kind of time, one whose cyclical patterns form a narrative whole of which we are a part.

If time is simply succession, what the Greeks called *chronos,* then it makes sense that we would develop technologies to maximize it, to extract more "value" from this scarce resource. Airplanes and highways transport us across more miles per hour (although, as Ivan Illich has shown, these technologies are much less efficient than we tend to think).[3] Fiber optics and the latest wireless networks transfer more megabits per second. Powerful combines harvest more acres per hour. Keyboards enable us to type more words per minute. This is our 24/7 economy, in which each second must be used efficiently.

In a related way, other technologies reinforce our perception of time as undifferentiated. Hidden air conditioning and heating systems flatten seasonal time—all seasons feel the same 68 degrees. Global agricultural and transportation systems bring fresh produce to our grocery stores year-round. In subtle ways, even the smartphone cameras we carry reinforce this sense of uniform time; we can "capture" any moment, store it, and access it later at our convenience. Hence, all times and experiences are at hand and present to us.

This way of experiencing time weakens our sense that we inhabit circadian, lunar, or seasonal cycles, much less theological patterns of redemptive time. In other words, it causes us to lose a liturgical feel for time as a meaningful cycle, a pattern that includes us in a greater whole. The Greek term for this kind of time was *kairos*.[4] Our industrial culture has commercialized what little remains of this patterned sense of time: pumpkin spice lattes and Black Friday sales must mean that it's fall, and Super Bowl Sunday provides a midwinter ritual that gathers us around our TVs. These are weak replacements, however, for a religious and natural sense of kairos that places individuals in a coherent narrative. Taylor explains how a Christian sense of "higher tim[e] gather[s] and re-order[s] secular time. [It] introduce[s] 'warps' and seeming inconsistencies in profane time-ordering. Events which were far apart in profane time could nevertheless be closely linked. . . . Good Friday 1998 is closer in a way to the original day of the Crucifixion than mid-summer's day 1997."[5] When this understanding of time as a patterned whole is lost, our understanding of memory changes. An industrial culture tends to understand memory by analogy to computer memory; it's a process by which we retrieve randomly stored bits of data. And increasingly we offload this process to computers themselves: we don't need to remember things anymore because we can just Google them. This leaves us with a dramatically flattened kind of memory.

When we experience time as kairos, however, our memories integrate and connect disparate events into a meaningful narrative whole.[6] As we lose this richer sense of memory, we lose also our sense of a continuous and coherent self, one rooted in a remembered past. In its stead, we get the malleable self of industrialism that can be updated, upgraded, and refashioned as desired.[7] Certainly ethnic, national, religious, and even ostensibly natural understandings of patterned time have been used oppressively—individuals have too often been conscripted into damaging narratives. But such abuse doesn't mean the solution is simply to discard all pattern and assert that time is a blank, undifferentiated succession on which individuals are free to impose whatever meaning they desire. Liturgical time is one of those "inherited cultural jigs" that Matthew Crawford notes "once imposed a certain coherence (for better and worse) on individual lives."[8] Without being anchored in such a patterned, remembered whole, the self is adrift, free to choose a new location, career, friendship, spouse, or gender. This is the self as organizing subject rather than grateful recipient, the iPhone self that swipes away the unpleasant parts of its past. This self is liberated, but its Dionysian freedom becomes lonely, imprisoning, and ultimately destructive, and its forgetfulness makes it particularly vulnerable to being conscripted into potent commercial or political narratives that promise at least a patina of meaning.[9]

A forgetful self, one that merely inhabits bits of sequential time, cannot recognize temporal patterns, much less understand itself as a member of these patterned wholes. Yet as I have already discussed, Berry thinks that this sense of wholeness, with its etymological connections to health and holiness, is essential to fostering a sustainable community.[10] It is through memory that we perceive the health—or the lack thereof—in both communities and individuals. Once we learn to perceive our community as a whole, whether in ecological, theological, or cultural terms, we can work to fit ourselves rightly into this whole. Memory thus subordinates the individual self to a larger whole, knitting us into a narrative of which we are a part. It is this work of memory and membership that makes possible repentance and forgiveness, for without memory, individuals cannot mature and change in any coherent way.[11]

Readers of Berry's fiction repeatedly listen to characters narrate this kind of remembered self. His first novel, *Nathan Coulter,* employs the voice of an older narrator looking back on his childhood, and though his next three novels are written in the third person, two of them have some form of the word *memory* in their titles—*The Memory of Old Jack* and *Remembering*—and follow protagonists who are looking back on their lives in an effort to make sense of them. All his subsequent novels and many of his short stories are narrated by older characters recollecting either their whole lives or particular episodes. And it is through this act of remembering that Berry's narrators come to understand their individual lives as members of a patterned whole.

Rather than trying to control linear time, then, Berry's exemplary characters learn to inhabit cyclical time. They articulate an understanding of time and memory that has rich theological and literary roots, reaching back to Augustine, Dante, and T. S. Eliot. As characters like Nathan Coulter, Jack Beecham, Jayber Crow, Hannah Coulter, and Andy Catlett look back over their lives and stitch meaning together from disparate events, they discern the communal and theological narratives to which they belong. In this chapter I will focus on the short story "Pray without Ceasing," in which this kind of memory enables Andy Catlett to learn from his grandmother and other members of Port William how to understand and love the whole pattern of which he is a part. Applying memory's ability to perceive the whole pattern to sustainable communities may enable us to make decisions on the basis not only of our immediate desires but of the whole order. In this way, cultivating memory is a countercultural, resurrecting practice that can tune our affections to the larger pattern of creation and liberate love, as Eliot would have it, "beyond desire."

Augustine, Eliot, and a Theology of Memory

In *The Trinity,* Augustine searches for analogies by which we might understand the doctrine of the Trinity. He proposes that the three primary faculties of the human mind—memory, understanding, and will or love—bear a certain likeness to the Father, Son, and Holy Spirit in their independence yet mutual dependence. As he develops his argument, however, Augustine refines this analogy, saying that only when these three mental faculties are directed toward the real Trinity does their analogical likeness to God become fully realized: "Hence, this trinity of the mind is not on that account the image of God because the mind remembers itself, understands itself, and loves itself, but because it can also remember, understand, and love Him by whom it was made. And when it does so, it becomes wise; but if it does not, even though it remembers itself, knows itself, and loves itself, it is foolish. Let it, then, remember its God, to whose image it has been made, and understand Him and love Him."[12] Memory is the first step in a three-part process by which the mind becomes aware of itself, recognizes itself as created, and finally chooses to worship and love the Creator, thus, as Augustine goes on to say, being a "partaker" of the divine love. Through this process of remembering, knowing, and loving our Creator, humans may be "reformed and renewed" by participating in the life of God.[13]

It's important to note that Augustine sees this memory that unites us to God's life as a particular kind of memory, one slightly different from our normal understanding of memory as that faculty by which we recollect past events. Memory of some external phenomenon always chronologically follows the actual reality itself, and thus constitutes a less divine use of memory because it is not eternal. The mind's memory of itself, however, what Augustine calls *memoria sui,* is coterminous with the mind's existence and is therefore eternal (with respect to the mind). In other words, the mind's memory of itself is a special case of memory in which the event does not precede its memory. This is the memory by which I know myself to be myself, by which I know that the "I" who was raised in a particular family and married a particular person is the same "I" who is now writing this sentence. It is in this memory as self-knowledge that Augustine glimpses the image of his Trinitarian Creator in himself, and this image is completed only when his self-knowledge is oriented toward his Creator.

Nevertheless, this particular kind of memory is related to memory more broadly: in book 10 of *The Confessions,* Augustine describes his memory as an expansive space: "I come to the fields and vast palaces of memory, where are the treasuries of innumerable images of all kinds of objects brought in by sense-perception."[14] He goes on to delineate many different kinds of memory and the ways that these various functions undergird thinking, learning, and ultimately love. Yet in all these storehouses, Augustine fails to discern the highest truth, so his reflection on memory concludes with a turn toward the God in whose memory he is held: "I can find no safe place for my soul except in you. There my dispersed aspirations are gathered together, and from you no part of me will depart."[15] Sorting through the "dispersed aspirations" of his life enables

Augustine to find the one in whom they are gathered, the one who gives Augustine his very self. Thus the self-knowledge memory makes possible is complete only when it rests in its Creator.[16]

There are at least two implications that Augustine's view of memory has for Berry's sustaining, redemptive mode of memory. The first is that the faculty of memory enables self-knowledge, and yet this is not a knowledge of ourselves as separate individuals, as organizing subjects, but as persons in relationship. Memory grounded in a relational, Triune Creator reveals our place in the larger narrative that includes all creation. Rather than a self-knowledge predicated on Descartes's *cogito ergo sum,* Augustine's relational identity begins with memory. This is why Augustine's *Confessions* is a prayer to his Creator that remembers the events of his life to better understand them and so express proper gratitude to and worship of the God who has led him.[17]

This sense of individual lives participating in a larger, divine narrative is a feature of the Judeo-Christian imagination. Israel's covenant, as Ellen Davis points out, is maintained by the Israelites' practice of "communal memory," which reminds individuals of their responsibilities to God and the land he has given their community.[18] Christians inherit this sense of their place within an ongoing covenantal narrative, which is why many older Bibles have space for a family tree between the Old and New Testaments—our individual family stories are part of God's story.[19] In an essay about Augustine's influence on this feature of Christian thought, Alan Jacobs calls such practices "thinking narratively about individual lives." As Jacobs explains, it is Augustine's "memoria"—"this active, interpretive, constructive faculty"—"that enables us to think of our lives in meaningfully narrative ways."[20] As we will see, this narrative understanding of the self made available through memory permeates Berry's fiction.[21]

By relating the individual self to this larger narrative whole, memory makes restoration and redemption possible, and this restorative power of memory is the second way that Berry's fiction draws on an Augustinian understanding of memory. Augustine's anthropology sees humans as broken and restless until they are restored to a right relationship with their Creator. This rest in God's love is the goal of Augustine's prayer and remembering in *Confessions,* and it is why he claims a mind can become wise only when it "remember[s], understand[s], and love[s] Him by whom it was made." This unity with the Creator begins to restore Augustine to a right relationship with Him and the rest of creation, thereby granting Augustine a foretaste of the final restoration of all things. Thus, for Augustine, the highest use of the faculty of memory is prayer: *Confessions* is his life remembered as a prayer of repentance and redemption. Berry draws on this connection between memory and prayer throughout his fiction and particularly in "Pray without Ceasing."

In some ways, this summary of Augustine merely reframes the good work done by Phillip Donnelly and John Leax on Berry and memory. Both scholars link Berry's view of memory to Augustine's and articulate how memory positions Berry's characters in a larger communal whole. As Leax claims, "Andy's memory is fruitful, able to shape his return and future, because it is not merely a personal memory; it is a memory participating in a communal memory that contains him quite apart from his actions."[22] Donnelly reads Berry's novella *Remembering* to trace the ways in which Andy's act of remembering heals the dismemberment precipitated by the loss of his right hand. As Andy remembers his familial, local, and biblical narratives, he is restored to his membership in these communities.[23] This understanding of Augustinian memory in Berry's fiction can be extended and clarified in two ways, however: first, by a consideration of T. S. Eliot's influence on Berry, and, second, by giving close attention to the way that Berry enacts this Christian view of memory in the form of his narration. I will consider these in turn.

T. S. Eliot acts as an important mediator between Augustine and Berry: I am not aware of any specific references to Augustine in Berry's writing, but Berry cites Eliot often, and his address accepting the T. S. Eliot Award (1994) pays tribute to Eliot's poetry of hope and redemption, a redemption grounded in honest love.[24] In *The Four Quartets,* Eliot provides a vision of the power of memory to restore healthy relationships. In this masterful sequence of poems, Eliot draws disparate elements from his cultural and personal past and seeks to discern a whole pattern within them. Eliot shares Augustine's belief that memory can enable us to perceive the redemptive pattern within which we belong. Near the end of "Little Gidding," Eliot writes, "A people without history / Is not redeemed from time, for history is a pattern / Of timeless moments."[25] Only by looking back through time can a people perceive the eternal pattern in which they are held and thus know themselves as members of a larger whole. This past, as Eliot writes elsewhere in *The Four Quartets,* is not "mere sequence" or "even development" but a "pattern," an order we can enter only by the "sharp compassion of the healer's art," one "whose constant care is . . . to remind of our, and Adam's curse."[26] Again, as Augustine does, Eliot employs memory to remind himself of his place in the narrative that includes not only Adam's curse, but also that Friday "we call . . . good."[27]

Eliot clarifies how memory can place us in this pattern when, in "Little Gidding," he reflects on the differences among "attachment," "indifference," and "detachment." Eliot distinguishes among attachment—which can be selfish and immature but is nonetheless part of love—detachment—which is needed so that we can see the whole—and indifference—which is a kind of distance that leads not to the flowering of healthy attachment but to jaded apathy. It is memory's task to refine these impulses into genuine love:

There are three conditions which often look alike
Yet differ completely, flourish in the same hedgerow:
Attachment to self and to things and to persons, detachment
From self and from things and from persons; and, growing between them,
　　indifference
Which resembles the others as death resembles life,
Being between two lives—unflowering, between
The live and the dead nettle. This is the use of memory:
For liberation—not less of love but expanding
Of love beyond desire, and so liberation
From the future as well as the past.[28]

This love, as Eliot explains, is "never indifferent," but its paradoxically attached detachment frees the rememberer to seek the good of the whole pattern, the whole community. It is this expansion of "love beyond desire" that many of Berry's narrators experience as they remember their lives: it is what Jayber experiences as he remembers his love for Mattie, it is what Hannah experiences as she allows her expectations for her children to be transformed into simple hope, and it is what Andy experiences in *Remembering* as he accepts the loss of his right hand and chooses to return to his place in his family and community. What Eliot seems to be getting at here is that memory, by allowing us to see the whole picture, gives us the opportunity to direct our affections and loves more intentionally and rightly. It's not the cold, objectifying distance sought by the organizing subject—memory is a deeply subjective experience—and so it doesn't lead to apathy and destruction, but it does provide the understanding of the whole that we need in order to be liberated from selfish desires and set free into the course of true charity.

The love that Eliot describes here is akin to an aesthetic experience in its simultaneous detachment and subjectivity. In commenting on this passage, Seamus Heaney explains how memory allows us to fit our experiences into an artistic whole: "When T. S. Eliot says in *Little Gidding* that the use of memory is 'for liberation,' he is not thinking of memory as an escape mechanism. What he has in mind is something more akin to that readjustment and repossession of the ability to understand experience which Aristotle called *catharsis*, that momentary release from confusion which comes from seeing a drama complete itself in accordance with its own inner necessities rather than in accordance with the spectator's wishes. The satisfaction which art gives resides in this sense of rightness."[29] Heaney describes the aesthetic experience aptly; perceiving beauty is liberating in the same way that memory can be because in both experiences we gain distance or perspective (Eliot's "detachment") without being personally removed ("indifference"). We experience beauty from a certain distance, it's an object "out there" that we perceive to be beautiful, and yet the desire beauty arouses is deeply subjective. In one essay, Eliot explains that he can appreciate and enjoy a live performance of a symphony better if he already knows it well: "I enjoy and 'understand' a piece of music better for knowing it well simply because I have at any moment during its performance a memory of the part that has preceded and a memory of the part that is still to come. Ideally I should like to be able to hold the whole of a great symphony in my mind at once."[30] As Dominic Manganiello explains in reference to this passage, Eliot's memory enables him to relate the parts to this whole.[31] If Eliot holds a symphony in his memory, he can love it *better* than other symphonies: he loves it more strongly than others and he loves it more richly and accurately. Through memory, and the conception of the whole it provides, Eliot's love for this beautiful piece of music has been refined and deepened.

The view of memory that Augustine and Eliot hand down, then, values memory because it allows us to see the whole pattern without removing ourselves from this pattern: we are not the organizing subjects standing over a world of commodities, swiping and tapping to meet our immediate desires, but nor are we so enmeshed in the present that we don't understand how our lives fit in the larger patterns to which we belong. Thus, memory liberates us to love and desire the health of our communities; we begin to think not only of our individual desires and preferences, but of the other members of the pattern. Memory allows us, to use Augustine's terms, to understand the whole and then to love it. In this way, memory leads to the renewal and transformation of the pattern in which we live, and it does this by enlarging and clarifying our affections, by, to use Eliot's phrase, changing "the ground of our beseeching."[32]

"Pray without Ceasing"

To demonstrate how such an understanding of memory works out in Berry's fiction, I will focus on his short story "Pray without Ceasing." This story is narrated by Andy Cattlet, the most autobiographical character of Berry's Port William fiction and the one he most often chooses as a narrator.[33] Andy is fifty-five years old in this story, and his opening reflections on time and memory lead him to remember a particular day, about twenty-five years earlier, when he listened to his grandmother recall for him the story of his great-grandfather's murder. Andy's narration thus shuttles between three times: the present, his conversation with his grandmother Margaret twenty-five years previously, and the death of his great-grandfather Ben seventy-eight years before the present. Interestingly, though, most of the story is actually a third-person, past-tense account of the events around Ben's death; when Andy narrates the story he heard twenty-five years earlier from his grandmother, he largely removes both her and himself and allows the characters to speak for themselves. The memory of this event has ceased to belong to any one individual and instead belongs to the community. At certain key junctures in the story, however, Andy breaks from this third-person voice to relate asides from Margaret or to describe how he responded that day to learning the fuller story of his great-grandfather's death. To understand the implications of this particular narrative structure, I'll first look at Andy's opening remarks about time and memory; then I'll examine the shifts between Margaret's narration to Andy and the actual events some fifty-three years earlier. By doing so, we can see how memory links all these individuals into an eternal, redemptive story, for even as Margaret tells Andy of two tragic deaths, she sees how the pain of this story has been, and is still being, redeemed by love. Her memory, the memory Andy comes to own for himself, liberates them into love and ultimately prayer.

Andy opens his story by defining his place in the family line: "Mat Feltner was my grandfather on my mother's side."[34] This past tense verb *was* then leads Andy into a reflection on the strangeness of time: the present tense *is* that he once used to refer to his grandfather became a *was* when Mat died. "This is part of the great mystery we call time," Andy says, "But the past is present also. And this, I think, is a part of the greater mystery we call eternity."[35] Here, at the outset of his story, Andy reveals his Augustinian understanding of memory as the faculty by which we participate in eternity.

And yet, as his first sentence indicates, the memory of his grandfather leads him to know his place in eternity through his particular place in his family line. Andy subtly compares this self-knowledge to the Old Testament understanding of a covenant that continues "generation to generation." Andy recalls that when he would sit down with his grandfather after returning from a longer absence, Mat would place his hand "lightly onto my leg above the knee. . . . The shape of his hand is printed on the flesh of my thigh as vividly as a birthmark."[36] As biblical scholars have observed, Hebrew covenants are passed down by placing a hand under the thigh.[37] Andy knows himself as a member of this continuing family narrative; his memory enables him to take his place in his covenant community.[38]

As Andy's reflections on memory continue, they become more explicitly Augustinian. Andy describes how his memories of his grandfather and of his place in his family's story unite him with the Creator who is always at work: "You work your way into the interior of the present, until finally you come to that beginning in which all things, the world and the light itself, at a Word welled up into being out of their absence. And nothing is here that we are beyond the reach of merely because we do not know about it. It is always the first morning of Creation and always the last day, always the now that is in time and the Now that is not, that has filled time with reminders of Itself."[39] Like Augustine, who views memory's ultimate purpose as uniting us with the life of the triune Creator, Andy here uses his memory to work his way into the presence of the eternal Word who created the world and time. Andy's movement in these opening paragraphs, from his memory of past events to his place in his family's lineage, to the presence of the creative Word, follows Augustine's movement from the memory of experiences to understanding how these fit into a whole narrative, to participatory worship and love of the Creator.

Andy goes on to explain memory's resurrecting power by articulating what he learned while watching his grandfather die: "I was experiencing consciously for the first time that transformation in which the living, by dying, pass into the living."[40] Theologically, this describes how death is the consummation of Mat's participation with the ever-living Word, and ecologically it describes the way his body will die, decompose, and feed new life. In other words, it is by watching his grandfather die that Andy first learns what it means to practice resurrection. And as he listens to his grandmother narrate his great-grandfather's death, Andy learns how he, though still living, can die to his selfish desires and pass into the living love, the love by which all that lives lives. Andy's grandmother Margaret teaches him the use of memory that Eliot wrote about, the liberating of desire into love. She is a fit teacher for Andy because she has undergone this redemptive liberation herself. Andy knows that as she sat each day in great pain from her arthritis, "she occupied her mind with thoughts. Or that is what she said she did. I believed, and I was as sure as if she had told me, that when she sat alone that way, hurting or not, she was praying."[41] She has turned her thoughts and memories into prayer, and so, like Augustine, employs memory to lead her into the love that created the world.

Andy's general musings on memory lead him to recall a specific day twenty-five years earlier when a neighbor brought him an old newspaper clipping about his great-grandfather Ben Feltner's death. On that day in 1912, Thad Coulter rode into town and shot Ben Feltner in the head before turning himself into the sheriff and telling him, "I've killed the best friend I ever had." Reading this clipping, Andy realizes that he doesn't know much more about this event than the bare facts. Seeing "how incomplete the story was as the article told it and as I knew it," Andy remembers, "I felt incomplete myself."[42] That day, when Andy went to visit his grandfather, who was slowly dying, his grandmother finally told him this painful family story. She knew it well, having "pondered" it over many years with her mother-in-law, Ben's wife.[43] Andy begins to relate the story as he heard it that day from his grandmother: " 'If it hadn't been for Jack Beechum, Mat would have killed him,' my grandmother said. That was the point. Or it was one of the points—the one, perhaps, that she most wanted me to see. But it was not the beginning of the story. Adam and Eve and then Cain and Abel began it, as my grandmother depended on me to know."[44] Like the imprint of his grandfather's hand on his thigh, this story places Andy, and the other participants in it, within the grand redemptive narrative of the Bible. Not only is his family tree probably written in the pages of the old family Bible, his family's stories are also continuations of the biblical story. Again we see memory connecting Andy and his family to a larger eternal narrative, a narrative that begins with pride and sin and murder but that will end in redemption and love. The point in Margaret's mind is that community, represented in this case by Jack Beechum, can slow us down and remind us of the eternal whole in which we participate, thus liberating us to understand and to will love toward someone who has hurt us deeply.

After beginning the story here in his grandmother's words, Andy shifts into a semi-omniscient, third-person point of view. It is as if by listening to his grandmother tell the story, a story she herself learned not only from her role in it but also from conversations with Ben's wife and other participants, Andy internalizes the story himself. He now shares this story with us from the narrative perspective of the community, a perspective that sees the whole, having understood and sympathized with the various individual perspectives.

Yet Andy punctuates this third-person narration with memories of his grandmother's telling the story to him that day twenty-five years before. For instance, after introducing Thad Coulter, the man who would kill Ben, and describing the familial and financial problems that shamed him and drove him to drink, Andy interjects this exchange: " 'Thad Coulter was not a bad man,' my grandmother said. 'I believed then, and I believe now, that he was not a bad man. But we are all as little children. Some know it and some don't.' She looked at me to see if I was one who knew it, and I nodded, but I was thirty then and did not know it yet."[45] Andy, looking back with the wisdom of twenty-five more years, knows himself as he was then better than he knew himself at the time. He sees now that he didn't even know his own ignorance, his own proclivity to weakness and failure, but in the remembered context of his grandmother's story, he knows himself more fully—he did not know it yet, but he does now.

These interjections by Margaret serve to drive home the point, or points, that she begins her story with: "If it hadn't been for Jack Beechum, Mat would have killed him." Jack was Mat's uncle, and on the day Thad rode into town and shot Ben, Jack was also in town on business. When he heard his brother-in-law had been shot, he ran toward the crowd, coming just as Mat, who had arrived first and seen his father's dead corpse, was running to find Thad and avenge his father's death. When Jack saw Mat, he simply "caught [him] and held him." Jack holds the enraged Mat, pinning his arms and restraining him:

They strove there a long time, heaving and staggering. . . . Something went out of [Jack] that day, and he was not the same again.

And what went out of Jack came into Mat. Or so it seemed, for in that desperate embrace he became a stronger man than he had been. A strength came into him that held his grief and his anger as Jack had held him. And Jack knew of the coming of this strength, not because it enabled Mat to break free but because it enabled Jack to turn him loose.[46]

Like his grandfather's hand clasped on Andy's thigh, this bear hug forcibly reminds Mat of the whole in which he is a part. At a moment when his anger had made "both [him] and his enemy . . . as clear of history as if newborn," Mat needs Jack's embrace to free him from his raw anger, to liberate him from the desire for revenge into the love of his family and community, a love that must now, somehow, include even his father's murderer.[47]

Mat, liberated by Jack's embrace from his violent anger, comes home to break the tragic news to his mother and his wife. Margaret realizes what has happened when Mat asks her to take their young daughter upstairs so he can tell Ben's wife in private: " 'I knew what it was then,' my grandmother said. 'Oh, I felt it go all over me before I knew it in my mind. I just wanted to crawl away. But I had your mother to think about. You always have somebody to think about, and it's a blessing.' "[48] This blessing is another one of the points of Margaret's story: remembering others, willing the good of others in love, liberates one from selfish desires, whether Mat's longing to kill Thad or Margaret's desire to isolate herself in her own private grief.

This same blessing is also revealed in the person of Thad's daughter, Martha Elizabeth. When Thad in his drunken rage sets out to kill Mat, Martha Elizabeth follows her father, trying to comfort him and bring him home, and even after he shoots Ben and then turns himself into the sheriff, Martha Elizabeth sits with him in jail, feeding him and being present with him. Tragically, the second night he is in jail, when she goes to sleep at the sheriff's house, Thad takes his own life. Repeatedly, Andy breaks from his third-person narration to repeat Margaret's memories of Martha Elizabeth: she "remembered how gentle Martha Elizabeth had been with [Thad]"; " 'Everybody loved Martha Elizabeth,' my grandmother said. 'She was as good as gold.' "[49] Near the end of the story, when recalling Thad's death in jail, Margaret takes great pains to convey to Andy the import of the love that Martha Elizabeth embodied:

"You see," my grandmother said, "there are two deaths in this—Mr. Feltner's and Thad Coulter's. We know Mr. Feltner's because we had to know it. It was ours. That we know Thad's is because of Martha Elizabeth. The Martha Elizabeth you know."

I knew her, but it came strange to me now to think of her—to be asked to see her—as a girl. . . . Miss Martha Elizabeth, we younger ones called her. Everybody loved her.[50]

Having known her only as an older woman, Andy can hardly imagine her as a young girl, faithfully following her father-turned-murderer. Andy's knowledge of this woman is, he now sees, incomplete, as all our knowledge inevitably is, but this story of her love for a wrecked father transforms Andy's understanding of her. He now glimpses the depths behind her smile and laughter, knowing more fully the pain it includes.

But his grandmother still isn't convinced that Andy has understood her point adequately:

Again she paused, looking at me. . . . "People sometimes talk of God's love as if it's a pleasant thing. But it is terrible, in a way. Think of all it includes. It included Thad Coulter, drunk and mean and foolish, before he killed Mr. Feltner, and it included him afterwards."

She reached out then and touched the back of my right hand with her fingers; my hand still bears that touch, invisible and yet indelible as a tattoo.

"That's what Thad saw. He saw his guilt. . . . But in the same moment he saw his guilt included in love that stood as near him as Martha Elizabeth and at that moment wore her flesh. It was surely weak and wrong of him to kill himself—to sit in judgment that way over himself. But surely God's love includes people who can't bear it." . . .

"It's a hard story to have to know," my grandmother said. "The mercy of it was Martha Elizabeth."

She had more to tell, but she paused again, and again she looked at me and touched my hand.

"If God loves the ones we can't," she said, "then finally maybe we can. All those years I've thought of him sitting in those shadows, with Martha Elizabeth standing beside him, and his work-sore old hands over his face."[51]

As she acknowledged, on the day Margaret heard that Thad had killed her father-in-law, her first thought was not about God's love or loving Thad; she just wanted to crawl away. And yet over the years, as she has pondered these events with Ben's wife and with Martha Elizabeth, Margaret has allowed herself, through memory, to be included in a divine love for all creation. She has been made able to love the enemy she couldn't love. Memory has liberated her into love, the love that as Augustine wrote was the proper end of all our memory and understanding and will.

One of the ways that this understanding and love are evidenced is in the sections where the narrator of the story attempts to enter into Thad's consciousness.

As I mentioned, while ostensibly Andy narrates the story to us as he remembers Margaret narrating it to him, much of the story is actually written in a sort of omniscient third person. It is as if the story belongs neither to Margaret nor to Andy, but to the collective memory of Port William itself, and thus at several junctures we are privy to Thad's emotions and thoughts. In particular, this happens as Thad, in his drunken state, rages against his financial failure and his perception that Ben Feltner has rejected him. Then, after he shoots Ben, we again follow Thad as he makes the slow journey to the sheriff's office to turn himself in. As he travels, the realization of what he has done becomes increasingly oppressive: "The walking . . . cleared his mind, and now he knew himself as he had been and as he was and knew that he was changed beyond unchanging into something he did not love. Now that his anger had drained away, his body seemed to him not only to be a burden almost too heavy to carry but to be on the verge of caving in. He walked with one hand pressed to his belly where the collapse seemed already to have begun."[52] Yet as Margaret says, the mercy of the story is that when Thad cannot love himself, the community can nevertheless include him in its love. Martha Elizabeth continues to love her father, to see him held within the divine love that "includes people who can't bear it."[53]

Martha Elizabeth, standing in love beside her broken father, is not the only standing figure whom Margaret asks Andy to see. The final scene Margaret describes to Andy is the lynch mob that arrived at Mat's door the night of Ben's murder and offered to raid the jail and kill Thad. As Mat stands on the porch to speak to these men who desire to enact the revenge he himself had wanted a few hours earlier, Jack takes his stand just behind Mat, still not certain if his earlier embrace of Mat has completed its work. But it has, and Mat calmly answers their offer to kill his father's murderer: "No, gentlemen. I appreciate it. We all do. But I ask you not to do that. . . . Come and be with us. We have food, and you are all welcome." Mat chooses peace, offering renewed fellowship and friendship rather than revenge: " 'I can see him yet,' my grandmother said, her eyes, full of sudden moisture, again turned to the window. 'I wish you could have seen him.' And now, after so many years, perhaps I have." Andy has taken Margaret's memory and made it his own, thus allowing him to see how forgiveness and concern for others can liberate us from wrong desires. And he knows this not only in his memory but also in his bones, for as he says, "I am blood kin to both sides of that moment when Ben Feltner turned to face Thad Coulter in the road and Thad pulled the trigger. . . . I am the child of [Mat's] forgiveness."[54] If it were not for Mat's choice to forgive that day, and the whole family's choice to heal the broken community, Andy's parents would never have married; his mother descended from the murdered man, but his father was a relation of the murderer. Knowing this story, he knows his identity as a member of a forgiving community. The

"incomplet[ness]" he felt at the beginning of the story has been healed, and joining in this history of love, Andy knows himself and his ancestors, in the words of
Eliot, "renewed, transfigured, in another pattern."[55]

His grandmother's example and her story show Andy that to maintain his
place in this pattern of love, he must learn to pray without ceasing. This titular
quotation is spoken in the narrative by Della Budge, Jack Beechum's old teacher
who tried unsuccessfully to "teach him the begats from Abraham to Jesus."[56] But
though she failed to implant these names in his memory, she seems to have succeeded in teaching Jack to understand his life as part of the redemptive narrative
these biblical names signify. When Della leaves the Feltner house after paying her
respects to Ben, she tells Jack that death will come unexpectedly for them all, "So
we must always be ready. . . . Pray without ceasing." Jack helped her down the
steps, then "stood and watched her going away, walking, it seemed to him, a tot-
tering edge between eternity and time."[57] As Andy discerns in his reflections at
the beginning of his story, so also Jack sees how memory directed toward the
Creator in prayer allows us to participate in an eternal pattern even as we live in
time. As memory "purifies the ground of our beseeching" and liberates us to live
in the renewed pattern of love, we begin to know ourselves in community, to
know the blessing, as Margaret says, of always having somebody to think about.

Practicing Memory

The narrative form of Andy's story enacts this process of remembering our place
within an eternal community. Andy does not see himself as an organizing subject who is free from his time and place; rather, he comes to understand himself
as a member of a narrative that stretches back to Adam and Eve, Cain and Abel.
This narrative continues in the life of his local community, and Andy is "incomplete" until he knows himself as a part of this larger story. Such a relational
understanding of the self is essential to a sustainable community because it positions individuals to understand and make decisions as members of a larger whole.

Not all remembered narratives lead to forgiveness and renewal. Unfortunately, many communities and individuals remember themselves in ways that
feed bitterness and resentment. Port William has its share of individuals who
remember the past in damaging patterns. Thad is driven to drink and eventually
to murder because he cannot reconcile who he has become—a destitute beggar—
with the memory of his role as a successful farmer and respected member of Port
William. If he had allowed Ben and others to renarrate how he understood his
son Abner's business failure, Thad might have been able to regain his place in the
community, but his shame and anger isolated him. And in *A Place on Earth*,
Roger Merchant's absurdly romanticized memory of his father "as a cultivated

and enlightened gentleman farmer" enables him to justify to himself his lazy, drunken way of life.[58] Margaret, however, models for Andy a mode of memory that, because it is rooted in the biblical narrative of redemption, heals and restores a damaged community.

It is memory's ability to perceive and mend the tattered patterns of our lives that makes it a sustaining virtue. Remembering the whole pattern of which we are a part focuses our attention on our particular place in this whole, and on the local, immediate steps we can take toward healing and restoring this order. All restorative ecology, for instance, depends on memory; not the memory of some pristine, Edenic, "perfect" ecological community, but the memory of other communities in this place, and how healthy communities follow from earlier healthy communities, a succession that in many places has been interrupted by sickly monocultures.[59] Like meaning, our perception of health emerges only in memory, a memory composed by the kind of communal pondering demonstrated in "Pray without Ceasing." As Eliot could better enjoy a symphony that he knew well because he held the whole work in his mind and could appreciate how each part fit into this whole, so cultivating a fuller memory of ecological health can enrich our understanding of this health, leading us to love the way that each member fits into this pattern.

Berry's remembering narrative voice also shapes readers in more personal ways. Memory offers us the opportunity to shape our affections and pursue wisdom. Berry's exemplary characters—whether Margaret sitting in pain from her arthritis and remembering and praying, or Della Budge still instructing Jack to pray without ceasing, or Andy himself thinking back to his grandmother telling him this story and seeking to impress on him the mysterious extent of God's love—have altered the "ground of their beseeching," their deepest longings, through carefully pondered memory. Reconfiguring the narratives of their lives leads these characters toward charity, toward thinking of somebody else. Memory, then, enables *metanoia* on the basis of understanding and loving a coherent whole.

In a culture whose technologies aim to control chronological time and use it more efficiently, we can nonetheless cultivate a kind of memory that locates us in patterned, cyclical time. We can practice a mode of memory that does not merely access past events—that is simply Google—or feed the self-serving fantasies of the organizing subject. Instead, we can practice memory as the process by which the given self understands what has been given and what this gift requires. Our parents and grandparents can narrate their stories in redemptive ways, working together to see how our lives might fit into the patterns of resurrection. Margaret takes great pains to tell this story of murder and loss in ways that enable Andy to see its redemptive possibilities. As Hannah Coulter would put it, Margaret "tell[s] the stories right." Hannah defines right storytelling in ways that resonate with Margaret's prayerful, redemptive narration: "You mustn't wish for another life. You mustn't want to be somebody else. What you must do is this: 'Rejoice evermore. Pray without ceasing. In every thing give thanks.' I am not all the way capable of so much, but those are the right instructions."[60] Remembering our lives in this grateful, prayerful mode can be a key countercultural practice that tunes our affections to the larger patterns of creation and thus prepares the way for redemptive action within our places and times. Through this kind of remembering, our love can be liberated "beyond desire" so that we participate in the love that, as Dante wrote, moves the sun and all the stars.

6

Fidelity

Margaret's mode of remembering and narrating the past involves grateful fidelity to those around her, a fidelity that resists the isolation loss so often causes. The sudden death of her father-in-law makes her want "to crawl away," but her four-year-old daughter requires her care. As she tells Andy, "You always have somebody to think about, and it's a blessing."[1] Years later, when her son is reported missing in action during World War II, her husband, Mat, articulates his deep sense of death's isolating power. "Loss," he tells Margaret, "singles us out." Margaret, however, refuses the false promise of negative freedom, of withdrawing from commitment in response to the pain that such commitment invariably causes. As she tells Mat, "I don't believe that when his death is subtracted from his life it leaves nothing. . . . What it leaves is his life. How could I turn away from it now any more than I could when he was a little child, and not love it and be glad of it, just because death is in it?" Mat's response to loss—feeling singled out, isolated—is probably more common than Margaret's. Yet Margaret's faithful love for both her missing son and her grieving husband makes healing and redemption possible in the midst of their suffering. As she tells Mat, "'We belong to each other. After all these years. Doesn't that mean something?' . . . 'I don't know what it means,' he says finally. 'I know what it's worth.'"[2]

For Mat, the isolation he feels as a result of his son's loss is painful, but one of the most remarkable achievements of the industrial culture has been to transform the meaning of such isolation so that we can experience it as a good thing. This is seen most clearly, perhaps, in the Romantic ideal of the isolated artist, a creative self free from constraints, free from traditions and norms, free to be true to himself. Such a self *wants* to be singled out and imagines that having "somebody to think about" is a burden rather than a blessing. For such an artist, isolation enables the creation of the "new." Beginning around the turn of the nineteenth century, as Charles Taylor observes, this kind of artist became the paradigmatic individual, "an agent of original self-definition": "No longer defined mainly by imitation, by *mimesis* of reality, art is understood now more in terms of creation." And because authentic persons wouldn't want to imitate others, they seek to break from the past and from their community and create themselves de novo. As Taylor puts it, "My self-discovery" entails "the making of something original and new."[3] Creating something new, on this view, requires freedom from confining relationships and obligations, and this understanding of creativity renarrates isolation as a prerequisite for growth and self-fulfillment rather than as a painful wound to be remedied by fidelity to one's place and community.[4]

I could point to any number of contemporary artists whose work celebrates this freedom from constraining relationships, but a more insidious result of such artistic freedom has been its acceptance in our broader economy and culture.[5] Richard Florida is the most prominent booster for this "creative" economy.[6] In a series of books and essays, he urges cities, regions, and individuals to find ways to profit from the rapidly expanding "Creative Class" that now drives economic growth.[7] Members of the Creative Class—"artists or engineers, musicians or computer scientists, writers or entrepreneurs"—are not tied to ancestral lands or large-scale manufacturing infrastructure but instead move about in search of cities that have the opportunities and amenities that will allow them to "leverage" their creative talents.[8]

The two defining features of Florida's Creative Class are their mobility and their creation of profitable new forms. To be a successful member of the Creative Class, you have to be willing to leave your family in pursuit of new career opportunities. Florida even offers a way to calculate "the monetary value of frequently seeing friends and relatives" so that individuals can better decide whether to take a higher-paying job far from home.[9] The biographical blurb on the back of his books indicates he's taken his own advice, as he somehow lives concurrently in three cities: "Toronto, New York, and Miami Beach."

Florida valorizes such geographical freedom by identifying it with tolerance or openness. Citing a study by Jason Rentfrow and Sam Gosling, Florida observes that individuals with more "open" personalities "were more likely to 'attempt to escape the ennui experienced in small-town environments by relocating to metropolitan areas where their interests in cultures and needs for social contact and stimulation are more easily met.' In other words, they move to and cluster in places that welcome them and offer them lots of exciting experiences and stimuli."[10] Built into Florida's understanding of "creativity" is the assumption that some places are inherently "boring" and cause "ennui," and that creative people need to be free from such uninteresting places so they can seek stimulation elsewhere.[11]

Florida is right that certain types of closed-mindedness are dangerous, so in critiquing his understanding of creativity and mobility, I don't want to oppose his Dionysian celebration of freedom and openness with an Apollonian preference for closure and fixed structures. Rather, the alternative posture that Berry models—and that is central to his understanding of creative renewal—is one of fidelity. Openness too often entails irresponsibility and a parasitic relationship to one's place and community: Florida's advice to members of the Creative Class is to move to a location where they can "reach [their] potential and find happiness."[12] These are not refugees driven from their places by political turmoil, economic devastation, or abusive families; they are boomers (in Stegner's sense of that term) looking to maximize self-fulfillment. So perhaps the boredom that "open" personalities experience in small towns is not caused primarily by some lack in the place itself, but by a culture that shapes people to seek to maximize individual self-fulfillment. If we are always looking to move somewhere that can make us happier, we are dooming ourselves to be restless consumers of places rather than members of them.

Further, Florida's Creative Class may not be as tolerant as he suggests; they may be open to people from different ethnic, sexual, or geographic backgrounds, but are they open to blue-collar workers, migrant farm laborers, or the custodians who clean their buildings? Are they open to lasting relationships with those who might be different from them? Like most people, Creative Class individuals tend to be tolerant of people who share their values, and their mobility leads them to more easily segregate themselves by class, occupation, and culture. Thus, Jamie Peck, in his broader critique of Florida, quips, "*Homo creativus* is an atomized subject, apparently, with a preference for intense but shallow and noncommittal relationships, mostly played out in the sphere of consumption and on the street."[13] Indeed, scholars such as Willie Jennings and bell hooks warn that geographic mobility tends to foster racial oppression, as privileged individuals exploit places and communities rather than belong to them.[14] Jennings astutely links mobility with a damaging form of creativity: deracinated European colonists developed a new understanding of human creativity, one in which the white outsider can come to a dark, blank place and freely inscribe his desired vision; like God, the colonist can create ex nihilo.[15]

This view of creativity brings us to the second defining feature of Florida's Creative Class: their ability to "create meaningful new forms." Berry would agree with Florida that formal intelligence is essential to a post-Fordist economy, but the standard by which Florida judges and values forms is quite different from Berry's standard of health or renewal. Florida's standard of value is how much profit new forms can generate: "I define the highest order of creative work as producing new forms or designs that are readily transferable and widely useful—such as designing a consumer product that can be manufactured and sold; coming up with a theorem or strategy that can be applied in many cases; or composing music that can be performed again and again."[16] The great irony is that these creative inventions must be mass-produced by non-creatives; these forms must be universally applicable in cookie-cutter fashion rather than being creatively adapted to particular locales.

It's no surprise, then, that Florida's understanding of creativity differs sharply from Berry's. Florida assumes that the new begets the new and so envisions people going to new places to create profitable new forms. As we will see, however, such a standard for art or for life is destructive and isolating. For Berry, there is a qualitative difference between the creativity that happens in the jostling of novelties and the creativity that emerges from faithful attention to the familiar. Sustainable cultures depend on people remaining faithfully in their places and fostering locally adapted, healing forms. A more sustainable mode of creativity would come from asking not "Is this new?" but, rather, "Is this renewing?" Margaret's example of faithfully thinking of others and working to creatively tend their needs challenges our industrial response to loss or damage, which is to throw the old away and make something new. Rather than seeking a clean break from all our painful relationships or boring places, Berry suggests that fidelity in the midst of loss and confusion leads to creative renewal—indeed, to resurrection.

While the Romantic self is true to its own potential and self-fulfillment, Berry models a way of being true to one's place and community. And whom we are faithful to determines, in large part, how we imagine creativity. The Romantic self sees creativity as an opportunity to reinvent the self, to make something radically new in opposition to the limits of our environments. Berry, however, imagines creativity as the ability to see again—to reenvision—and so renew life within the bafflement that formal constraints impose. Berry's practice of careful revision, particularly evident in his early novels *Nathan Coulter* and *A Place on Earth,* exemplifies this creative fidelity. In the case of *Nathan Coulter,* his revisions reimagine the death of Nathan's grandfather and make Nathan himself a more faithful inheritor of loss. In *A Place on Earth,* Berry's changes similarly focus the novel on questions of fidelity. In the first edition, his prose provided too much explication and context for readers, exempting them from the difficult ignorance his characters endure. The revision more successfully portrays the mystery that Berry's characters live with; his spare writing forces us to read without knowing the full context, to be faithful in the midst of uncertainty. These revised novels do not sugarcoat the difficult work of fidelity; rather, they portray how fidelity enables individuals and communities to prepare the way for redemption in the midst of confusion and loss.

The Renewing Power of Faithful Creativity

How we understand the human self will determine, to a large extent, whether we see creativity as a faculty that frees us from prior constraints in order to discover something new, or whether we see it as a faculty that submits to formal constraints and seeks to renew life within those limits. So the root difference between

Berry's sustainable creativity and the industrial creativity promoted by Florida is their contrasting views of the self. To use a pair of terms from Charles Taylor, Berry understands the self as fundamentally *dialogical,* whereas Florida imagines the self as *monological.*[17] Creativity is important for Florida because it enables individuals to "realize our truest selves."[18] Florida is merely echoing the bromides of an industrial culture that tells me to be "true to myself" and envisions creativity as a matter of expressing this "true" or "authentic" me. This is the deeply American view of the self that Huck Finn voices when he decides to "light out for the Territory" if he can't handle the challenges of living with Aunt Sally.[19]

Yet as Taylor points out, the very notion of being true or faithful implies a relationship. Thus, for Taylor, authenticity entails being faithful to what he calls "demands emanating beyond the self": "Only if I exist in a world in which history, or the demands of nature, or the needs of my fellow human beings, or the duties of citizenship, or the call of God, or something else of this order *matters* crucially, can I define an identity for myself that is not trivial. Authenticity is not the enemy of demands that emanate from beyond the self; it supposes such demands."[20] For Taylor the self is always already "dialogical"—a term he borrows from Mikhail Bakhtin—and forming one's identity entails faithfully working out this conversation between self and others.[21] It is this view of the self that is implicit in Margaret's assertion that "it's a blessing" to "always have somebody to think about."[22]

Indeed, if the self is fundamentally dialogical, if our relationships to those around us—to our community, place, history, and God—are what shape our identity, then it's actually self-defeating to cast aside these relationships in the mistaken belief that they are limiting our self-fulfillment. As Taylor puts it, "My identity-defining relationships can't be seen, in principle and in advance, as dispensable and destined for supersession. If my self-exploration takes the form of such serial and in principle temporary relationships, then it is not my identity that I'm exploring, but some modality of enjoyment."[23] Viewing these relationships as merely instrumental to my self-discovery, as Florida does in making one's personal happiness and success his only rubric for where to live, leads ironically to dissatisfaction.

Sustainability and resurrection, however, require that we subordinate our individual desires to pursue relational goods like health and love. Being faithful serves these intrinsic goods and enables genuine authenticity. Berry describes the posture necessary to maintain such authenticity as a kind of "double fidelity": "This word-keeping, standing by one's word, is a double fidelity: to the community and to oneself. . . . The individual is thereby at once free and a member. To break one's word in order to be 'free' of it, on the other hand, is to make and enforce a damning equation between freedom and loneliness."[24] The deep paradoxical insight of Berry's work is that when we stop trying to maximize our own desires, when we stop trying to be free from all constraints, we may find ourselves more fulfilled and liberated. As Jesus puts it, in a passage Berry particularly notes, "Except a corn of wheat fall into the ground and die, it abideth alone: but if it die, it bringeth forth much fruit. He that loveth his life shall lose it; and he that hateth his life in this world shall keep it unto life eternal."[25] If we refuse this self-giving, we will be trapped inside the echo chamber of a hollowed-out self, restlessly tapping the walls in search of some meaning and significance.

Beyond locking us in the narrow confines of a monological self, Florida's treatment of relationships as instrumental leads to parasitic forms of creativity. Instead of the creativity of the given self that aims to be true to its place and community, the creativity of the organizing subject is self-serving. This is the kind of creativity referred to by the oxymoron "creative destruction." It does take creativity, of an infernal sort, to turn a mountain into coal, topsoil into corn, rainforests into beef, financial transactions into massive profit, the labor of distant people into cheap commodities, and friendships into digital platforms from which to sell advertising. These forms of creative destruction are mirrored in the kinds of avant-garde art represented by Nam June Paik's "One for Violin Solo," in which the performer slowly raises a violin and, after five minutes of silent, suspenseful buildup, smashes the instrument. Such industrial forms of "creativity" bring temporary profit or meaning only by destroying the sources of their abundance.

This industrial, Romantic mode of creativity is a cop-out. If we're confronted by an intractable problem, it's easier to "disrupt" the situation and make a quick buck than it is to deal with the problem in all its messy complexity. Romantic creativity, then, functions as a kind of self-defense, isolating us from responsibilities and promising us freedom from painful entanglements and commitments. Yet sustaining, renewing creativity depends on faithfully grappling with an intractable reality and finding ways to work fruitfully within its constraints. Matthew Crawford critiques Florida from this perspective, arguing that creativity is not "what happens when people are liberated from the constraints of conventionality" but rather "is a by-product of mastery of the sort that is cultivated through long practice. It seems to be built up through *submission* (think a musician practicing scales, or Einstein learning tensor algebra). Identifying creativity with freedom harmonizes quite well with the culture of the new capitalism, in which the imperative of flexibility precludes dwelling in any task long enough to develop real competence."[26] Building on this idea elsewhere, Crawford describes watching a virtuoso bluegrass guitarist and having the sensation that he could do whatever he wanted with his instrument. Yet this musical freedom was the fruit, paradoxically, of long, formative submission to the physical demands of the guitar and to musical traditions. Thus, Crawford makes the bold claim that "membership in a community is a prerequisite to creativity. . . . These communities and aesthetic traditions provide a kind of cultural jig, within which our energies get ordered."[27] For Crawford creativity can happen only after we submit to the limits of formal constraints.

Berry makes a similar point about the relationship between limits and creativity in his essay "Poetry and Marriage." While the two forms named in his title may seem quite different, both set bounds to an individual's freedom, bounds that can spur creativity. As he explains, "It may be . . . that form serves us best when it works as an obstruction to baffle us and deflect our intended course. It may be that when we no longer know what to do we have come to our real work and that when we no longer know which way to go we have begun our real journey. The mind that is not baffled is not employed. The impeded stream is the one that sings."[28] Frustration, when we respond to it by redoubling our commitment to our craft, leads to creative insight. Bafflement, faithfully encountered, can lead to renewal. But if we respond to difficulties simply by leaving and finding a less challenging task, then we'll never learn to sing the song of the impeded stream.

The theme of this song, one that Berry has tuned himself to hear in its many variations, is the grace of unexpected renewal. When we submit ourselves to the formal limits of poetry or marriage—or to the constraints of our places and communities—we open ourselves to receive the gifts of inspiration, renewal, and resurrection. As Berry writes, "Form, like topsoil (which is intricately formal), empowers time to do good."[29] This is why fidelity is a prerequisite to creative renewal; we have to stick it out even when we can't foresee any possibility of resolution: "That necessity to 'stay there for a while' is the gist of the meaning of form. Forms join us to time, to the consequences and fruitions of our own passing." In other words, forms teach us to live well in the midst of death and loss. Such fidelity "has nothing to do with what is usually called optimism. . . . The faith, rather, is that by staying, and only by staying, we will learn something of the truth, that the truth is good to know, and that it is always both different and larger than we thought."[30] We can be faithful within the constraints of formal limits when we trust that such a commitment prepares us to receive grace.

In another essay, Berry describes such a receptive, faithful posture through the image of topsoil slowly forming in the bottom of an abandoned metal bucket. Inside the narrow walls of this bucket, "the greatest miracle that I have ever heard of" is taking place: "it is making earth." Leaves, nuts, animal droppings, dead insects, and more have fallen into it, and they have been transformed. Berry marvels at the remarkable renewal that has taken place inside this humble bucket: "I look into that bucket with fascination because I am a farmer of sorts and an artist of sorts, and I recognize there an artistry and a farming far superior to mine, or to that of any human." This is the creative process that "all creatures die into . . .

and . . . live by."[31] The bucket is "creative" because it digests whatever odds and ends and garbage are given to it and transforms them into new life.

If Florida's Creative Class moves about in search of a good bar scene, hip recreation amenities, and better career opportunities, Berry's creative class stays put and attends to death. Parasitic creativity takes complex forms of life, finds some new way to transform them into a profitable commodity, and leaves waste. But creativity modeled on this bucket takes dregs and dead ends and, by faithfully holding them in place, transforms them into forms that can sustain new life. One telling result of these contrasting modes of creativity is that members of Florida's Creative Class probably do not know where they want to be buried or who will come to their funerals, but Berry's faithfully creative characters certainly do.

From Revision to Revision

What difference does this mode of creativity actually make for Berry's writing? There are several formal traits I could point to, but for the sake of conserving space I will focus on just one: his penchant for revision. In a broad sense, Berry's entire body of work demonstrates his commitment to re-vision, to seeing again from different perspectives. Reading through *The Unsettling of America,* his first major nonfiction book, one finds sentences that form the seeds of essays written decades later. Similarly, each novel or short story about Port William opens up new vistas on the place and its many inhabitants; new characters retell old stories or offer backstories that deepen our understanding of characters we thought we already knew. We see the whole better for having seen it again and again from different perspectives. And of course each of Berry's genres provides a complementary mode of perception: his poems, for instance, re-vision images and ideas from his essays and fiction.

Through these acts of reenvisioning, Berry practices his faith that the subject of his writing—his place—is inexhaustible; there is always more to see. Hence, he revises his written works as part of his more fundamental commitment to live his entire life "from revision to revision":

> Living and working in the place day by day, one is continuously revising one's knowledge of it, continuously being surprised by it and in error about it. And even if the place stayed the same, one would be getting older and growing in memory and experience, and would need for that reason alone to work from revision to revision. One knows one's place, that is to say, only within limits, and the limits are in one's mind, not in the place. This is a description of life in time in the world. A place, apart from our now always

possible destruction of it, is inexhaustible. It *cannot* be altogether known, seen, understood, or appreciated.[32]

Faithfully working to revise his understanding of his place is Berry's way of honoring its complexity and richness. In this way, he seeks to follow his own claim about the purpose of literature, which "is to renew not only itself but also our sense of the perennial newness of the world and of our experience; it is to renew our sense of the newness of what is eternally new."[33] Revision is a form of renewal; like the bucket that grows topsoil, it takes what seems old and stale and creatively transforms it to sustain new meaning and life.[34]

Revision, then, is one example of how fidelity in the midst of confusion cultivates space for redemption. When we make a mistake, when we experience loss or death, when we are baffled by a seemingly insurmountable problem, we can be tempted to escape these frustrations and make a clean start. But Berry argues that sustainable art and lives will recognize that true freedom lies not in escaping the consequences of error, but in creatively re-seeing the problem and then going to work again:

> Because we must be always correcting our errors, art and science always need to be free to shift their ground and start again. The unenviable, the necessarily ongoing problem of justice to the world and to one another thus enforces practically the requirement of freedom. . . . Freedom in both science and art probably depends upon enlarging the context of our work, increasing (rather than decreasing) the number of considerations we allow to bear upon it. This is because the ultimate context of our work is the world, which is always larger than the context of our thought. . . . If we could faithfully commit ourselves to the principle that nothing whatever can safely be said to lie outside the context of our work, then artists and scientists would have to be ready at any time to see that they have been wrong and to start again, making yet larger the context of the work. *That* is true freedom. It means simply that beyond all error we can begin again; redemption is possible. . . . Work that diminishes the possibility of a new start, of "making it new," is bad work.[35]

Berry's faithful creativity entails remaining within the limits of one's place and working to do ever greater justice to its beauty and complexity. This is the creativity of a dialogical self, a self committed to sustaining life and beauty in relation to its place and community. In the remainder of this chapter, I will show how this mode of creativity plays out in Berry's first two novels, both of which were republished in significantly revised form. Comparing the different versions of these novels allows us to read them as a kind of palimpsest that reveals his process of revision and the maturation of his understanding of creativity.

Revising Nathan Coulter's Fidelity

Berry's early novels have rather complex publication histories. In part, this is because he switched from working with major publishers like Houghton Mifflin and Harcourt (which later merged) to publishing with Jack Shoemaker's various presses: North Point, Pantheon, Shoemaker & Hoard, and Counterpoint. As Shoemaker reissued Berry's early novels, Berry took the opportunity to revise them, sometimes extensively. So portions of *Nathan Coulter* first appeared in a set of three short stories in 1956; the full novel was then published in 1960; and a drastically revised version—with the last four chapters excised—was published in 1985. Excerpts from *A Place on Earth* came out in 1966; the novel was published in 1967; it was shortened by one-third for the 1983 edition; and further changes were made for a 2001 edition.[36]

In each of these novels, Berry's revisions foreground the challenges of responding to death and loss in redemptive, faithful ways. *Nathan Coulter* is a bildungsroman, and Nathan matures in the presence of many deaths. Besides the central deaths of his mother and grandfather, a series of smaller deaths litter the pages of this short novel: his grandfather Dave gets annoyed with a cat and hangs it from a tree by their porch; a neighbor woman dies; Chicken Little drowns; an out-of-town visitor dynamites the river to kill fish; Burley and Nathan hunt coons and ducks. In the first version, Nathan responds to loss by fleeing from his place and family, but in the revised version we see him learn to patiently tend his place in spite of its scars and difficulties. Near the beginning of the novel, Nathan recalls his Uncle Burley's countercultural warning that life isn't easier somewhere else: "Uncle Burley said hills always looked blue when you were far away from them. That was a pretty color for hills; the little houses and barns and fields looked so neat and quiet tucked against them. It made you want to be close to them. But he said that when you got close they were like the hills you'd left, and when you looked back your own hills were blue and you wanted to go back again. He said he reckoned a man could wear himself out going back and forth."[37] Burley's sage observation serves as a warning to Florida's Creative Class who migrate from place to place looking for greener pastures. What Nathan must learn to do—and his Uncle Burley is his primary teacher—is to recognize the beauty of his own hills, and then to tend this beauty in the midst of pain and death.

Nathan's ancestors haven't been as migratory as many Americans, but they haven't exactly been exemplary inhabitants of their place. Perhaps the clearest indicator of this is their bitter response to death. Modern Americans tend to avoid loss and death by moving away, and though the Coulter family hasn't had that luxury, their selfish reactions to death aren't much better. Near the beginning of his narrative, Nathan tells readers that "the first thing anybody remembered about our family" was Aunt Mary's death and burial. Nathan's great-great-grandfather Jonas Coulter had a property-line dispute with a neighbor, and when his daughter Mary died of scarlet fever, Jonas insisted on burying her where he thought the boundary line was: "His wife never would speak to him or even look at him after that; but it settled the argument over the fence."[38]

Using death as an opportunity to selfishly manipulate others seems to run in the Coulter family. Nathan's great-grandmother Parthenia bought a giant granite tombstone from a traveling salesman, and it took her son Dave five years to pay it off. Even more galling, she had Dave's name and birth year inscribed on the stone so he could be buried next to her and her husband. But "the last thing [Dave] wanted was to have his name carved in four-inch letters on a tombstone. . . . It was as if she'd expected him to write his other date up there and die right away to balance things." As Fritz Ohlschlaeger recognizes, "What rankles [Nathan's] Grandpa is the thought of mortality, limitation"; Dave is so annoyed by the giant monument that he buys another lot in the cemetery to spite his mother: "He'd be damned if anybody was going to tell him where to be buried."[39] Both Jonas and Parthenia try to use death for their own benefit: to settle a boundary dispute or to assert their rights over an ungrateful son.

In the first edition, Nathan is clearly an heir to his family's bitter responses to death—responses that entail running away either emotionally or physically—but in the revision, Berry portrays Nathan as gradually learning a better, more faithful response that makes room for renewal. This shift can be seen in several scenes, but I will focus on just four. The first initially appeared in a short story Berry published as a graduate student. Nathan and his brother Tom visit a boy from out of town and stuff a dynamite cap up his pet crow's "bunghole." Tom lights the fuse, the crow flies frantically up, and "feathers and guts" rain down. In the first version of the story, Nathan callously watches the other boy's response to this wanton violence: "The tears was running down along side his nose. He looked sillier than hell."[40] In both editions of the novel, however, Berry portrays Nathan as more remorseful, altering these lines accordingly: "He started to cry. I felt sorry for him when I saw that, but there was nothing to do but run."[41] In these later versions, Nathan learns that cruelty and senseless death cause real pain to people. He learns there are consequences to death, and that he will need to find better ways to deal with death than merely inflicting it on others and running away. But at this point, his response to their mistake is simply to leave: "There was nothing to do but run."

The second key scene contrasts two inchoate responses to the tragic death of Nathan's mother: her sons' bewildered sorrow and her husband Jarrat's bitter withdrawal. The boys, only nine and seven, are understandably confused by the death of their mother, and when Jarrat catches them playing over their washing-up, he shakes them violently.[42] Tom and Nathan then decide to run away from home and try to live with a neighbor. The only way they know to respond to death and conflict is to run away. Jarrat doesn't run away from death, as his sons do, but he closes up, firmly rejecting all possibility of redemption or renewal. He stays put, but only doggedly, and his stoic self-enclosure blinds him to any creative way that he might turn the painful loss of his wife to some healing end.

The revisions Berry makes between his initial short story and both editions of the novel soften Jarrat's character, rendering his grief-stricken response more sympathetically while still critiquing his stoicism as inadequate. In the original story, Jarrat destroys a rosebush that symbolizes his wife's hope for renewal: "Our mother had planted it and watered it with water from the well. She said when she saw it bloom in the spring it made her feel like winter never would come back again. He cut the rose bush down with one lick, all of its stems with one lick."[43] Jarrat's violent decimation of the rose is a rejection of seasonal cycles; after the winter of his wife's death, he cannot imagine the return of spring. If the rose's blooms made his wife naively feel that "winter never would come back," Jarrat's act of anger and grief seeks to make winter eternal. Both are oversimplifications. In revising this scene for the novel, Berry has Jarrat chop wood rather than the rosebush. He is still unable to receive comfort from his neighbors or offer comfort to his sons, but his grief appears less a morally culpable rejection of renewal, and more a raw and inarticulate expression of pain. Jarrat doesn't so much reject renewal as he simply lacks the vocabulary to even imagine it.[44] He has been singled out by loss, and because he cannot find a way to be faithfully present to those who still belong to him, his sons move in with their grandparents and Uncle Burley.

Berry articulates the possibility of renewal, a possibility needed to sustain faith through difficult loss, in a third scene that underwent subtle but significant revisions between the first and second editions of the novel. A lightening strike catches Jarrat's barn on fire, and though the neighbors gather quickly to try to save the barn, they are unsuccessful. While the first edition stresses their failure, the second edition emphasizes the limited good their efforts accomplish and thus finds grounds for hope even in the terrible loss. In the first edition Nathan states that throwing their small bucketfuls of water on the fire "was like throwing rocks at a mad dog; you couldn't hurt it and you couldn't stop it."[45] In the second edition, though, Berry replaces that description with a much more hopeful one: "We worked to keep the fire away from the pump, and to save the crib and the granary and the wagon shed."[46]

In the same vein, the second edition lacks Nathan's claim that their efforts were completely futile: "The fire had beaten us. We'd worked hard all night, and there hadn't been a single straw or splinter that we'd been able to put out before it burned out. The fire had ignored us and burned in spite of us. It was as if we'd never been there at all."[47] In the older version, their efforts are in vain, and they fight with a stoic sense of inevitable defeat.[48] The revision cuts this evaluation, however, and adds that they "saved the outbuildings"; this small victory ameliorates the fire's damage. So while both versions conclude in the same way, the meaning of Nathan's assessment has shifted: "We hadn't accepted the fire; we'd been able to fight that as long as it burned. But now, in the daylight, in our tiredness, as if we'd fought all night in a dream, we accepted the ashes."[49] In these two taut sentences, Nathan lays out the tension he is learning to inhabit faithfully and creatively: the forces of evil that cause death and loss are to be fought, but we need to accept their consequences, the ashes they leave, to have any hope of participating in their redemption. If we emotionally or physically run away from the ashes of death, we lose the opportunity to creatively and faithfully cultivate the life that remains.

The final scene that demonstrates the novel's revised understanding of Nathan's fidelity is also the most significant one. In the first edition, Nathan is walking his ailing grandfather back to the house when Dave has a sudden stroke. Nathan carries him the rest of the way, and Dave lingers on for two weeks before dying. The night Dave dies, Nathan slips out to visit Mandy, a young, attractive neighbor who is married to an older man. Mandy's husband finds out about their adultery, and he comes several days later to exact vengeance, barging into Dave's wake with a knife. Nathan and his family fend him off, but Nathan is forced to leave his family and community. Because he copes with his grandfather's death by running away and seeking satisfaction for his own desires, the result is further discord and his own departure.

The second edition cuts the last twenty-two pages and thus ends in starkly different fashion. Nathan's final memory is bearing his grandfather's dying body: "I called his name, but he didn't stir. I picked him up in my arms and I carried him home."[50] This line marks the end of Nathan's boyhood. In this revised version, he has learned to faithfully bear the deaths of his place, to accept their ashes and creatively tend life in the midst of suffering and loss. The first sentence of *Hannah Coulter,* published in 2004, begins with Nathan speaking this same line as the conclusion of a story to their children, and Hannah says that Nathan thought of that day "as the last day of his boyhood." After his grandfather's death, he was ready to take his place in the family lineage: "[He] expect[ed] to go on working in the same place at the same work for the rest of his life. . . . Tom had left home, but Nathan wanted to stay. He had not thought of going away."[51] Hannah's description clearly matches the Nathan of the revised edition, the Nathan who does not try to break free from the constraints of his family and community but instead commits himself to working creatively within these relationships, damaged though they are. And the great paradox is that the Nathan of the first edition, the one who commits adultery and sets out to seek his fortune, is not more liberated or fulfilled or authentic than the Nathan of the second edition; he is more isolated and damaged.

Perhaps in the first edition Berry could not yet imagine how Nathan might remain faithful to his withdrawn father, dead grandfather, and warped family heritage, and so he has him abandon this place at the novel's conclusion. But because Berry himself did not abandon the novel, he was able to reimagine Nathan's narrative in a more redemptive light. Like the Nathan of the second edition, Berry stayed put, working from "revision to revision" to find the possibilities of renewal within the novel's formal limits. It also seems probable that Berry's own return to Kentucky, five years after *Nathan Coulter* was first published, inspired this revision process. Recommitting himself to his physical place helped him tell the stories of his Port William membership right, to forgo the merely new in order to cultivate renewal.[52]

Revising Readers' Fidelity

If Berry's revisions to *Nathan Coulter* reimagine Nathan as a more faithful member of his place, his revisions to *A Place on Earth* invite readers to practice this difficult fidelity themselves. Unlike the changes to *Nathan Coulter,* particularly its altered ending, the revisions to *A Place on Earth* don't substantially change the content of the novel. That doesn't mean, however, that the revisions are insignificant. As Berry writes in his preface to the 1983 revision, he cut "perhaps a third of the text of the first edition." The result of these changes "is not a new book, but a renewed one. As a writer and a conservationist, I am pleased to think it possible, as suggested by the shortening of my text, that improved literary judgment can save trees."[53] Berry's wry humor intuitively links his artistic revisions with sustainable living. Perhaps his improved literary judgment saves trees not only by reducing the novel's page count, but also by training readers to be faithful to their places and communities. When characters in *A Place on Earth* experience death and loss, they must choose whether to remain faithful to their communities and creatively work for their renewal, or to respond to death by running away. Death brings uncertainty, and those who do remain have to sustain life while working on the basis of incomplete knowledge. So in the revised edition of *A Place on Earth,* Berry puts his readers in a place of greater uncertainty and challenges them to consider how they might practice fidelity in the midst of death and ignorance.[54]

In revising the novel, Berry's "only rule was to do the work so far as possible by cutting."[55] The effect of these cuts is to reduce much of the context that helps readers of the first edition make sense of characters' motivations and actions. The revised text uses shorter, more direct sentences and relies on the reader to fill in connections; it gives an image or describes an action and moves on without explaining the scene for the reader. Often the revision deletes the last sentence or phrase of a paragraph that in the first edition evaluates the scene. The lack of these transition phrases does not make the story hard to follow, but it puts a greater burden of interpretation on the reader.

The changes go beyond these paragraph-level reductions. Throughout the first edition, Berry includes several stories about minor characters or community events that flesh out the life of Port William. The revision cuts these as well as sections from the lives and histories of the main characters. The background and context of nearly every important character are reduced, including Gideon Crop, Burley Coulter, and Ernest Finley.[56] An entire chapter that tells the history of Mat Feltner's boyhood, courtship, education, and return to his farm and marriage is taken out.[57] Also removed is the journal Mat begins as he works through his emotions over the loss of his son Virgil.[58] These cuts in the revision are large-scale parallels to the paring that occurs on the paragraph level. Berry removes many of his characters' thoughts on, and internal evaluations of, the novel's action. It is a subtle shift, but one that withholds from the reader much of the characters' history and thoughts and motivation. Instead, readers experience the action of the novel without its being explicitly evaluated for them.

One way to understand the effect of this shift is through an image Berry develops at the beginning of the novel. The Feltners haven't heard from their son Virgil, fighting in World War II, for three weeks, so when Mat sees a government envelope addressed to Virgil's wife, Hannah, he fears the worst. Steadying himself before going inside with the letter, he looks out over the puddle that the yard has become: "The rain is falling slowly in large drops so that the circles it makes striking the surface of the pool remain intact. For a moment at the center of each circle the black branches of the trees are mirrored perfectly, and then distorted and fragmented as the circles interlink and subside and renew."[59] From where he stands, Mat can see the reflection clarified, distorted, and clarified again, and he can see the continual mingling and fading and beginning again of the pattern the drops make. But this is because he himself is not a part of this pattern, but outside and above it. From this external perspective he has glimpses of clarity and renewal, but he cannot view his own life in this way. In the midst of his own loss and uncertainty, how can he *know* that renewal will come, the pattern be restored?

He can't. And in fact, none of us are granted an external, bird's-eye perspective on our lives; rather, it is in the confusion and bewilderment of loss that we all must choose whether to remain faithful to the part of the pattern we can still see, or to reject the pattern as fatally broken and meaningless. The effect of Berry's revisions, then, is to shift readers from a bird's-eye perspective where we can see the disruptions and healings from above, to a more ground-level perspective, where we experience the uncertainty, loss, and pain that the characters do, and so wrestle with them through their difficult decisions to remain faithful, or not, in the midst of loss. To borrow terms from an essay Berry wrote praising Norman Maclean's writing, the earlier edition sought to master its subjects, laying their thoughts and motivations bare to us readers, but the revised edition approaches Maclean's style, a style that Berry writes is "vulnerable to bewilderment, mystery, and tragedy—and a style, therefore, that is open to grace."[60]

The letter Mat carries informs them that Virgil is missing in action, and his uncertain fate mirrors another loss in the community. The rain that Mat watches falling into the puddle causes severe flooding, including a flash flood that sweeps away Gideon and Ida Crop's young daughter Annie. Gideon watches her get caught by the waters, and his attempts to rescue her turn into a seven-day vigil in search of the body he cannot find. He clings desperately to the possibility that she may be alive, but when the water recedes, he leaves Ida and their farm: "He goes, it seems to him, through the opening at the end of his life as it was. To stay, now that the end has come, would be to plant and reap in the very earth of his ruin."[61] The flood is a violent disruption of the orderly pattern he was a part of, and to continue his faithfulness to that pattern would require a greater faith than he can now muster. How can the planting and reaping of his land, or the love and life of his marriage to Ida have any meaning in the presence of their daughter's senseless loss? His desertion of Ida results from his inability to imagine that his fidelity to the order that remains might bring renewal from the very earth of his ruin.

Gideon's departure after Annie's death provides a clear illustration of how Berry's revisions shift the reader's experience of the narrative. In the first edition, Berry foreshadowed Gideon's departure by explaining his tendency to grow depressed and leave the farm for a week or two at a time: "Once or twice a year his mind seems to turn over like a boat in rough water, forced toward a consuming darkness. He's afraid then that . . . there's not enough left of his life to buy itself back out of the land."[62] This context helps the reader understand Gideon's departure, but in its absence there is no precedent for Gideon's departure, and the reader of the revised edition is left more uncertain about whether Gideon will return.

In spite of this uncertainty, his wife, Ida, remains faithful to Gideon and to their place. Though Gideon cannot revise his understanding of what responsibility to his place might entail after the loss of his daughter, Ida remains in the very earth of their ruin, grieving her daughter and caring for what remains. And Ida's fidelity makes renewal possible. She carries on the work of the farm, relying on the generous help of their neighbors, and she continues to hope for Gideon's return. She doesn't hear anything from him and has no way of knowing that he will come back, but when Gideon does finally return, Ida's fidelity has sustained his place.

Although Mat does not physically run away after he finds out his son is missing, he does withdraw emotionally. And perhaps the most drastic changes to the revised novel involve limiting readers' insight into his grieving processes. Besides eliminating a thirty-page chapter that details his life history, the revision cuts the deeply personal and philosophic journal entries that illuminate his sorrow and slow growth. These entries in the first edition explicate the action of the novel and tell the reader precisely what Mat thinks:

> Maybe the whole meaning of my life is in—or dependent on—the possibility that I can learn, by the time I die, to give it up freely.
> *But* I wanted to be able to give it up freely to my son. The final selfishness of wanting to know, arrange and understand in advance, the transition from life to life—to get past that. . . .
> I must learn the love of an old man that accepts freely the changing and passing of what is loved, as a condition of the loving. Though I've long understood the need of it, I've never learned it. . . .
> I've learned the patterns [the land's] lives make, from its men to its weeds, and I have grown ever less willing to set myself against any of them, or to turn aside from them. I see that none are separate or different from it and that I'm not.[63]

By telling readers how to understand his life, Mat does the difficult work for them: he spoon-feeds the pattern he is learning to see instead of allowing readers to piece the deaths and lives together for themselves in order to imagine what faithful action might look like. In the revision, the characters and the reader are on a more equal footing, and both are subject to ignorance and mystery. The characters, in spite of the uncertainty and pain in which they live, can choose to be faithful to their marriages, their farms, the part of the pattern they can still see; the readers of the revised text share in their ignorance, empathize with their loss, and hope for their fidelity.

The final scene in both versions of the novel portrays Mat's renewed commitment to his place. The loss of his son has forced him to accept that he does not have a panopticon perspective on his life. Mat is learning to relinquish both this Apollonian gaze, which seeks to master and control, and the Dionysian embrace of meaningless chaos. Unlike Mat's position at the beginning of the novel, where he stood on his porch and looked down at the reflective surface of the puddle marred by raindrops, Mat's situation is now amid an order he only vaguely senses, one that is deeply damaged and yet still brings life from death. Coming into the woods in search of a calving heifer, Mat tends to her and her calf and then walks farther on and sits down among the trees:

> He feels the great restfulness of that place, its casual perfect order. It is the restfulness of a place where the merest or the most improbable accident is

made a necessity and a part of a design, where death can only give into life. And Mat feels the difference between that restful order and his own constant struggle to maintain and regulate his clearings. Although the meanings of those clearings and his devotion to them remain firm in his mind, he knows without sorrow that they will end, the order he has made and kept in them will be overthrown, the effortless order of wilderness will return.[64]

His perception of the patterns to which he belongs will remain partial and inadequate, but this limit does not absolve him from the responsibility of tending the part he can perceive. Instead, it requires him to be always willing to revise his "clearings," the orders that he makes and tends, to more faithfully honor the greater pattern of which he is a part.[65]

Practicing Fidelity

Reading the revised edition of *A Place on Earth* can train readers in this kind of faithful, renewing creativity. Readers confront grievous losses alongside the novel's protagonists, and they too struggle to imagine what it might look like to plant and reap in the very earth of one's ruin. Like Nathan Coulter, they learn not to run away from pain and bewilderment, but to accept the ashes of death in faithful, creative, and redemptive ways. Fittingly, these portrayals of fidelity's hard-won rewards are the fruit of Berry's own commitment to return to his early novels and see them again.

Berry's revisions to these two novels invite us to practice a faithful creativity that dramatically differs from the Romantic kinds of creativity that boomers like Richard Florida celebrate. Rather than responding to difficulty and loss by moving away in search of more interesting, fulfilling opportunities, Berry challenges us to stay put. Such a faithful stance responds to frustrating limits not by turning inward and seeking some elusive, self-referential authenticity, but by looking outward and finding new ways to care for those to whom we belong. Though such faithful service can be incredibly difficult, Berry's work bears testimony to its rich rewards: "It may be that when we no longer know what to do we have come to our real work and that when we no longer know which way to go we have begun our real journey. The mind that is not baffled is not employed. The impeded stream is the one that sings."[66] Maybe, as Margaret says, it is indeed a blessing to always have someone to think about, someone to pull us out of our solipsistic grief and call us back to the work of creatively tending our broken places.

7

Convocation

The life story of Burley Coulter bears witness to the fact that tuning oneself to faithfully hear the needs of others can be radically redemptive. The young Burley was a wayward Don Juan, yet by the end of his life, he had become the most vocal defender of the Port William "membership," welcoming many others into its sustaining community. Burley's surprising transformation happens through a process that Berry calls *convocation*—a multifaceted term that names both the fact of our membership and the process by which we come to know ourselves as members of an orchestrated, patterned whole. Convocation is obviously not a virtue that an individual can practice in isolation (and, in reality, none of the other virtues I've examined are); rather, it's a formal characteristic of sustainable communities. Convocation, then, is one way of describing the culmination or effect of the virtues examined in this book: attention and gratitude, humility and hope, memory and fidelity enable communities to practice healthy convocation.

This concluding chapter draws together many of the various threads I've woven through my argument. It incorporates Berry's poetry, essays, and especially his fiction to illuminate his understanding of convocation, and it refers to many of the theorists whose work I've used to help clarify Berry's vision. But the focus of this chapter is the life of one of the central figures in the Port William membership: Burley Coulter. In the form of Burley's life, narrated both by him and by many other members of his community, the sustainable, resurrecting forms I have been tracing come sharply into focus. Burley is a man who has suffered many deaths, he is a man who has failed in many ways, and yet he submits to a way of life and membership that sustains both him and, more importantly, his place. Thus, to borrow a description from one of Berry's poems, Burley's story

> is not the story of a life.
> It is the story of lives, knit together,
> overlapping in succession, rising
> again from grave after grave.[1]

So it is impossible to narrate Burley's story without narrating the convocated membership to which he belongs. As Burley himself puts it, "The way we are, we are members of each other. All of us. Everything. The difference ain't in who is a member and who is not, but in who knows it and who don't."[2]

Knowing Oneself as a Convocated Member

In an industrial culture, most of us fall into the latter category: those who don't know that they are members of each other. We are encouraged to imagine ourselves as autonomous individuals, organizing subjects free to direct our attention in whatever ways we think will maximize our pleasure. This fond belief is nurtured by what may seem like the most innocuous of sources: Disney. Disney's stories, oriented toward children and teenagers, proclaim that you can "be who you wanna be / Anyone you wanna be."[3] As one critic observes about the arc of Disney's typical narrative, "It's the naysaying authority figures who need to be enlightened about the importance of never giving up on your dreams, no matter how irrational, improbable, or disruptive to the larger community." The result is "an ethos that privileges self-fulfillment over the communal good."[4]

Disney-esque bromides promising that "you can do anything you set your mind to" are patently false. Where and when you are born—things you don't choose—determine much of your identity. Cervantes warns us that a man living in the fifteenth century who has read too many chivalric romances might want to be a knight, but his desperate attempts to fulfill this ambition will only make him the laughingstock of everyone he encounters. As Christopher Lasch wryly notes, "What we are is largely inherited, in the form of gender, genetic endowment, institutions, predispositions—including the universal predisposition to resent these constraints on our freedom and to dream of abolishing them."[5] Recognizing this, as we have seen, leads Jean-Luc Marion to describe the self as a gifted recipient rather than a buffered, autonomous agent.

Furthermore, it's not just an innocent lie to tell children that their identity originates deep within themselves and that they have to pursue it in opposition to their benighted families. Such narratives have negative consequences for our communities and our children.[6] As William Cavanaugh argues, Disney's call to follow your inner self ends up being self-defeating. Young people "who have been marinated in this type of cultural messaging" can be "paralyz[ed]" when they try to figure out who their true self is and what it wants to do.[7] This search for a true self underlies the popularity of various personality tests and career quizzes, yet these are inadequate replacements for thick, constitutive relationships. Cavanaugh argues that the better alternative to a Disneyfied sense of self is to receive our identities and callings as gifts from our communities: "We need others to tell us what

·we can give to the world, which is a quite different question from what will give us pleasure. We need families to make demands upon us, to limit the places that we will consider living. We need to prepare one another for suffering, for running up against limitations, for caring for a special-needs child decade after decade. We need to make commitments to one another that are not reversible."[8] Cavanaugh's assessment parallels Charles Taylor's argument that true authenticity is developed not by throwing off all outside voices but by engaging in a dialogical relationship with one's community. As Taylor puts it, drawing on Mikhail Bakhtin, "Human beings are constituted in conversation." What this means is that the "self never preexists all conversation, as in the old monological view; nor does it arise from an introjection of the interlocutor; but it arises within conversation, because this kind of dialogical action by its very nature marks a place for the new locutor who is being inducted into it."[9] And if, as Burley Coulter claims, we are all inescapably members of each other, then denying this dialogical reality doesn't negate it.

Hence, Berry critiques those who insist on denying their status as members and who try to peer within themselves to find their true identity. Writing in 1977, he proposes that the reasonable way to treat the "so-called identity crises" would

> consist in the restoration of . . . connections: the lost identity would find itself by recognizing physical landmarks, by connecting itself responsibly to practical circumstances; it would learn to stay put in the body to which it belongs and in the place to which preference or history or accident has brought it; it would, in short, find itself in finding its work. But "finding yourself," the pseudo-ritual by which the identity crisis is supposed to be resolved, makes use of no such immediate references. . . . The fashionable cure for this condition, if I understand the lore of it correctly, has nothing to do with the assumption of responsibilities or the renewal of connections. The cure is "autonomy," another illusory condition, suggesting that the self can be self-determining and independent without regard for any determining circumstance or any of the obvious dependences. This seems little more than a jargon term for indifference to the opinions and feelings of other people. There is, in practice, no such thing as autonomy. Practically, there is only a distinction between responsible and irresponsible dependence.[10]

The distinction Berry makes here between responsible and irresponsible dependence parallels exactly Burley's distinction between those who know they are members and those who don't. And as Berry argues, ignorance of one's identity as a member doesn't enable one to escape this membership; it merely exposes one to be formed less consciously by distant, disembodied voices.[11]

In spite of the myths Disney tells us, then, our identities are convocated, and the question we should be asking is *Who* is convocating us? Which voices constitute our selves and desires? Denying our dependencies and proclaiming ourselves to be self-made individuals only makes us more susceptible to being unconsciously formed by the voices of mass media. We all narrate our lives through the voices of others, the voices we hear and take up, but many of us come to know who we are through disembodied voices—Disney characters, advertisers, politicians, and celebrities. With a smartphone in our pocket, we always have access to these abstract voices, voices that will happily narrate our lives for us in exchange for our attention and money. Entertainers and advertisers are expert at shaping our desires. As an advertising manual written at the turn of the twentieth century puts it, "Advertising aims to teach people that they have wants, which they did not recognize before."[12] In a similar fashion, flipping through a celebrity profile or scrolling down an Instagram feed educates our desires, teaching us who we should want to be.

As I have been arguing, convocation is both a fact and a process: it describes the fact of our membership as well as the process by which we come to inhabit our roles within this membership. And when we deny the fact of convocation, we inhibit our ability to participate redemptively in the process of convocation. One of the chief reasons we are tempted to deny the reality of convocation is that we fear our dependence on others will constrain or limit us. But Berry embraces these dependencies because of his faith that the bonds that convocate us can be bonds of love. These bonds, Berry believes, constitute us in at least three overlapping contexts: religious, ecological, and communal. Our identity is given and received in a dialogue with the God who called us into being by his creative word and is renewing us by his incarnate and resurrected word, a dialogue with our physical place and the other creatures who share it, and a dialogue with our local and cultural communities. In each context, Berry challenges us to look for ways to lovingly assume our responsibilities and renew our connections.

Berry's commitment to convocation and membership begins with his theological belief that we are created and sustained in love. In one poem he bluntly states his dissatisfaction with our culture's way of imagining identity—"I think the issues of 'identity' mostly / are poppycock"—and then goes on to offer convocation as an alternative paradigm for understanding the sources of our lives:

> Each one who speaks speaks
> as a convocation. We live as councils
> of ghosts. It is not "human genius"
> that makes us human, but an old love,
> an old intelligence of the heart
> we gather to us from the world,
> from the creatures, from the angels
> of inspiration, from the dead.[13]

It is through "an old love" that we gather our lives from the voices of our places, our fellow creatures, the dead who have gone before us, and even the angels. And though in this poem the nature of this love remains somewhat ambiguous, elsewhere Berry confesses his faith in its divine source: "I believe that the world was created and approved by love, that it subsists, coheres, and endures by love, and that, insofar as it is redeemable, it can be redeemed only by love. I believe that divine love, incarnate and indwelling in the world, summons the world always toward wholeness, which ultimately is reconciliation and atonement with God."[14] It is this faith in an incarnate love summoning us toward wholeness that underlies Burley's declaration that we are all members of each other.

As Burley's use of the term suggests, Berry derives his understanding of "membership" from Saint Paul's description of the church as the body of Christ.[15] In an interview, Berry explains his expansive understanding of this metaphor:

> When St. Paul said that "we are members of one another," he was using a far more inclusive "we" than Christian institutions have generally thought. For me, this is the meaning of ecology. Whether we know it or not, whether we want to be or not, we are members of one another: humans (ourselves and our enemies), earthworms, whales, snakes, squirrels, trees, topsoil, flowers, weeds, germs, hills, rivers, swifts, and stones—all of "us." The work of imagination, I feel, is to understand this. . . . For us, it is not a question of whether or not we shall be members one of another, but of whether or not we shall know that we are and act accordingly.[16]

As he often does, Berry here emphasizes the need to imaginatively accept and honor the fact of our membership. For Berry, this imaginative recognition of membership begins by seeing Christ, as Saint Paul has it, as "the head of the body."[17] Our membership in creation is determined not just by God's act of loving creation, but also by his ongoing work of redemption, which flows from Christ's incarnation and resurrection. Berry articulates this in his poem on Piero's *Resurrection* that I discussed in the first chapter.[18] When confronted with the face of the risen Christ, the poem's narrative voice shifts from first-person singular to first-person plural. In the light of Christ's resurrected countenance, the poet realizes that he is a member of all those who have been seen by the resurrected Word, the Word whose risen presence makes the bare trees green.

Piero's portrayal of the resurrected Christ as the source of creation's fertility aligns with Berry's understanding of convocation as at once religious and ecological. In an essay that traces the figure of Dame Nature through Western literature, Berry emphasizes our physical interdependence on the other creatures with whom we share our convocated life: "We have our lives by no right of our own, but instead by the privilege of sharing in the life that sustains all creatures. This great convocation is the work of Nature."[19] It is simply a biological fact that we live with and from others, that we share even our bodies with other organisms. Quite literally, we "live as councils / of ghosts." This is why Berry dislikes the term *environment*—because it means simply " 'surroundings,' a place that one is *in* but not *of*."[20] Ecologically, then, convocation names the way that Nature calls together diverse members to live in interdependence.

The membership that sustains and convocates us is not only divine and ecological; it is also cultural. Berry makes this point in many places, but one of the most beautiful is in his short novel *Remembering*. When Andy loses his right hand, this physical dismemberment leads him to resent the conditions of his belonging to his place and community, and the novel traces the process by which he is re-membered into his community. In an excellent essay, Phillip Donnelly demonstrates the formal resonance between Andy's story and the novel's structure. The novel itself is a convocation that orchestrates biblical texts, literary forebears like Dante and Milton, and the voices of Andy's neighbors and family members, and it is through this convocation that Andy renews his commitment to his fellow members.[21]

Moreover, this convocation is inherently a kind of renewal. Near the beginning of the book, Andy is at an academic conference listening to professors who haven't farmed in years pontificate about the "Future of the American Food System." In contrast to these abstracting voices, Andy remembers the many neighbors he has known and farmed alongside. One of these farmers, Elton Penn, would tell Andy, "If you're going to talk to me, Andy, you'll have to walk," but he always said this phrase in Old Jack Beecham's voice, the originator, as far as anyone in Port William knew, of this saying:

> Elton's mind had been, in part, a convocation of the voices of predecessors saying appropriate things at appropriate times . . . ; and he was a good enough mimic that when he recalled a saying its history would come with it. When he would tell Andy, "If you're going to talk to me, you'll have to walk," it would not be just the two of them talking and listening, but Old Jack would be saying it again to Mat, and Mat to his son-in-law, Wheeler, Andy's father, and Wheeler to Elton, and Elton to Andy all the times before; and an old understanding and an old laughter would renew itself then, and be with them.[22]

Elton models for Andy the ongoing convocation of a healthy membership, a convocation that brings dead voices to life so they can sustain those who follow. As Berry explains in the context of writing poetry, "Any poem worth the name is a product of a convocation. It exists, literally, by recalling past voices into presence. . . . As a new poem is made, not only with the art but within it, past voices are convoked—to be changed, little or much, by the addition of another voice."[23]

Convocation is a form of resurrection; it brings dead voices to life so that they can guide and instruct us. But to hear these voices and be guided by them, we must gratefully recognize our belonging rather than resent it or try to avoid the voices that remind us of our membership.

Healthy cultural convocation is always threatened by our human proclivity to ignore the voices that make uncomfortable demands on us, and cultures often develop systems that silence certain groups of people. One of the forms this tendency has taken in Berry's Kentucky community is the racial silencing of African American voices. Such historical and ongoing injustices cause some people to view rooted communities as inherently oppressive: hence Richard Florida's claim that the mobility of the Creative Class makes them more tolerant. Berry's multifaceted understanding of convocation, though, offers a different corrective to racism, patriarchy, and other ways that we silence certain voices.[24] According to Berry's view of membership, if our cultural convocation is rooted in a theology of belonging and an ecological recognition of those with whom we share our biological lives, it is more likely to be open to diverse voices. In *The Christian Imagination: Theology and the Origins of Race,* Willie Jennings beautifully describes the way his parents and community convocated him into a narrative identity rooted in the dirt and woven from their family and biblical narratives, but he also traces how colonialism violates such belonging and obscures certain voices.[25] As Joseph Wiebe argues, Jennings "rehabilitat[es] the spatial aspects of identity" in ways that are consonant with Berry's vision of placed convocation.[26] Though she does not write from a theological perspective, bell hooks makes a similar argument in *Belonging,* a book that includes a long conversation between her and Berry.[27] To return to the example of Andy Cattlet, two of the voices that shaped him as a young boy were those of Dick Watson and Sarah Jane, an African American couple who worked for his grandfather. As an old man, Andy reflects on how the racial divide in his community influenced his friendship with these two in ways he only vaguely sensed at the time. Nevertheless, Andy says about Aunt Sarah Jane: "She too I loved. She too is a knot in the net that has gathered me up and kept me alive until now."[28] So instead of seeking different voices by traveling to far-off places, Berry suggests we should listen first to those who share our places and communities, being particularly attentive to those whom our culture tends to marginalize.[29]

Belonging to one another is messy and painful. But it is through faithful, attentive listening that we can begin to inhabit our memberships redemptively, healing what Jayber Crow describes as "the frayed and always fraying, incomplete and yet ever-holding bonds of the various sorts of affection." As Jayber attests, our communities will "always be marred by members who are indifferent to [them] or against [them], who are nonetheless [their] members and maybe nonetheless essential to [them]. And yet I saw them all as somehow perfected, beyond time, by one another's love, compassion, and forgiveness, as it is said we may be perfected by grace."[30] By submitting to the dialogical process of convocation, we can participate in the grace that Jayber envisions and contribute to the "assumption of responsibilities [and] the renewal of connections."[31]

Such healing depends, however, on responding to the fact of our membership with gratitude rather than resentment. Our Disneyfied culture shapes us to be like Milton's Satan, who resents his dependence on the Creator and strives to "quit / The debt immense of endless gratitude, / So burthensome, still paying, still to ow[e]." Because Satan resents the burden of gratitude, he fails to experience the liberating paradox by which "a grateful mind / By owing owes not, but still pays, at once / Indebted and dischargd."[32] Through grateful convocation—through allowing our desires and identities to be shaped by the voices of those to whom we belong—we receive a different kind of self, one that is not a container to be filled (pursue self-fulfillment!), software to be updated (be the best version of yourself!), or an investment in individual happiness (don't sell yourself short!) but, rather, a gift that we can only fully receive when we turn around and offer it to others. Convocation invites us to attend to the needs of those around us—to be, indeed, grateful for those needs—rather than pursuing our own elusive, internal desires.

Andy Catlett reflects on these mysteries through a haunting line composed by Maze Tickburn, who, in his drunken songs, would proclaim himself Port William's "onliest" stonemason.[33] Maze was a member whose belonging was certainly frayed, yet decades later Andy remembers Maze's lonely song and weaves his marginal voice into the membership of love:

> Time, then, is told by love's losses, and by the coming of love, and by love continuing in gratitude for what is lost. It is folded and enfolded and unfolded forever and ever, the love by which the dead are alive and the unborn welcomed into the womb. The great question for the old and the dying, I think, is not if they have loved and been loved enough, but if they have been grateful enough for love received and given, however much. No one who has gratitude is the onliest one. Let us pray to be grateful to the last.[34]

When we are grateful for the voices of others, even those voices that make painful demands on our lives, we open ourselves to participate in the grace of sustaining membership. And we may find ourselves wanting to be not just "anyone," but a member of those to whom we are grateful to belong.

Burley Coulter's Convocation

Burley Coulter is one of Port William's most famous, or infamous, inhabitants. As one of his neighbors tells the preacher's wife, "That Burley, now, he's in a class by hisself. There's stories about him that nobody's going to tell you, Mrs. Milby, or anyhow I ain't, but I wish you could know him."[35] Yet Burley is not the focus of any novel and is the narrator of only four short stories.[36] For the most part, readers learn who Burley is through the same process of convocation by which Burley comes to know himself. We listen to others tell of Burley's "escapades [that] have now, by retelling, worn themselves as deeply into that countryside as its backroads."[37] And as Burley contributes and listens to the community's ongoing conversation, he finds that his youthful desires to be "free as a bird" are altered.[38] Listening to others and attending to their needs transforms his identity and desires, causing his "heart [to grow] bigger inside" and eventually making him the "presiding elder" of the Port William membership, one who invites others into the joy of belonging.[39] It is by knowing himself as a convocated member and welcoming others into this convocation that Burley discovers he is "practicing up" for resurrection morning.[40]

Berry describes the ongoing conversation in towns like Port William as "the unceasing meandering of its story of itself by which it diverted, amused, and consoled itself."[41] And he goes on to say that you could understand the "consciousness"—a word whose etymology literally denotes shared knowledge—of such places "as the continual, continually wandering story that in one way or another included everybody, carrying them through time like the current of the river."[42] Members of this conversation learn that attending to this current of talk can teach us "where needs" are and how we might respond to them.[43] Readers of Berry's Port William fiction are invited to listen in on this meandering conversation: we hear the same stories told from different perspectives and in different contexts, we learn the background of characters we've come to love, and we gradually come to know the place by eavesdropping on its convocation.

The stories and novels about Port William come to function as interdependent voices within a larger conversation. Berry's method is in some ways like that of Athey Keith, who, according to Jayber Crow, tells stories in "odd little bits and pieces, usually in unacknowledged reference to a larger story that he did not tell because (apparently) he assumed you already knew it, and he told the fragment just to remind you of the rest."[44] It is only by listening to Athey over the course of many years that Jayber learns to stitch the various stories together into a coherent whole. Writing about one of Berry's short-story collections, Matthew Horton makes a claim that can, I think, be usefully extended to all of Berry's fiction: "Like the inhabitants of a community, each story has independent value, is able to stand alone, and asserts its own level of influence on its surroundings; however, understood in light of its relationship to the other parts, each story gains significance, is strengthened and enriched by its context, and is shaped by the influence of those around it. . . . [*The Wild Birds*, a collection of six short stories,] contains interrelated stories that structurally embody the interdependence of individuals in a unified community.["45] In other words, Berry's stories exist in a dialogical relationship with one another, and listening in on their dialogue shapes us in the habits of attention, gratitude, humility, hope, memory, and fidelity needed to hear the conversation to which each contributes. As Horton concludes, "'Remembering' disparate, smaller wholes into a unified vision . . . emphasizes the tenuous interdependence that preserves and perpetuates those cycles."[46] Reading Berry's stories, then, can train us in the virtues needed to participate in loving convocation.

Burley Coulter is an exemplary participant in Port William's conversation, and one of the telltale results is that his speech incorporates the sayings of others. To use Bakhtin's term, Burley's is a "dialogical imagination," one composed from the voices of those with whom he shares his place. His understanding of the world is filtered through the descriptions of his friends and neighbors, and Berry suggests that this kind of convocated consciousness is one way of practicing resurrection. In one of the few stories that Burley narrates, "Burley Coulter's Fortunate Fall," Burley is roped into painting a large barn roof for a nearby landowner, Miss Charlotte. The story begins with Burley giving us a description of Miss Charlotte's history and personality, a description that ventriloquizes the voices of other community members, particularly Miss Charlotte's tenant Grover Gibbs:

> She would come riding in, always unexpectedly, in the back seat of her long green car that was about the same color as folding money. It would be shined so slick, Grover said, that a housefly couldn't stand up on it. She would be wearing a dress that was like a cloud or like a flower bed in full bloom or like a pool with a goldfish—this is Grover talking. And she would have on white gloves and a hat with a veil, and if the weather was the least bit cool she would have a fox or a mink fur piece around her neck and her hands stuck into a fur muff with every hair standing on end. And she would be sitting straight up like a queen in a picture, in reference strictly to herself.[47]

Miss Charlotte, unlike Burley, refuses to accept her membership in this place. She thinks of herself "in reference strictly to herself" and doesn't willingly participate in the community's talk, but that doesn't stop the community from including her in its talk:

> It's a mystery how the voices gather. Our talk at row ends or in the barn or stripping room would call up the voices of the absent and the dead. Somebody maybe would wonder what old Uncle Bub would think of Miss Charlotte, and though we never knew him and he never knew her he would say about her what he said about everybody: "Hell and dammit, boys! She's a ring-tailed twister!" About everybody knew of Miss Charlotte and took some

interest in her. She was surrounded, you might say, with observation. And of course also, as Wheeler said, with her own glitter.[48]

For all her aloofness, Miss Charlotte remains a member of this community; she is one of those members "who don't" know the fact of their belonging. But Burley's narration of her, weaving together the voices of Grover, Uncle Bub, and Wheeler, attests to his self-understanding as a member.

When Miss Charlotte decides that her barn roof needs to be painted, Grover flatly refuses to do it, citing a grave fear of heights. Jarrat, however, could use the money, so he agrees to paint it with his brother, Burley. Burley wasn't party to this agreement, and he's rather disgruntled when Jarrat announces that he's signed them up to paint this roof. Nevertheless, Burley joins his brother, and so he finds himself spending long, hot summer days doing a job that he didn't want or choose. One sweltering afternoon, when they are finally nearing the end of the task, they hear an airplane fly low overhead. Burley leans back to look at it and loses his balance. He drops his bucket, takes a step back to steady himself, puts his foot on the freshly spilled paint, and skis down the slope of the metal roof, riding a layer of slick paint. As he slides down, he envisions his imminent death, but he happens to fall into a solitary old cedar growing at the edge of the barn: "When I came to the outreaching lower branches, they just bent and tumbled me from one to the next, sort of gently, maybe gracefully, until the bottom one dropped me without too much of a thump onto the ground."[49]

While Burley sits on the ground and collects himself, Jarrat climbs down the roof, looks over the eave and asks, "Well, are you practicing up for something, or was that it?" Still rather stunned, Burley simply recalls, "It came to me I was alive."[50] As Oehlschlaeger comments about this scene, "Unknowingly Burley has just practiced being interrupted by the unexpected, the unwanted, and yet discovering something 'saving' in it."[51] Oehlschlaeger is right to see this as a moment of unexpected redemption; while stuck in a job he didn't want to do, Burley experiences grace. But perhaps even more specifically, Jarrat's question points back to an earlier line in the story when Burley looked at the roof and knew "that if you fell from so high onto that old ledgy hillside you wouldn't get up again maybe until resurrection morning."[52] Well, Burley did indeed fall from so high, and in getting up after his fall, he is "practicing up" for resurrection morning. His exploit and Jarrat's wry remark certainly enter the talk of Port William, becoming part of the unceasing meandering that carries the community through time. And Burley's contribution to this conversation is composed from the redemptive fruits of his eavesdropping—both listening in on his community's conversation and quite literally falling from eaves. On resurrection morning, Burley will experience the same sort of unexpected grace that he receives when he falls into the old cedar tree and when he allows his identity to be shaped in response to the voices and needs of those around him.

Receiving grace through unexpected means isn't always easy, though, which is why we have to practice up for it. In another story, "Stand by Me," Burley reflects on some of the difficult experiences through which he gave up his dreams of autonomy and learned to be grateful for the gift of membership. In the story's opening sentence, Burley reflects on the gap between how we imagine our lives and how they in fact turn out: "When Jarrat married Lettie in 1921 and bought the little place across the draw from our home place and started to paying for it, in that time that was already hard, years before the Depression, he had a life ahead of him, it seemed like, that was a lot different from the life he in fact was going to live."[53] This difference between what his life seemed to have in store and what it in fact held will be a hardship not only for Jarrat, but for all those who belong to him. In 1921, just back from fighting in World War I, Burley had a lot of things on his mind, and belonging to Jarrat wasn't too high on the list. Yet like his brother, Burley is also ignorant of "the life he in fact was going to live" and of the way this life would reshape his desires and identity. Through the fact of his membership, Burley discovers that who he wants to be changes in response to the needs of those around him. While this impinges on Burley's freedom to be whoever he wants to be, knowing himself as a member gives him an identity larger and, in a paradoxical way, more fulfilling, than he could have imagined.

His second cousin Wheeler Catlett remembered that as a young man, Burley acted like he was "free as a bird," and he resented anything that might limit that freedom.[54] Burley's nephew Nathan recalls his uncle similarly: "He said land was worse than a wife; it tied you down, and he didn't want to be in any place he couldn't leave. He never did go anyplace much, except fishing and hunting, and sometimes to town on Saturday. But he wanted to feel that he could leave if he took the notion."[55] As his kin attest, Burley was under the illusion of autonomy, and yet time and again he discovers that he belongs to people who need him, and that while this belonging ties him down, it ties him with bonds of love.

Burley survived his service in World War I—which included a brief time in jail for striking an officer—without having his autonomy seriously damaged; the imposed, Apollonian order of the military couldn't tame him.[56] But shortly after he returns home, his sister-in-law suddenly dies and leaves behind two young sons. In response to this tragedy, Burley allows himself to be constrained by these two nephews whom he loves: "The boys all of a sudden, instead of belonging just to her and Jarrat, belonged to us all. . . . And I was one of the ones that they belonged to. They belonged to me because I belonged to them. . . . I belonged to them because they needed me."[57] We have already seen, in *Nathan Coulter,* how Jarrat is so wounded by the loss of his wife that he struggles to care for his sons, so the boys come to live with their grandparents and Uncle Burley. Burley admits having the boys living with him inhibited his freedom to go hunting or fishing or visiting his women friends, but he nevertheless responds to their need by offering them his care.

And the great paradox of membership is that when he consents to the loss of autonomy entailed by belonging to his nephews, Burley receives the unexpected grace of a given self. He finds himself—and his *vocation*—by losing himself.[58] As Burley puts it, "They changed me. Before, I was oftentimes just on the loose, care-free as a dog fox, head as empty as a gourd. Afterwards, it seemed like my heart was bigger inside than outside."[59] Responding to these needy boys actually changes Burley's desires, his identity. In a different story, Burley explains this process in terms of a transformation from others' *needs* to his own *wants*:

> I might have gone somewhere else when I got mustered out in 1919, but I come back, and looked like I was in the habit of staying, so I stayed. I thought of leaving, but the times was hard and Pap needed me—or needed somebody better, to tell the truth—and I stayed. I stayed to help bring up Tom and Nathan after their mother died. And then Pap died and Mam was old, and I stayed on with her. And when she died I stayed on and done my part with Jarrat; the boys was gone then, and he needed me. And somehow or other along the way, I began to stay because I wanted to. I wanted to be with Jarrat, and Nathan and Hannah here, and Mat and you and the others. And somewhere or other I realized that being here was the life I had because I'd never had another one any place else, and never would have.[60]

By attending and responding to the needs of others, Burley participates in the process of convocation and comes to know himself as a loving member of his community and place. Burley's responses are certainly not perfect; his most prominent failure is waiting to formally acknowledge his "all-but-marriage" to Kate Helen Branch until after her death, a failure Burley comes to regret deeply.[61] Even so, in his peculiar, wayward fashion, Burley answers the claims that others make on him, and by doing so, he receives a given identity that is bigger and richer than the one he imagined for himself as a young man with a "head empty as a gourd." As one of Berry's favorite lines from *King Lear* has it, Burley "losest here, a better where to find."[62]

Relinquishing one's dreams and expectations can be very hard, however, and Burley's brother, Jarrat, resents being forced to do so. The result of this resentment is pain and frustration, both for himself and those he belongs to. After the death of Lettie, Burley describes how Jarrat resists receiving comfort from others: "He didn't want kindness for himself, though of course he needed it. He didn't want to be caught needing it."[63] Participating in the process of convocation requires us to accept our need for others, but Jarrat clings to the illusion of self-sufficiency and so cuts himself off from any unexpected grace that might come through the love of his kin and neighbors.

In clinging to his autonomy, Jarrat also hinders the development of his sons' voices. Healthy convocation depends on individual members listening to the voices of others and contributing their own voice in response; it is a dance that involves give-and-take. But Jarrat crowds out his sons. According to Burley, "Jarrat was hard for his boys to get along with. He just naturally took up too much of the room they needed to grow in." He didn't say much to them, but when he spoke it was most often to urge them back to work, "Let's go! Let's go!"[64] Things come to a head one hot afternoon in the tobacco field when Tom challenges Jarrat, trying to outpace his father in the harvest. Jarrat wins the race and mercilessly taunts Tom, inciting a fight. In recalling that day, Burley can only say, "It was awful." Tom leaves home that night: "He had to get out from under his daddy's feet and onto his own."[65] Jarrat wouldn't give Tom the space to find his voice in the community's conversation, so Tom's anger and departure are certainly understandable. This tragic rending of the membership is ameliorated somewhat by Tom's extension of forgiveness: before he leaves to fight in World War II, where he will be killed, he visits home a few times and reconciles with Jarrat.[66]

Jarrat's silencing of his sons is one example of how members too often abuse those to whom they belong, ignoring them or drowning out their voices in ways that mar genuine convocation. Often, as in Jarrat's case, it is those who have been wounded in some way by their membership with others, and so come to resent their own belonging, who in turn fail to attend to others. The loss of his wife wounds Jarrat, and he in turn wounds his sons. But such abuses of membership don't negate its reality or the need to cultivate its health. In advocating for membership, Burley is not defending either an Apollonian imposition of one voice over the community—"My way or the highway!"—or a Dionysian pursuit of antinomian freedom—"I can do whatever the heck I want to do!" In fact, as we have seen time and again, these industrial diseases are two sides of the same coin: both are predicated on suppressing the voices of those to whom we belong.

In contrast, Burley endeavors to listen to the diverse, sometimes discordant voices of those who share his place and do what he can to orchestrate them into a harmonious whole. This process is difficult, and it will never be complete, but it's the ongoing work of loving convocation.[67] Participating in the process of convocation—attending to the needs and voices of those around you—doesn't mean that you make yourself into a blank slate on which others can inscribe their voices. Rather, it means that you give priority to the health of the whole membership over the voice of any one individual, your own or another's. Sometimes this will entail speaking up forcefully in defense of those whose voices are marginalized. Jayber Crow remembers a day in his barbershop when a man came in and insulted the appearance of "niggers." Jayber is speechless and doesn't know what to say, but an elder in the community, Athey Keith, exercises "prompt, regardless courage" and makes a withering reply. Out of the silence that results, Athey concludes, "It might prove out to be . . . that if we can't live together, we can't live atall."[68] Healthy convocation depends on members who stand up for each other and work toward a harmony that includes everyone's voice.

This means it includes even the voices of those who fail to listen and who silence others. So Burley continues reaching out to Jarrat, refusing to allow him to remain in his self-imposed isolation. When Jarrat receives a letter from the government informing him that Tom has been killed in action, he hands it to Burley. Burley reads it, and an "awful, awful silence" descends on them. Out of this incredibly painful loss, Burley calls to Jarrat, inviting him back to the work at hand: "For the first and last time I said it to him, I said, 'Let's go.' The day's work was only half finished. Having nothing else we could do, we finished it." Burley transforms Jarrat's saying by inflecting it with love and compassion rather than impatience, and in so doing he offers Jarrat a redeemed version of his voice. And Burley stands by his words. After working together the rest of the day, Burley goes to Jarrat's house that evening and sits, silently, in the kitchen until bedtime: "If it had just been me and I needed company, which I did, I could have walked to town and sat with the talkers in the pool room or the barber shop. But except that I would go to sit with him, Jarrat would have sat there in his sorrow entirely by himself and stared at the wall or the floor. I anyhow denied him that." And each night after that, "for a long time," Burley returned to sit quietly with his brother.[69] Jarrat has known the fact of his membership with others primarily through loss—most prominently the loss of his wife to disease and the loss of his son first to his own hardness and then to war—and these losses are painful reminders that as much as he would like to be self-sufficient, he is connected to others through bonds of dependence and love. But Burley's faithful presence testifies that this membership can also be a consolation.[70]

Working on with Jarrat after the death of Tom, Burley reflects on the way that grieving for those he has loved and lost reminds him of the other world, the eternal world, that is the ultimate source of our mutual belonging: "As your heart gets bigger on the inside, the world gets bigger on the outside. If the dead had been alive only in this world, you would forget them, looks like, as soon as they die. But you remember them, because they always were living in the other, bigger world while they lived in this little one, and this one and the other one are the same."[71] So though all of us can be tempted to respond to loss by withdrawing from the world, as Jarrat does, Burley comes to know that

You can't stop just because you're carrying a load of grief and would like to stop, or don't care if you go on or not. Jarrat nor I either didn't stop. This world was still asking things of us that we had to give.

It was maybe the animals most of all that kept us going, the good animals we depended on, that depended on us: our work mules, the cattle, the sheep, the hogs, even the chickens. They were a help to us because they didn't know our grief but just quietly lived on, suffering what they suffered, enjoying what they enjoyed, day by day. We took care of them, we did what had to be done, we went on.[72]

Burley has come to the same conclusion that Margaret Feltner does: "You always have somebody to think about, and it's a blessing."[73] The bodily needs of others remind us of our mutual interdependence, our mutual belonging that is certainly biological and ecological, but that is ultimately rooted in the divine love that created us and is redeeming us. Burley continues to cultivate membership, in spite of the load of grief it places on him, because of his faith in "the other, bigger world" to which we all belong.

By allowing his desires and identity to be reshaped in response to the needs of those to whom he belongs, Burley participates in the life of this bigger world. Thus, at the end of his life his friends testify that he was "a faithful man."[74] And they, in turn, are faithful to him. One of Berry's most beautiful short stories, "Fidelity," narrates Burley's rather unusual last days. In doing so, it sharply illustrates the contrast between the freedom sought by the industrial mind, a freedom that is ultimately lonely and sterile, and the faithful, redemptive bonds of loving convocation. So what to the industrial mind appears to be a kidnapping is in fact the bonds of loving membership holding Burley's death in place so that it can serve life.

At the beginning of the story, Burley has grown so sick that he reluctantly allows his son and daughter-in-law, Danny and Lyda, to take him to the hospital. Once there, he is trapped in the bureaucratic procedures of the medical industry. Hooked up to tubes and surrounded by machines, Burley looks lost: "He did not, in fact, appear to belong to his name at all." Shortly after being admitted to the hospital, Burley becomes disoriented and incoherent: "He was no longer in his right mind . . . because he was no longer in his right place." His friends and family members visit him, gathering at his bed and "reconstructing their membership around him in that place that hummed, in the lapses of their talk, with the sound of many engines." In its dystopian parody of Saint John's heavenly vision—in which Christ's voice carries "the sound of many waters"—Berry's description contrasts the membership's convocation with the hospital's ineffectual imitation of redemption.[75] The hospital's engine-like order is too narrow to account for

Burley's beloved "bigger world." When the doctor gives Burley's prognosis, he speaks "fluently from within the bright orderly enclosure of his explanation, like a man in a glass booth. And Nathan and Hannah, Danny and Lyda stood looking in at him from the larger, looser, darker order of their merely human love."[76] For the doctor, death is merely a quantity to be forestalled by industrial procedures, but those within the larger order of love seek to discern opportunities within Burley's death to practice up for resurrection.

Realizing that he has consigned his father to the mechanical, quantified order that Burley's way of life cheerfully rejected, Danny slips out of bed in the middle of the night and returns to the hospital to reclaim him. Knowing the doctors wouldn't release Burley in his condition, Danny commandeers a gurney, cuts his father free from the tubes, and surreptitiously wheels him out to his waiting truck. The hospital staff are understandably alarmed when they discover their patient is missing, and they inform Lyda that her father-in-law has "disappeared."[77] Lyda and the other members know quite well what has happened, but they work together to foil Detective Kyle Bode in his efforts to prove that Danny has kidnapped his father.

Detective Bode, defender of hospital policies and the legal order, is the story's main representative of the industrial mind. He seeks to impose a rigid, black-and-white, Apollonian order onto his world, and when that imposed structure inevitably fails to contain reality's complexity, he resorts to Dionysian violence. He imagined himself in a noble career: he would be "a man who—insightful, alert, and knowing—stepped into the midst of confusion and made clarity and order that people would be grateful for." Unfortunately, Bode found his work as a detective rather more complicated than he had imagined. The people he worked with "had motives that were confusing, and they left evidence that was confusing." And the frustration that marks his professional aspirations also dogs his personal life. His father was born in a place called "Nowhere" and moved to the city to make something of himself. Kyle, in turn, "had higher aims, which made him dangerous to those he considered to be below him. . . . Kyle was an idealist, with a little bit of an ambition to be a hero. Perhaps by the same token, he was also a man given to lethargy and to sudden onsets of violence by which he attempted to drive back whatever circumstances his lethargy had allowed to close in on him." This unstable vacillation between idealized order and chaotic violence haunts his marriages. When he "began to feel that [his first wife] was limiting his development, . . . he divorced her in order to be free to be himself." He married again, but his second wife always seemed dissatisfied:

> He, too, was dissatisfied; he could not see what he had because he was always looking around for something else that he thought he wanted. And so

perhaps it was out of mutual dissatisfaction that their divorce had come, and now they were free. Perhaps even their little daughter was free, who was tied down no more than her parents were, for they sent her flying back and forth between them like a shuttle-cock, and spoiled her in vying for her allegiance, and gave her more freedom of choice than she could have used well at twice her age. They were all free, he supposed.[78]

Detective Bode has clung to his freedom, but in doing so, he has excluded himself from any bonds that would hold him in the larger order of love. Trying to be whoever he wants to be, he has been unable to discover who he wants to be, and he has become merely lonely.

Burley, by contrast, is not free; he is held in the "room of love," kidnapped back into it, you might say.[79] And from the outset, this kidnapping is figured in redemptive, freeing terms. When Danny wheels Burley out of the hospital, he passes two janitors leaning against the wall "as stupefied, apparently, as the soldiers at the Tomb."[80] Danny is rescuing Burley from the tomblike hospital, and though Burley's death is imminent, he is being carried toward resurrection. Danny drives back to Port William and pulls down a little-used track. He then carries his father—as Nathan had carried his dying grandfather at the end of *Nathan Coulter*—into an abandoned barn a quarter mile away. Throughout their journey, Burley is unresponsive, but Danny continually narrates for him where they are and what he is doing. His voice invites Burley back into his place and the self he has received from this place. When he finally lays him down in the old barn and makes him comfortable, Danny turns his flashlight on Burley's face to check on him, and Burley seems restored to himself: "It was, as it had not been in the hospital, unmistakably the face of the man who for eighty-two years had been Burley Coulter. Here, where it belonged, the face thus identified itself and assumed a power that kept Danny standing there, shining the light on it."[81] What is this power? Perhaps it is akin to that of the face that Berry witnesses in Piero's painting of Christ:

> But for his face and countenance
> I have found no words: powerful beyond life
> and death, seeing beyond sight or light,
> beyond all triumph serene.[82]

As Danny digs a grave for Burley, he periodically returns to the barn to check on his father. On one of these visits, he is surprised to find Burley's eyes open, and he asks him if he knows where he is. Burley smiles and says, "Right here."[83] When "Fidelity" was first published in *Orion* and then later collected with four other stories in *Fidelity,* it included a brief explanatory paragraph about Burley's reply: "He was quoting himself as the hero of an old joke and an old story in which, lost on a night hunt, his companions had asked where they were, and he had told them, 'Right here.'"[84] In the version collected in *That Distant Land,* however, Berry takes out this paragraph. In the stand-alone versions, he had to step in and supply the history for readers, but at the end of *That Distant Land,* readers have read about this "old story" three times already, and Berry can count on us to recall it along with Danny and Burley.[85] Rather than being treated as outsiders in need of an explanation, readers are invited to become participants in the convocation of those who know where they are.

The next time Danny returns to check on him, Burley has died. Danny finishes the grave, carefully lines the bottom and sides with stones brought up from the creek, and carries Burley's body from the barn. When he gently lays the body in the grave, it "seemed to accept again its stillness and its deep sleep, submissive to the motion of the world until the world's end." This is a radical acceptance of death, but it is also a hopeful one; by burying Burley in the place he so loved, Danny is participating in Burley's hope that at the world's end—on "resurrection morning"—this place will be redeemed and made whole.[86] Danny covers Burley's body with armloads of wildflowers, lays broad stones across the tops of the upright stones, and speaks a benediction over the grave: "Be with him, as he has been with us."[87] As he proceeds to bury his father, Danny, in a very literal sense, rises from the dead: "As he filled the grave and thus slowly rose out of it, he felt again that the living man, Burley Coulter, was near him, watching and visible, except where he looked. The intimation of Burley's presence was constantly with him, at once troubling and consoling; in its newness, it kept him close to tears."[88] By accepting his father's death and finding a way to hold it in place, Danny is practicing up for resurrection.

While Danny is burying his father, Wheeler and Henry Catlett have gathered the membership together at their law office, and Detective Bode is there trying to find proof that Danny has kidnapped Burley. The only evidence he has to go on is that a man wearing a blue shirt was seen pushing a gurney out of the hospital. Unbeknown to the others, when Nathan heard that, he took one of his shirts, found where Danny had hidden his truck, and left it on the front seat. Their communal resistance to Detective Bode's efforts bears witness to Henry's claim that "people belong to each other and to God" rather than to the legal system.[89] It is in defense of this belonging that the membership has gathered to hold a sort of wake, remembering Burley, sharing stories, being present together. Against his will, Bode is drawn by the beauty of their convocation: he is "tempted over and over again to leave . . . the small, clear world of the law and its explanations and to enter the larger, darker world not ordered by human reasons or subject to them, in which he sensed obscurely that something might live that he, too, might be glad to have alive."[90] Wheeler, a man who has had his differences with

Burley, then offers a sort of eulogy for Burley. He begins with some of Burley's wild escapades, but concludes by reflecting on the ways that Burley matured in response to the needs of others:

> Though he never gave up his love of roaming about, he had become a different man from the one he started out to be. I'm not sure when that change began. Maybe it was when Nathan and Tom started following him around when they were little boys, after their mother died. And then, when Danny came along, Burley took his proper part in raising him. He took care of his mother until she died. He was a good and loyal partner to his brother. He was a true friend to all his friends. . . . We'll not forget his laughter. He looked at the world and found it good.
>
> "I've never learned anything until I had to," he often said, and so confessed himself a man like other men. But he learned what he had to, and he changed, and so he made himself exceptional.
>
> He was, I will say, a faithful man.[91]

As Wheeler concludes his account of Burley's remarkable life, the gathered membership hears Danny's step outside the door. Fearful of Danny's entrance, of whether he will enter with mud on his shoes and wearing a blue shirt, they all sit silent "as under a stone." But Danny "stepped into the room, wearing a shirt green as the woods, his well-oiled shoes as clean as his cap. He was smiling. To those seated around the book-lined old walls, he had the aspect and the brightness of one who had borne the dead to the grave, and filled the grave to the brim, and received the dead back into life again."[92] The stone is rolled away, and by remaining faithful to Burley, they all receive again the gift of his life, even in his death.

Burley has been rescued from the order of engines and brought back into the larger, looser order of topsoil, the order of a convocated membership. He was going to die in both orders, but in the one his death would have been just a number blinking out; in the other, his memory continues to serve his beloved community. And in his death, he practices resurrection not through his own virtuous action, but through the faithful love of his kin and neighbors. Like the time he fell from Miss Charlotte's barn roof, Burley is caught by a grace he doesn't expect or deserve. His irregular faithfulness to his community is matched by its members' unlawful fidelity to him, but Burley hasn't been faithful in expectation of some return. He was faithful because he listened to what were, at the time, the unwanted claims their voices made on him, and he responded as best he could. In turn, his friends respond to his needs, and together they form a sustaining, redemptive convocation.

Listening in on their conversation, we, like Detective Bode, are invited to turn from our lonely pursuit of power and freedom and join in the larger, looser, darker order of love to which they remain faithful. We are invited to put off the industrial mind that treats death as an infringement on our freedom and something to be avoided at all costs, and to enter a sustaining membership that accepts death, holds it in place, and waits for life to come, "if it will."[93] We are invited into a way of happening that might make a vineyard of the curse. The trees, once bare, are green.

Practicing Convocation

Most families won't have the opportunity or need to kidnap their relatives from the hospital, but there are less sensational ways that we can situate death in a more communal context. Some developments in hospice care have made it easier for people to experience a good death with their families.[94] In the case of my own grandfather, we knew well in advance that he was dying from cancer. Our extended family gathered often in the months before his death, and the night before he died, he gave a personal blessing to each of his children, children-in-law, and grandchildren. The following week, many of us stayed at my grandparents' home and built a coffin for him using his own woodworking tools. The circumstances in which our loved ones die will vary, but we can find ways to hold these losses in place so that the death of each member sustains the convocation to which he or she belongs.

By doing so, we will remind ourselves and those around us that even in death we cannot be whoever we want to be, that the demands others make on us, while often frustrating and difficult, are opportunities for sacrificial love. And in faithfully responding to these demands, we come to know ourselves as "members of each other. All of us. Everything."[95] Dying in the company of those to whom we belong is one way of bearing witness to Berry's faith that

> this is the morning
> of Christ's resurrection.
> The tomb is empty. There is
> no death. Death is our illusion,
> our wish to belong only
> to ourselves, which is our freedom
> to kill one another.
> From this sleep may we too
> rise, as out of the dark grave.[96]

Epilogue

Practicing Resurrection

Reading Wendell Berry's poetry, essays, and stories won't provide us with a simple solution to our cultural and ecological challenges. He doesn't give us a set of techniques for swiping away intractable problems. But practicing the virtues of renewal that his literary forms model can enable us to begin inhabiting our places more sustainably. These virtues, like poetry, won't *make* anything happen, but they lead us into a way of happening that is healing, redemptive, and ultimately resurrecting.

This redemptive way of happening, this sustainable form of life, looks different for different people in different places, but these different local adaptations are analogous to one another. These analogies also hold across different scales, so that there are formal affinities between sustainable selves, households, neighborhoods, churches, and poleis. In each of these spheres, members of sustaining communities hold death in place, practice virtues of renewal, and lovingly give of themselves to others. Sustaining members act according to the agrarian and theological principle that "except a corn of wheat fall into the ground and die, it abideth alone: but if it die, it bringeth forth much fruit."[1]

In a world organized according to industrial principles, such sustainable forms will necessarily be worked out on the cultural and economic margins. But as we have seen, while Berry is not optimistic about the spread of sustaining forms of life, he is hopeful, and hope depends not on probabilities or expectations, but on practicable examples. Burley Coulter's son, Danny Branch, stands as one such example of how we might make do—in a Certeauian sense—on the margins of an industrial economy. In the short story, "The Branch Way of Doing," Andy Catlett does his best to distill the "economic principles" of Danny's sustainable way of life:

1—Be happy with what you've got. Don't be always looking for something better.

2—Don't buy anything you don't need.

3—Don't buy what you ought to save. Don't buy what you ought to make.

4—Unless you absolutely have got to do it, don't buy anything new.

5—If somebody tries to sell you something to "save labor," look out. If you can work, then work.

6—If other people want to buy a lot of new stuff and fill up the country with junk, use the junk.

7—Some good things are cheap, even free. Use them first.

8—Keep watch for what nobody wants. Sort through the leavings.

9—You might know, or find out, what it is to need help. So help people.[2]

Danny's principles are eminently practicable, even for those of us who aren't small-scale farmers in rural Kentucky. His example shows us how we might begin living redemptively right now, in the midst of a broken and messy world. And if we faithfully live out Berry's virtues of renewal, we might discover that we, like Burley, have been practicing up for resurrection morning.

At the end of Milton's *Paradise Lost,* Adam testifies that "to the faithful, death [is] the gate of life."[3] Berry has spent his life creatively working to be faithful in a faithless culture—he has been faithful to his wife, his place, his community, his art, and his religious tradition. And the words he has written from these complex and difficult fidelities bear witness that to the faithful, death is indeed the gate of life.

Acknowledgments

Writing this book has provided many tangible reminders of my membership in communities that care deeply about sustainable forms of life. Spring Arbor University has provided one of these communities, and I'm grateful for my students and colleagues who have questioned, conversed, and lived many of the ideas in this book. I tried out an early version of my argument in a special-topics course titled "Wendell Berry and the Study of Form," and a thoughtful group of students made that class a rich and fruitful place: Kaylee Anderson, Kayla Chenault, Kat Cooper, Salina Delarosa, Molly Gorczyca, Katlyne Heath, Jill Heine, April Holmes, Kyle Huizenga, Jordan Moore, and Carly Thompson. Katlyne Heath went on to write an insightful honors thesis on the revisions in *Nathan Coulter,* and her research significantly deepened my own understanding of that novel. Kerry Wade and Alison Westra did further research, providing me with meticulous records of the revisions Berry made to several of his published works.

Working and writing with Jack Baker has been an incredible blessing; I no longer know which ideas about Berry I developed and which ones I stole from Jack. I'm also grateful for long conversations with other colleagues and friends, many of whom read and commented on portions of this manuscript: Robbie Bolton, Tim Burbery, Brent Cline, Andrew Harvey, Bethany Hebbard, Matt Hill, Sebastian Holder, Tom Holsinger-Friesen, Millard Kimery, Josh Mabie, Ethan Mannon, Eric Miller, Cameron Moore, Robert Moore-Jumonville, Scott Moore, Lucas Nossaman, Gracy Olmstead, Jason Peters, Steven Petersheim, Ingrid Pierce, Jonathan Rinck, and Jamie Skillen. Josh Skinner graciously helped me compile the index.

My department chair, Kimberly Moore-Jumonville, has been fiercely supportive of my research, even when that's made more work for her. She embodies the virtues of academic leadership, and I could not imagine working under a better chair. I'm grateful for a course release Spring Arbor University granted to provide time for research and for a three-month Writer's Retreat hosted by the Issachar Fund. White Library, and the interlibrary loan skills of Kami Moyer, gave me access to any books I needed.

A substantial portion of chapter 5 first appeared in *Christianity and Literature* as "The Ecology of Memory: Augustine, Eliot, and the Form of Wendell Berry's Fiction." *Southern Literary Journal* published "A Form for Living in the Midst of Loss: Faithful Marriage in the Revisions of Wendell Berry's *A Place on Earth*," from which a portion of chapter 6 came.

My wife, Melissa, and daughter, Hannah, joined me in Grand Rapids for a summer of writing and have put up with my Wendell Berry obsession for many years. My gratitude for them is beyond words.

Notes

Preface

Epigraph drawn from Wendell Berry, "Notes: Unspecializing Poetry," in *Standing by Words: Essays* (1983; repr., Washington, D.C.: Shoemaker & Hoard, 2005), 89.

1. W. H. Auden, *Collected Poems* (1976; repr., New York: Vintage, 1991), 248.

2. Vandana Shiva, *The Vandana Shiva Reader* (Lexington: University Press of Kentucky, 2014), 273.

3. Marshall McLuhan, *Understanding Media: The Extensions of Man [1964]: Critical Edition*, ed. W. Terrence Gordon (Corte Madera, Calif.: Gingko Press, 2003), 25.

4. In fact, Berry repeatedly cautions young people who are inspired by his writings *not* to go into farming, given the economic difficulties of getting started. See Wendell Berry, "The Making of a Marginal Farm," in *Recollected Essays: 1965–1980* (San Francisco: North Point Press, 1981), 338; Berry, "The Whole Horse," in *Citizenship Papers* (Washington, D.C.: Shoemaker & Hoard, 2003), 121; Sarah Leonard, "Nature as an Ally: An Interview with Wendell Berry," *Dissent,* Spring 2012, www.dissentmagazine.org /article/nature-as-an-ally-an-interview-with-wendell-berry.

5. For a typical assessment, see Andrew J. Angyal, *Wendell Berry* (New York: Twayne Publishers, 1995), 99, 104. Ethan Mannon rightly challenges this way of understanding Berry's work in different genres; see Mannon, "Leisure and Technology in Port William: Wendell Berry's Revelatory Fiction," *Mississippi Quarterly* 67, no. 2 (2014): 171–72. Jack Baker and I discuss the reception of Berry's different genres in our introduction to Jack R. Baker and Jeffrey Bilbro, eds., *Telling the Stories Right: Wendell Berry's Imagination of Port William* (Eugene, Ore.: Front Porch Republic Books, 2018), xiii–xviii.

6. Mannon makes a similar analogy between Berry's generic diversity and the diversity of a healthy ecosystem: "In much the same way that Berry advocates a diversified agricultural system on a single farm, he seems to value a varied writing practice. By applying himself to poetry, fiction, and nonfiction, Berry asks critics to take seriously the generic boundaries he erects between his works: though particular themes might appear in multiple genres, one should not read any one genre as representative of the whole or suggest that he is at the same task regardless of genre." Mannon, "Leisure and Technology in Port William," 189.

7. Berry, *This Day: Collected and New Sabbath Poems* (Berkeley, Calif.: Counterpoint, 2013), 154. Copyright 2013; reprinted by permission of Counterpoint.

8. Benjamin Franklin, *The Autobiography of Benjamin Franklin* (Boston: Houghton, Mifflin, 1886), 101–14.

9. Jared Diamond, "What's Your Consumption Factor?" *New York Times,* January 2, 2008, www.nytimes.com/2008/01/02/opinion/02diamond.html. See also Roddy Scheer and Doug Moss, "Use It and Lose It: The Outsize Effect of U.S. Consumption on the Environment," *Scientific American,* September 14, 2012, www.scientificamerican.com/article /american-consumption-habits/.

10. David R. Montgomery, *Dirt: The Erosion of Civilizations* (Berkeley: University of California Press, 2007); Gail A. Eisnitz, *Slaughterhouse: The Shocking Story of Greed, Neglect, and Inhumane Treatment inside the U.S. Meat Industry,* 2nd ed. (Amherst, N.Y.: Prometheus Books, 2006); Michael Pollan, *The Omnivore's Dilemma: A Natural History of Four Meals* (New York: Penguin, 2006).

11. Robert D. Putnam, *Bowling Alone: The Collapse and Revival of American Community* (New York: Simon & Schuster, 2000); J. D. Vance, *Hillbilly Elegy: A Memoir of a Family and Culture in Crisis* (New York: Harper, 2016); Matthew Desmond, *Evicted: Poverty and Profit in the American City* (New York: Crown, 2016). Berry's essay on race perceptively explores these problems as well: *The Hidden Wound* (1970; repr., Berkeley, Calif.: Counterpoint, 2010).

12. Marshall McLuhan analyzes technologies as extensions in *Understanding Media.* Kentaro Toyama considers technology as an amplifier of human intentions and desires in Toyama, *Geek Heresy: Rescuing Social Change from the Cult of Technology* (New York: Public Affairs, 2015), which offers a persuasive account of how technological solutions on their own are unable to solve complex problems.

13. Berry is not alone in this view. As the British environmental author Robert Macfarlane writes, "I remain drawn to the idea that, as Wendell Berry put it, environmentally we require not 'the piecemeal technological solutions that our society now offers, but . . . a change of cultural (and economic) values that will encourage in the whole population the necessary respect, restraint, and care.' In my experience, Berry—a farmer and a writer—speaks only the crash-tested truth, and I suspect he has got it right again in this case." Macfarlane, "Rereading: Robert Macfarlane on The Monkey Wrench Gang," *Guardian,* September 25, 2009, www.theguardian.com/books/2009/sep/26/robert -macfarlane-monkey-wrench-gang.

14. White House, Office of the Press Secretary, "Remarks by the President on Opportunity for All and Skills for America's Workers," January 30, 2014, www.whitehouse.gov /the-press-office/2014/01/30/remarks-president-opportunity-all-and-skills-americas -workers; and "President Obama to Award 2010 National Medal of Arts and National Humanities Medal," March 1, 2011, https://obamawhitehouse.archives.gov/the-press -office/2011/03/01/president-obama-award-2010-national-medal-arts-and-national -humanities-m.

15. Berry, "In Defense of Literacy," in *A Continuous Harmony: Essays Cultural and Agricultural* (New York: Harcourt Brace Jovanovich, 1972), 169–73.

16. Berry, "The Responsibility of the Poet," in *What Are People For? Essays* (San Francisco: North Point Press, 1990), 89.

17. William Major's excellent book translates many of the terms favored by New Agrarians, like Berry, into the parlance of academic discourse; Major, *Grounded Vision: New Agrarianism and the Academy* (Tuscaloosa: University of Alabama Press, 2011).

18. As will become clear, I disagree with critics like Kimberly Smith who think that despite Berry's reliance on religious language, the "highest ideal achievable" for Berry is "common grace—a secular grace—that keeps the world and preserves us in it." See Smith, *Wendell Berry and the Agrarian Tradition: A Common Grace* (Lawrence: University Press of Kansas, 2003), 176. To be fair, however, Berry's articulation of his Christian faith has changed over the course of his writing, so readers who rely on his earlier work find fewer explicitly Christian terms. For more on Berry's relationship with Christianity, see Smith, *Wendell Berry and the Agrarian Tradition*, 171–75; Phillip Donnelly, "Biblical Convocation in Wendell Berry's *Remembering*," *Christianity and Literature* 56, no. 2 (2007): 275–96; Fritz Oehlschlaeger, *The Achievement of Wendell Berry: The Hard History of Love* (Lexington: University Press of Kentucky, 2011), 77–116; Joel James Shuman and L. Roger Owens, eds., *Wendell Berry and Religion: Heaven's Earthly Life* (Lexington: University Press of Kentucky, 2009); J. Matthew Bonzo and Michael R. Stevens, *Wendell Berry and the Cultivation of Life: A Reader's Guide* (Grand Rapids: Brazos Press, 2008); Ragan Sutterfield, *Wendell Berry and the Given Life* (Cincinnati: Franciscan Media, 2017).

19. Wendell Berry and Gary Snyder, *Distant Neighbors: The Selected Letters of Wendell Berry & Gary Snyder*, ed. Chad Wriglesworth (Berkeley, Calif.: Counterpoint, 2014), 56–57.

20. Berry, for instance, criticizes the introduction of *Gaia* as a replacement for *Nature*. Although it trades on the religious import of a Greek goddess, "no modern humans, let alone modern scientists, have even pretended to believe" in her. Such disingenuous attempts to bridge science and religion sidestep the real work of bringing these conversations together. Berry, *A Small Porch: Sabbath Poems 2014 and 2015, Together with "The Presence of Nature in the Natural World: A Long Conversation"* (Berkeley, Calif.: Counterpoint, 2016), 90.

21. Berry, "The Conservation of Nature and the Preservation of Humanity," in *Another Turn of the Crank: Essays* (Washington, D.C.: Counterpoint, 1995), 73.

22. Taylor doesn't use the term *postsecular*, but his work has been influential in this discussion. See Charles Taylor, *A Secular Age* (Cambridge: Belknap Press of Harvard University Press, 2007). See also Peter L. Berger, ed., *The Desecularization of the World: Resurgent Religion and World Politics* (Grand Rapids: Eerdmans, 1999); Philip Gorski et al., eds., *The Post-Secular in Question: Religion in Contemporary Society* (New York: New York University Press, 2012).

23. For an overview of religious approaches to the environment, see Roger S. Gottlieb, ed., *The Oxford Handbook of Religion and Ecology* (Oxford: Oxford University Press, 2006). I argue for the importance of a religious ecological ethic, particularly in an American context, in Jeffrey Bilbro, *Loving God's Wildness: The Christian Roots of Ecological Ethics in American Literature* (Tuscaloosa: University of Alabama Press, 2015). For a creative approach to how faith communities might help us reimagine sustainable living, see Michael S. Northcott, *Place, Ecology and the Sacred: The Moral Geography of Sustainable Communities* (London: Bloomsbury Academic, 2015).

24. For one essay in which Berry makes this case at length, see the title essay in Berry, *It All Turns on Affection: The Jefferson Lecture and Other Essays* (Berkeley, Calif.: Counterpoint, 2012), 9–39. See also Shiva, *The Vandana Shiva Reader*, 7.

25. Berry, "Conservation of Nature," 74–76. See also Berry, *A Small Porch*, 106, and Berry, foreword to Jack R. Baker and Jeffrey Bilbro, *Wendell Berry and Higher Education: Cultivating Virtues of Place* (Lexington: University Press of Kentucky, 2017), xi–xiii.

26. Though Berry's writings have always been marked by his theology, his earlier economic essays tend to focus on the difference between how an agricultural, contemporary-sunlight economy uses energy and how an industrial, fossil-fuel economy uses energy; see Berry, "The Use of Energy," in *The Unsettling of America: Culture & Agriculture*, 3rd ed. (San Francisco: Sierra Club Books, 1996), chap. 6, and "Energy and Agriculture," in *The Gift of Good Land: Further Essays, Cultural and Agricultural* (1981; repr., Berkeley, Calif.: Counterpoint, 2009), 125–33. "Two Economies," written in 1983, begins with Berry recounting a conversation with Wes Jackson in which Wes said, "An energy economy [is not] comprehensive enough." When Berry asked what would be comprehensive enough, Wes replied, "The Kingdom of God." Berry, "Two Economies," in *Home Economics: Fourteen Essays* (San Francisco: North Point Press, 1987), 54. In the decades since, Berry has increasingly turned to religious language to describe sustainable economies.

Introduction

1. Berry, "Solving for Pattern," in *The Gift of Good Land: Further Essays Cultural and Agricultural* (Berkeley, Calif.: Counterpoint, 2009), 136.

2. As John Ehrenfeld and Andrew Hoffman argue, "'Hybrid cars, LED light bulbs, wind farms, and green buildings . . . are all just the trappings that convince us that we are doing something when in fact we are fooling ourselves, and making things worse.'" John Ehrenfeld and Andrew Hoffman, *Flourishing: A Frank Conversation about Sustainability* (Stanford: Stanford University Press, 2013).

3. Berry, "Solving for Pattern," 137.

4. Wendell Berry, *New Collected Poems* (Berkeley, Calif.: Counterpoint, 2012), 173. Copyright 2012; reprinted by permission of Counterpoint.

5. The Canadian philosopher George Grant defines the "technological society" in similar terms: "This is a society in which people think of the world around them as mere indifferent stuff which they are absolutely free to control any way they want through technology. I don't think of the technological society as something outside us, you know, like just a bunch of machines. It is a whole way of looking at the world, the basic way Western men experience their own existence in the world. Out of it come large organizations, bureaucracy, machines, and the belief that all problems can be solved scientifically, in an immediate quantifiable way. The technological society is one in which men are bent on dominating and controlling human and non-human nature." George Grant, *Collected Works of George Grant,* vol. 3, *1960–1969,* ed. Arthur Davis and Henry Roper Roper (Toronto: University of Toronto Press, 2005), 595.

6. In his 2007 commencement address at Bellarmine University, Berry told the graduates that they "cannot live in a career." Berry, "Bellarmine Commencement Address," 2007, http://christianstudycenter.org/wp-content/uploads/2009/10/WendellBerry -BellarmineCommencement.pdf. For an extended discussion of Berry and education, see Baker and Bilbro, *Wendell Berry and Higher Education.*

7. Nicholas Carr expands on the connections between an industrial economy and the Internet, arguing, "In Google's view, information is a kind of commodity, a utilitarian resource that can, and should, be mined and processed with industrial efficiency." Nicholas Carr, *The Shallows: What the Internet Is Doing to Our Brains* (New York: W. W. Norton, 2011), 152.

8. David A. Graham, "'Alternative Facts': The Needless Lies of the Trump Administration," *Atlantic*, January 22, 2017, https://www.theatlantic.com/politics/archive/2017/01/the-pointless-needless-lies-of-the-trump-administration/514061/.

9. Berry, "Local Knowledge in the Age of Information," in *The Way of Ignorance: And Other Essays* (Berkeley, Calif.: Counterpoint, 2005), 121.

10. Patrick J. Deneen, "Wendell Berry and the Alternative Tradition in American Political Thought," in *Wendell Berry: Life and Work,* ed. Jason Peters (Lexington: University Press of Kentucky, 2010), 301.

11. Berry, *The Unsettling of America,* 8–10. See also Vandana Shiva, *Staying Alive: Women, Ecology, and Development* (1999; repr., Berkeley, Calif.: North Atlantic Books, 2016), xvi.

12. Wendell Berry, "God, Science, and Imagination," in *Imagination in Place: Essays* (Berkeley: Counterpoint, 2010), 188–89; Wendell Berry, "Foreword," in Greg Abernathy et al., *Kentucky's Natural Heritage: An Illustrated Guide to Biodiversity* (Lexington: University Press of Kentucky, 2010), xi–xii.

13. Wendell Berry, "The Total Economy," in *Citizenship Papers: Essays* (Washington, D.C.: Shoemaker & Hoard, 2004), 63.

14. Berry, *Unsettling of America,* 82. Berry's argument here parallels that of Ivan Illich, *Energy and Equity* (New York: Harper & Row, 1974).

15. Scholars who articulate these links include Willie James Jennings, *The Christian Imagination: Theology and the Origins of Race* (New Haven: Yale University Press, 2010), and Shiva, *Staying Alive.*

16. See, for instance, Patrick Deneen's description, and critique, of liberalism in *Why Liberalism Failed* (New Haven: Yale University Press, 2018). See also the late thought of Christopher Lasch, who, "over against either the left or right species of liberal individualism, . . . proposed a civic ideal rooted in long-term membership in particular communities rather than a world of 'individual rights, contractual relations, and the primacy of justice.'" Eric Miller, *Hope in a Scattering Time: A Life of Christopher Lasch* (Grand Rapids: Eerdmans, 2010), 308. For the expansion of rights to nature, see Roderick Frazier Nash, *The Rights of Nature: A History of Environmental Ethics* (Madison: University of Wisconsin Press, 1989). See also the work of the Community Environmental Legal Defense Fund, "Rights of Nature," 2016, http://celdf.org/rights/rights-of-nature/.

17. For an account of how rights language has weakened our understanding of the common good, see Mary Ann Glendon, *Rights Talk: The Impoverishment of Political Discourse* (1991; repr., New York: Free Press, 1993). Nicholas Wolterstorff makes a compelling argument in defense of inherent natural rights. He admits that in a society of "possessive individualists . . . each will claim his own rights while neglecting or refusing to honor the rights of others. In no way does this alter the structure of rights themselves"; it merely distorts our understanding and practice of these rights. In advocating for a view of justice predicated on rights, though, Wolterstorff defends a rather thin understanding of justice. He defines "a social order as just in so far as its members enjoy the goods to which they have rights." Nicholas Wolterstorff, *Justice: Rights and Wrongs* (Princeton: Princeton University Press, 2008), 7, 10. This may be true, but such an account of justice has no way of articulating the need for selfless giving *beyond* what is owed to another—gifts are intrinsically gratuitous and not obligatory; in this regard, see William Cavanaugh's reading of *Caritas in Veritate* in *Field Hospital: The Church's Engagement with a Wounded World* (Grand Rapids: Eerdmans, 2016), 122–24. Such giving, as I will argue, is a constitutive

feature of Berry's sustainable, resurrecting forms. For instance, Christians do not think that humans had a right to Christ's incarnation, passion, and resurrection; this redemption is pure gift, and human self-giving imitates and participates in this gift.

18. As Robert Nisbet argues, "The real conflict in modern political history has not been, as is so often stated, between State and individual, but between State and social group." As the modern state gained power, it hollowed out other intermediary authorities—"guild, village community, class, and religious body"—liberating individuals from these allegiances and constituting them ever more fully as individual subjects of the state. Robert Nisbet, *The Quest for Community: A Study in the Ethics of Order and Freedom* (New York: Oxford University Press, 1953), 109.

19. Charles Taylor traces a related tension, between the ideal and the real, the spiritual and the secular (in Taylor's secular₁ sense), to the various reform movements that arose at the end of the medieval period; see Taylor, *A Secular Age*, 77–81. As James Smith puts it, "Reform unleashes both Puritanism *and* the '60s." James K. A. Smith, *How (Not) to Be Secular: Reading Charles Taylor* (Grand Rapids: Eerdmans, 2014), 37. Puritanism and the 1960s are pretty good stand-ins for Nietzsche's Apollo and Dionysius. For a similar diagnosis, see Christopher Lasch: "It is this coexistence of hyper-rationality [Apollonian] and a widespread revolt against rationality [Dionysian] that justifies the characterization of our twentieth-century way of life as a culture of narcissism. These contradictory sensibilities have a common source. Both take root in the feelings of homelessness and displacement that afflict so many men and women today." Christopher Lasch, *The Culture of Narcissism: American Life in an Age of Diminishing Expectations* (New York: W. W. Norton, 1991), 248.

20. Friedrich Nietzsche, *The Birth of Tragedy* (1872), trans. Douglas Smith (Oxford: Oxford University Press, 2000), 131.

21. David Bentley Hart, *The Beauty of the Infinite: The Aesthetics of Christian Truth* (Grand Rapids: Eerdmans, 2004), 36. Hart's reading of postmodernity's "ontology of violence" draws on John Milbank, *Theology and Social Theory: Beyond Secular Reason*, 2nd ed. (Oxford: Wiley-Blackwell, 2006).

22. Interestingly, John Crowe Ransom also compares an industrial economy to an internal combustion engine in *Land! The Case for an Agrarian Economy*, ed. Jason Peters (Notre Dame, Ind.: University of Notre Dame Press, 2017), 51.

23. Berry, *Unsettling of America*, 21.

24. Ibid., 19. Berry makes a related point in another essay: "Specialization . . . is little more than a euphemism for moral loneliness; morally, the specialist is a man out of control, an erratic particle." Berry, "The Loss of the Future," in *The Long-Legged House* (Washington, D.C.: Shoemaker & Hoard, 2004), 61.

25. Berry, *Unsettling of America*, 82.

26. For more on the lure of the technological sublime, its ethical shortcomings, and Wendell Berry's alternative mode of beauty, see Jeffrey Bilbro, "Sublime Failure: Why We'd Better Start Seeing Our World as Beautiful," *South Atlantic Review* 80, no. 1–2 (2015): 133–58. For a history of America's attraction to big technology, see David E. Nye, *American Technological Sublime* (Cambridge: MIT Press, 1996).

27. Berry, *New Collected Poems*, 173. Copyright 2012; reprinted by permission of Counterpoint.

28. Robert Farrar Capon articulates this distinction between seeing the natural order as based on coercion and seeing it as founded on love: "God, if we believe the Scriptures,

created the world out of delight; and he runs it, not by shoving things around with main force, but by attraction—by desire for Himself as the Highest Good." Robert Farrar Capon, *Food for Thought: Resurrecting the Art of Eating* (New York: Harcourt Brace Jovanovich, 1978), 28. For a fuller treatment of this in a theological key, see Hart, *The Beauty of the Infinite,* esp. 346–94. Given Berry's careful study of Milton, Milton's view of creation as a gift and right reason as peaceful participation in this gift probably shaped Berry's thinking on these matters. See Berry, "The Gift of Good Land," in *The Gift of Good Land: Further Essays, Cultural and Agricultural* (Berkeley, Calif.: Counterpoint, 1981), 267–81; Wendell Berry, "Poetry and Place," in *Standing by Words: Essays* (Washington, D.C.: Shoemaker & Hoard, 2005), 106–213; Phillip J. Donnelly, *Milton's Scriptural Reasoning: Narrative and Protestant Toleration* (Cambridge: Cambridge University Press, 2009).

29. Lynn White Jr., "The Historical Roots of Our Ecologic Crisis," *Science* 155, no. 3767 (1967): 1203–7, doi:10.1126/science.155.3767.1203. For Berry's response to White's thesis, see Berry, "Gift of Good Land."

30. Wendell Berry, "Health Is Membership," in *Another Turn of the Crank: Essays* (Washington, D.C.: Counterpoint, 1995), 89.

31. Berry, *It All Turns on Affection.*

32. Alfred, Lord Tennyson, *In Memoriam A.H.H.* (1850) (London: Bankside Press, 1900), 60.

33. Charles Darwin, *On the Origin of Species by Means of Natural Selection; or, The Preservation of Favoured Races in the Struggle for Life* (1859) (London: John Murray, 1873), 3; Charles Darwin, *The Autobiography of Charles Darwin and Selected Letters* (1887), ed. Francis Darwin (New York: Dover, 1958). See also Norman Wirzba, *The Paradise of God: Renewing Religion in an Ecological Age* (Oxford: Oxford University Press, 2007), 101; Norman Wirzba, "On Learning to See a Fallen and Flourishing Creation: Alternate Ways of Looking at the World," in *Evolution and the Fall,* ed. William T. Cavanaugh and James K. A. Smith (Grand Rapids: Eerdmans, 2017), 160–63; Emiliano Salvucci, "Selfishness, Warfare, and Economics; or Integration, Cooperation, and Biology," *Frontiers in Cellular and Infection Microbiology* 2, no. 54 (2012): 1–12, doi:10.3389/fcimb.2012.00054.

34. Peter Godfrey-Smith and Kim Sterelny, "Biological Information" (rev. ed.), in *Stanford Encyclopedia of Philosophy Archive,* ed. Edward N. Zalta, Summer 2016, http://plato.stanford.edu/archives/sum2016/entries/information-biological/.

35. Raymond John Pierotti, *Indigenous Knowledge, Ecology, and Evolutionary Biology* (New York: Routledge, 2011); Bert Hölldobler and Edward O. Wilson, *The Ants* (Cambridge: Harvard University Press, 1990); Lee Alan Dugatkin, *Cooperation among Animals: An Evolutionary Perspective* (Oxford: Oxford University Press, 1997). Robert W. Sussman, Paul A. Garber, and Jim M. Cheverud, "Importance of Cooperation and Affiliation in the Evolution of Primate Sociality," *American Journal of Physical Anthropology* 128, no. 1 (2005): 84–97; Peter Wohlleben, *The Hidden Life of Trees: What They Feel, How They Communicate—Discoveries from a Secret World* (Vancouver: Greystone, 2016).

36. By defining sustainability as cycles of renewal, Berry and other agrarians offer a way of understanding the inherent tension that *sustainability* implies between continuity or stability on the one hand, and change and development on the other. For more on the debates about the term *sustainability* in literary contexts, see John P. O'Grady, "How Sustainable Is the Idea of Sustainability?" *Interdisciplinary Studies in Literature and Environment* 10, no. 1 (2003): 1–10; Hubert Zapf, *Literature as Cultural Ecology: Sustainable Texts* (London: Bloomsbury, 2016), 15–26.

37. Sir Albert Howard and Yeshwant D. Wad, *The Waste Products of Agriculture: Their Utilization as Humus* (Oxford: Oxford University Press, 1931).

38. Franklin Hiram King, *Farmers of Forty Centuries; or, Permanent Agriculture in China, Korea and Japan* (Madison, Wisc.: Mrs. F. H. King, 1911).

39. Shiva, *The Vandana Shiva Reader,* 108.

40. Berry, "Foreword," in Shiva, *The Vandana Shiva Reader,* vii–viii.

41. Kevin Lowe provides a clear outline of the differences between traditional and industrial agriculture, and he traces how the industrial model came to dominate in twentieth-century America. Kevin Lowe, *Baptized with the Soil: Christian Agrarians and the Crusade for Rural America* (Oxford: Oxford University Press, 2015).

42. For one treatment of this colonial logic, see Jennings, *The Christian Imagination,* 38–59.

43. Wendell Berry, "The Long-Legged House," in *The Long-Legged House,* 108–69; Berry, "A Native Hill," in *The Long-Legged House,* 170–213; Berry, *The Hidden Wound.*

44. Berry, "It All Turns on Affection," 23.

45. Wendell Berry quotes this passage—originally from Howard's *An Agricultural Testament*—in "New Introduction," in Albert Howard, *The Soil and Health: A Study of Organic Agriculture* (Lexington: University Press of Kentucky, 2006), xv.

46. Berry, *Unsettling of America,* 82.

47. Ibid., 81–82.

48. Ibid., 85–86.

49. "Cryonics Institute," www.cryonics.org/; Jeff Bercovici, "Peter Thiel Is Very, Very Interested in Young People's Blood," *Inc.,* August 1, 2016, www.inc.com/jeff-bercovici /peter-thiel-young-blood.html.

50. The movie *In Time* takes this conception of time one step further, imagining it as a commodity individuals can sell. Andrew Niccol, writer and director, *In Time* (2011).

51. Theorists like Timothy Morton would cringe at Berry's use of *health,* thinking it overly hierarchical and oppressive. Timothy Morton, *The Ecological Thought* (Cambridge: Harvard University Press, 2010). I've critiqued Morton's view at length elsewhere—see Bilbro, "Sublime Failure"—and the indigenous scholar Raymond Pierotti offers a compelling defense of such language, arguing, "Indigenous perspectives are most effective in observing and describing wholes, because they operate at the level of human perception and concentrate on functional relationships and co-evolutionary processes rather than structure." Pierotti, *Indigenous Knowledge, Ecology, and Evolutionary Biology,* 73

52. Berry, *Unsettling of America,* 103.

53. Berry, "New Introduction," xxii; Berry, "Discipline and Hope," in *A Continuous Harmony: Essays Cultural and Agricultural* (New York: Harcourt Brace Jovanovich, 1972), 164.

54. For a related contrast, see Vandana Shiva's essay "Soil, Not Oil," in *The Vandana Shiva Reader,* 239–76.

55. Berry, "Poetry and Marriage," in *Standing by Words: Essays* (Washington, D.C.: Shoemaker & Hoard, 2005), 97. Berry also contemplates the mysteries of soil in "A Native Hill," 204, calling it "Christ-like" in its form. For other places where Berry discusses topsoil, see Berry, "Letter to Wes Jackson," and "The Work of Local Culture," in *What Are People For? Essays* (San Francisco: North Point Press, 1990), 3–5; 153–69.

56. Berry, "Two Economies," 54–56.

57. Ibid., 62–63.

58. Ibid., 65.

59. Ellen Davis describes the Israelite's manna economy in similar terms in *Scripture, Culture, and Agriculture: An Agrarian Reading of the Bible* (New York: Cambridge University Press, 2008), 69–75.

60. Berry, "Two Economies," 65.

61. Ibid., 63.

62. Ibid., 62.

63. Ibid., 67.

64. Ibid., 62.

65. Berry, *This Day*, 321.

66. For background on Berry's connection to the Orthodox tradition, see Andrew J. Harvey, "Curriculum and Culture according to Wendell Berry," in *Faith, Freedom, and Higher Education: Historical Analysis and Contemporary Reflections*, ed. P. C. Kemeny (Eugene, Ore.: Wipf and Stock, 2013), 149–64.

67. Berry, "Manifesto: The Mad Farmer Liberation Front," in *New Collected Poems*, 173–74. Copyright 2012; reprinted by permission of Counterpoint

68. John Lang, writing about Berry's early poetry, states that "Berry returns almost obsessively" to the question of death's meaning, and he traces the sacramental role that nature plays in mediating resurrection to humans. John Lang, "'Close Mystery': Wendell Berry's Poetry of Incarnation," *Renascence* 35, no. 4 (1983): 258–68.

69. Wendell Berry, "The Brothers," *Carolina Quarterly* 8, no. 3 (1956): 9–10. Fritz Oeschlaeger provides an extended discussion regarding the centrality of death to *Nathan Coulter* in *Achievement of Wendell Berry*, 157–66.

70. Berry and Snyder, *Distant Neighbors*, 123.

71. Berry, "Health Is Membership," 105. Phillip Donnelly provides a helpful reading of this passage in the context of Berry's understanding of death. Donnelly, "Biblical Convocation in Wendell Berry's *Remembering*," 277.

72. Berry, "The Morning's News," in *New Collected Poems*, 124.

73. Norman Wirzba considers this question at greater length and with appropriate nuance in *Food and Faith: A Theology of Eating* (Cambridge: Cambridge University Press, 2011), 133–35.

74. See, for example, the calls by some environmentalists for governments to reduce birthrates since each human "costs" a fixed quantity of natural resources. Sarah Conly, *One Child: Do We Have a Right to More?* (New York: Oxford University Press, 2015).

75. Berry expands on this distinction in his poem "For the Hog Killing," in *New Collected Poems*, 230, and his essay "The Pleasures of Eating," in *What Are People For?* 151–52.

76. John 12:24; Berry, *Unsettling of America*, 193.

77. Berry, "The Whole Horse," 118; Berry, "Foreword," in *The Holy Earth* (1915), by Liberty Hyde Bailey, ed. John Linstrom (Berkeley, Calif.: Counterpoint, 2015), x.

78. Berry explores this connection between death and renewal in the context of agrarian and religious and sexual cycles in "Discipline and Hope," 159–61.

79. Hans Urs von Balthasar, *Love Alone Is Credible*, trans. D. C. Schindler (San Francisco: Ignatius Press, 2005), 139. See also Paul Griffiths's claim that "the witness of the tradition is unanimous, or almost so, that wounds are healed by transfiguration rather than removal." Griffiths, *Decreation: The Last Things of All Creatures* (Waco: Baylor University Press, 2014), 288. This insight lies behind Adam's testimony at the end of *Paradise*

Lost that "to the faithful, death [is] the gate of life"; John Milton, *Paradise Lost,* in *The Riverside Milton,* ed. Roy Flannagan (Boston: Houghton Mifflin, 1998), 12.571.

80. Hans Urs von Balthasar, *Epilogue,* trans. Edward T. Oakes (San Francisco: Ignatius Press, 2004), esp. 109–123.

81. Berry, "Gift of Good Land," 281.

82. Wirzba, *Food and Faith,* 121.

83. Berry, "Prayer after Eating," in *New Collected Poems,* 169.

84. For more on the way that sacramental eating runs counter to an industrial economy, see William T. Cavanaugh, *Being Consumed: Economics and Christian Desire* (Grand Rapids: Eerdmans, 2008). This way of thinking is not exclusive to Christians; Raymond Pierotti discerns a similar view of eating in indigenous cultures: "By eating parts of other organisms, you demonstrate empirically that they are made of the same material of which you are made. . . . Christianity employs a similar principle in its communion rituals as a way of establishing links between their 'savior' and contemporary humans." Pierotti, *Indigenous Knowledge, Ecology, and Evolutionary Biology,* 62. See also Gary Snyder, *The Gary Snyder Reader: Prose, Poetry, and Translations* (1999; repr., Washington, D.C.: Counterpoint, 2012), 237–38.

85. In a fine essay on marriage and Berry's "sacramental imagination," P. Travis Kroeker describes Berry's view of love and marriage: "Love is . . . an act of giving ourselves away unconditionally, as God does." P. Travis Kroeker, "Sexuality and the Sacramental Imagination: It All Turns on Affection," in *Wendell Berry: Life and Work,* ed. Jason Peters (Lexington: University Press of Kentucky, 2007), 120–21. See also Anne Husted Burleigh, "Marriage in the Membership," in *The Humane Vision of Wendell Berry,* ed. Mark Mitchell and Nathan Schlueter (Wilmington, Del.: ISI Books, 2011), 7–18; Bonzo and Stevens, *Wendell Berry and the Cultivation of Life,* 106–15; Daniel Cornell, " 'The Country of Marriage': Wendell Berry's Personal Political Vision," *Southern Literary Journal* 16, no. 1 (1983): 59–70; Roger Lundin, "Wendell Berry and the Poetics of Marriage and Embodiment," *Christianity and Literature* 56, no. 2 (2007): 333–42.

86. Berry writes about marriage often. For two paradigmatic essays, see Berry, "Sex, Economy, Freedom, and Community," in *Sex, Economy, Freedom and Community: Eight Essays* (New York: Pantheon Books, 1993), 117–73; Berry, "Poetry and Marriage." One of the central features of marriage in these essays is its fertility, so many readers were confused when Berry published "Caught in the Middle," in *Our Only World: Ten Essays* (Berkeley, Calif.: Counterpoint, 2015), 73–96, an essay in which he argues homosexual couples should be allowed to marry. The best articulation of this confusion may be by Scott Moore, in remarks he gave when Berry presented an early version of his essay, in *Wendell Berry Speaks at Georgetown College,* 2013, https://www.youtube.com/watch?v=MnfZOLEb7p4. My best understanding of this apparent shift is that Berry's support for homosexual marriage stems from his reading of our political situation in which marriage rights have become just another sphere for conflict between individuals. I address this issue at greater length in a review of *Our Only World:* Jeffrey Bilbro, "Wendell Berry Opts Out of the 'Culture of Violence,'" *Front Porch Republic,* April 6, 2015, www.frontporchrepublic .com/2015/04/wendell-berry-opts-out-of-the-culture-of-violence/. For a more theological description of the ways that "marriage is a kind of holy dying," see Wesley Hill, "Jigs for Marriage and Celibacy," *Comment,* Winter 2016, www.cardus.ca/comment/article/4987 /jigs-for-marriage-and-celibacy/.

87. Berry, "Sex, Economy, Freedom, and Community," 138.

88. Ibid.

89. I'm thinking here especially of Burley Coulter and Jayber Crow. See, for instance, the description of Jayber's "ideal of marriage" in Berry, *A Place on Earth: A Novel* (1967; repr., Washington, D.C.: Counterpoint, 2001), 72.

90. Berry, "Sex, Economy, Freedom, and Community," 139.

91. Wirzba, *Food and Faith,* 112.

92. Ibid., 129. Oehlschlaeger makes a similar claim: "For Berry, our most important freedom lies not in what we do or make, but in what we are given, for what we most need to be free of is ourselves. Learning this is the lifelong work of love, the everyday practice of resurrection in making the self a gift." Oehlschlaeger, *Achievement of Wendell Berry,* 116.

93. The apparent suppression of the individual perspective is part of why Richard Pevear criticizes what he calls Berry's "Stoic deification of Nature." Richard Pevear, "On the Prose of Wendell Berry," *Hudson Review* 35, no. 2 (1982): 344–45. As Phillip Donnelly persuasively argues, however, Berry's work will not sustain Pevear's reading. Donnelly, "Biblical Convocation in Wendell Berry's *Remembering,*" 276–79. One possible way of understanding Berry's view of individual redemption is through Irenaeus's doctrine of recapitulation: because Christ recapitulates the human race in himself, all participate in his death and resurrection. As Irenaeus writes in *Against Heresies,* Christ is "in His own person the first-fruits of the resurrection of man; that, as the Head rose from the dead, so also the remaining part of the body—[namely, the body] of everyman who is found in life . . . may arise." Alexander Roberts et al., eds., *Ante-Nicene Fathers: The Writings of the Fathers Down to A.D. 325* (1867–73) (Peabody, Mass.: Hendrickson Publishers, 2004), 3.19.3; see also 3.18 and 5.9. For further reflection on the implications this joining to the body of Christ has for overcoming displacement and racism, see Jennings, *The Christian Imagination,* 248–49.

94. Berry, *A Small Porch,* 107.

95. Edmund Spenser, *The Works of Edmund Spenser,* ed. R. Morris (London: Macmillan, 1899), 8:2. For more on Berry's engagement with the conclusion of *The Faerie Queene,* see Lucas Nossaman, "The Wisdom of 'The Farm': Sabbath Theology and Wendell Berry's Pastoralism," *Renascence,* forthcoming.

96. Berry, "Manifesto: The Mad Farmer Liberation Front," 174. Copyright 2012; reprinted by permission of Counterpoint.

97. Berry, "Renewing Husbandry," in *The Way of Ignorance: And Other Essays* (Berkeley, Calif.: Counterpoint, 2005), 93. Alasdair MacIntyre, in his seminal work *After Virtue,* makes a parallel argument when he claims, "The creation and sustaining of human communities" was understood by the "ancient and medieval worlds" to itself "be a practice," a practice with its own internal goods and the virtues to pursue these goods. Alasdair MacIntyre, *After Virtue: A Study in Moral Theory,* 2nd ed. (Notre Dame, Ind.: University of Notre Dame Press, 1984), 187–88. In later works, MacIntyre further develops the connections between virtues and local communities, even referring to Berry's work. See in particular his essay "Politics, Philosophy, and the Common Good" in *The MacIntyre Reader,* ed. Kelvin Knight (Notre Dame, Ind.: University of Notre Dame Press, 1998).

98. Berry, "Notes: Unspecializing Poetry," 89.

99. Berry, "Renewing Husbandry," 104.

100. Berry, "The Responsibility of the Poet," 89.

101. Corby Kummer, "Last Word with Farmer-Author Wendell Berry," October 20, 2015, http://modernfarmer.com/2015/10/last-word-with-farmer-author-wendell-berry/.

Berry's comments in this interview echo earlier essays in which he has reflected further on the connections between art and farming. See Berry, *Unsettling of America*, 87; Berry, "Renewing Husbandry," 102–3. See also a joint interview with Wes Jackson and Wendell Berry in which Jackson expands on this comparison: Joshua Yates, "A Conversation with Wendell Berry and Wes Jackson," *Hedgehog Review* 14, no. 2 (2012), www.iasc-culture .org/THR/THR_article_2012_Summer_Interview_Berry_Jackson.php.

102. Berry, "Renewing Husbandry," 102.

103. Berry, *Unsettling of America*, 85.

104. C. S. Lewis, *The Abolition of Man; or, Reflections on Education with Special Reference to the Teaching of English in the Upper Forms of Schools* (1943; repr., San Francisco: Harper, 2001), 83.

105. Berry, *Unsettling of America*, 94.

106. James K. A. Smith, *Imagining the Kingdom: How Worship Works* (Grand Rapids: Baker Books, 2013), 143.

107. See also Matthew Crawford's analysis of the moral affects of technologies that buffer us from the material world, *The World beyond Your Head: On Becoming an Individual in an Age of Distraction* (New York: Farrar, Straus and Giroux, 2015).

108. For a rich and tragic analysis of how ecological consequences manifest themselves, see Rob Nixon, *Slow Violence and the Environmentalism of the Poor* (Cambridge: Harvard University Press, 2011).

109. Wendell Berry, "Agriculture from the Roots Up," in *The Way of Ignorance: And Other Essays* (Berkeley, Calif.: Counterpoint, 2005), 106–9.

110. Berry, *Unsettling of America*, 121.

111. Berry, "It All Turns on Affection," 23.

112. Berry, "Two Economies," 73. See also Berry, *Unsettling of America*, 91.

113. For further analysis of the links between Berry and MacIntyre, see Smith, *Wendell Berry and the Agrarian Tradition*, 161; Oehlschlaeger, *Achievement of Wendell Berry*, 12–14; Baker and Bilbro, *Wendell Berry and Higher Education*, 91–94.

114. Berry, "Work of Local Culture," 168–69.

115. Berry, "Standing by Words," in *Standing by Words: Essays* (1983; repr., Washington, D.C.: Shoemaker & Hoard, 2005), 29. See also Berry, "The Specialization of Poetry," ibid., 3–23.

116. Wendell Berry, *Life Is a Miracle: An Essay against Modern Superstition* (Washington, D.C.: Counterpoint, 2000), 77–89.

117. Berry, "Sex, Economy, Freedom, and Community," 153–62.

118. C. S. Lewis, *An Experiment in Criticism* (Cambridge: Cambridge University Press, 1961), 19.

119. Rich Cohen, "They Taught America How to Watch Football," *Atlantic*, October 2012, www.theatlantic.com/magazine/archive/2012/10/they-taught-america-to -watch-football/309083/.

120. In an essay charting this trend, Paul Reitter and Chad Wellmon coin the term *bibliotherapy* to describe how the humanities have been co-opted to individualistic, utilitarian ends. "Better Living through Bibliotherapy," *Hedgehog Review* 18, no. 2 (2016), www.iasc-culture.org/THR/THR_article_2016_Summer_ReitterWellmon.php.

121. Lewis, *An Experiment in Criticism*, 20.

122. Ibid., 104.

123. I'm aware that it's rather ironic to draw on Auden's poem to exemplify Berry's view of literature because Berry harshly critiques this poem, claiming it displays "cuteness," "self-conscious and presumptuous modernity," "wearied and belittling sophistication," and "compulsive disparagement and begging off." Berry, "Poetry and Place," 108. The core problem, for Berry, seems to be the way that Auden separates Yeats's poetry from Yeats himself. Yet I think Berry fundamentally misreads Auden's poem: it is not a unified and presumptuous dismissal of Yeats's life and work, but, rather, the articulation of Auden's own struggle with the usefulness of poetry. As Yeats himself states, "We make out of the quarrel with others, rhetoric, but of the quarrel with ourselves, poetry." W. B. Yeats, *Per Amica Silentia Lunae* (New York: Macmillan, 1918), 29.

124. Berry, "In Defense of Literacy," 172.

125. I first developed this reading of Auden's poem in Jeffrey Bilbro, "A Way of Happening," *Curator*, December 14, 2015, www.curatormagazine.com/jeffrey-bilbro/a-way-of-happening/.

126. W. H. Auden, "In Memory of W. B. Yeats," in *Collected Poems*, 247.

127. Ibid., 248.

128. Ibid.

1. Attention

1. Eric Schmidt and Jared Cohen, *The New Digital Age: Reshaping the Future of People, Nations and Business* (New York: Knopf, 2013). Toyama cites this line, and provides a thorough demonstration of its naïveté, in *Geek Heresy*, 21–22.

2. Berry, *This Day*, 292–93. Copyright 2013; reprinted by permission of Counterpoint.

3. I explored some of these themes—in greatly truncated form—in Jeffrey Bilbro, "Review of *This Day: New and Collected Sabbath Poems*," *Christianity and Literature* 65, no. 4 (2016): 524–28.

4. Berry, "Our Deserted Country," in *Our Only World: Ten Essays* (Berkeley, Calif.: Counterpoint, 2015), 115–18.

5. Cory Doctorow, "Writing in the Age of Distraction," *Locus Magazine*, January 2009, www.locusmag.com/Features/2009/01/cory-doctorow-writing-in-age-of.html, quoted in Alan Jacobs, "Habits of Mind in an Age of Distraction," *Comment*, Summer 2016; Linda Stone, "Continuous Partial Attention," November 29, 2009, https://lindastone.net/qa/continuous-partial-attention/. See also Carr, *The Shallows;* Crawford, *The World beyond Your Head.*

6. Bernard E. Harcourt, *Exposed: Desire and Disobedience in the Digital Age* (Cambridge: Harvard University Press, 2015), 110.

7. Berry, *Sabbaths 2013* (Monterey, Ky.: Larkspur Press, 2015), 29. Copyright 2015; reprinted by permission of Counterpoint.

8. For more on this danger, see Sherry Turkle, *Alone Together: Why We Expect More from Technology and Less from Each Other* (New York: Basic Books, 2011).

9. Bernard Harcourt provides an overview of these practices in *Exposed.*

10. Berry offers a chilling critique of this gaze in his novel *Remembering* when Andy Catlett passes through airport security. The surveillance of the state fosters a universal

suspicion among the passengers as "all turned inward." Berry, *Remembering: A Novel* (Berkeley, Calif.: Counterpoint, 2008), 78.

11. Alan Jacobs, "Attending to Technology: Theses for Disputation," *New Atlantis,* Winter 2016, 16–45.

12. For a study backing up this last example, see John M. Jakicic et al., "Effect of Wearable Technology Combined with a Lifestyle Intervention on Long-Term Weight Loss: The IDEA Randomized Clinical Trial," *JAMA* 316, no. 11 (2016): 1161–71.

13. Nicholas Carr, *The Glass Cage: Automation and Us* (New York: W. W. Norton, 2014), 219.

14. For some recent examples, see Radley Balko, "And Now: The Criminalization of Parenthood," *Washington Post,* July 14, 2014, https://www.washingtonpost.com /news/the-watch/wp/2014/07/14/and-now-the-criminalization-of-parenthood/; Donna St. George, "'Unsubstantiated' Child Neglect Finding for Free-Range Parents," *Washington Post,* March 2, 2015, https://www.washingtonpost.com/local/education/decision-in -free-range-case-does-not-end-debate-about-parenting-and-safety/2015/03/02/5a919454 -c04d-11e4-ad5c-3b8ce89f1b89_story.html.

15. Gracy Olmstead, "Is 'Free-Range Parenting' Bad?" *American Conservative,* March 4, 2015, www.theamericanconservative.com/olmstead/is-free-range-parenting -bad/.

16. Berry, *A Small Porch,* 6. Copyright 2012; reprinted by permission of Counterpoint.

17. Berry, *Sabbaths 2013,* 29. Copyright 2013. Reprinted by permission of Counterpoint.

18. Marion's account is part of his larger project—a theology without Being—but I use him here for the way he articulates a long tradition of how the icon works. For an excellent analysis of how Marion's description of idols and icons might apply to ecological ethics more broadly, see Norman Wirzba, *From Nature to Creation: A Christian Vision for Understanding and Loving Our World* (Grand Rapids: Baker Academic, 2015).

19. Jean-Luc Marion, *God without Being: Hors-Texte,* trans. Thomas A. Carlson (Chicago: University of Chicago Press, 1995), 12.

20. Ibid., 17–18.

21. Ibid., 19; emphasis in original.

22. Jean-Luc Marion, "The Saturated Phenomenon," *Philosophy Today* 40, no. 1 (1996): 120.

23. Andrew Harvey notes Berry's references to the Orthodox theologian Philip Sherrard, and in a personal conversation with Harvey, Berry recalled "the intense time he devoted to understanding Sherrard's arguments through the 1980s and early 1990s." Harvey, "Curriculum and Culture according to Wendell Berry," 155–57.

24. Marion claims that saturated phenomena are common—"The saturated phenomenon must not be understood as a limit case, an exceptional, vaguely irrational—in short, a 'mystical'—case of phenomenality"—and, in fact, that all historical events are saturated. Marion, "The Saturated Phenomenon," 120–21.

25. Berry, "Elegy," in *New Collected Poems,* 275.

26. This distinction parallels Norman Wirzba's contrast between seeing the world as "Nature" and seeing it as "Creation" in *From Nature to Creation.*

27. Berry, *The Unforeseen Wilderness: Kentucky's Red River Gorge,* photos by Ralph Eugene Meatyard, rev. ed. (San Francisco: North Point Press, 1991), 15–16. See also Wallis's analysis of this passage and its broader context in Bryan Wallis, "More Real Than

Real: The Weird Localism of Ralph Eugene Meatyard and Wendell Berry," *Australasian Journal of Ecocriticism and Cultural Ecology (AJE)* 2 (2012/2013): 87.

28. The term comes from Marshall Van Alstyne and Erik Brynjolfsson, "Global Village or Cyber-Balkans? Modeling and Measuring the Integration of Electronic Communities," *Management Science* 51, no. 6 (2005): 851–68. Toyama cites this study and develops its implications in *Geek Heresy*, 46–47. See also Cass R. Sunstein, *#Republic: Divided Democracy in the Age of Social Media* (Princeton: Princeton University Press, 2017).

29. Other critics have described the kind of mutual attention that Berry's poetry models. Leonard Scigaj, for instance, draws on Maurice Merleau-Ponty to trace how Berry's poems emphasize that "the eye cannot help but be implicated in what it sees, be of it and in it." Leonard M. Scigaj, *Sustainable Poetry: Four American Ecopoets* (Lexington: University Press of Kentucky, 1999), 138.

30. Berry, *Life Is a Miracle*, 142.

31. Jean-Luc Marion, *The Idol and Distance: Five Studies*, trans. Thomas A. Carlson (New York: Fordham University Press, 2001), 158.

32. Berry, *A Small Porch*, 14, 128–29.

33. Berry, *This Day*, xxi.

34. Ibid., 11.

35. Ibid., 252.

36. Berry, *New Collected Poems*, 151. Copyright 2012; reprinted by permission of Counterpoint.

37. Robert Macfarlane, *Landmarks* (London: Penguin, 2015), 24.

38. Berry, *New Collected Poems*, 236. Copyright 2012; reprinted by permission of Counterpoint.

39. In responding to the bird's call, Berry receives a vocation to sing in praise of his place and its beauties. This form of call-and-response follows Marion's account of the recipient in *Being Given*, an account I will consider more fully in the next chapter. Jean-Luc Marion, *Being Given: Toward a Phenomenology of Givenness* (Stanford: Stanford University Press, 2002), 282–96.

40. G. K. Chesterton, *Orthodoxy* (1908; repr., San Francisco: Ignatius Press, 1995), 65–66. Later Chesterton expands on the way that litanies or inventories testify to the great wonder of the quotidian—and I should acknowledge that I'm indebted to my colleague Robert Moore-Jumonville for bringing this quote to my attention. Chesterton writes that his favorite part of *Robinson Crusoe* "is simply the list of things saved from the wreck. The greatest of poems is an inventory. Every kitchen tool becomes ideal because Crusoe might have dropped it in the sea. It is a good exercise, in empty or ugly hours of the day, to look at anything, the coal-scuttle or the bookcase, and think how happy one could be to have brought it out of the sinking ship on to the solitary island. But it is a better exercise still to remember how all things have had this hair-breadth escape: everything has been saved from a wreck." Ibid., 69.

41. Berry, *This Day*, 232. Copyright 2013; reprinted by permission of Counterpoint.

42. Wallis, "More Real Than Real," 88–89.

43. Wallis's focus on how Berry's attention to the familiar results in surprise and rupture contrasts with Scott Slovic's argument, based largely on Berry's essay "The Long-Legged House," that reads Berry as becoming more and more at home in or comfortable with his place. Scott Slovic, *Seeking Awareness in American Nature Writing: Henry Thoreau, Annie Dillard, Edward Abbey, Wendell Berry, Barry Lopez* (Salt Lake City:

University of Utah Press, 1992), 115–19. So although Slovic contrasts Berry to a writer like Annie Dillard, the reciprocal mode of attention both articulate may be more similar than their differing styles would suggest. And Dillard records the sense of being seen that Berry also expresses in many of his poems: "Then one day, walking along Tinker Creek, thinking of nothing at all, I saw it—the tree with the lights in it. It was the same backyard cedar where the mourning doves roost, only charged and transfigured, each cell buzzing with flame. . . . It was less like seeing than like being for the first time seen, knocked breathless by a powerful glance. . . . I had been my whole life a bell, and never knew it until at that moment I was lifted and struck." Annie Dillard, *Pilgrim at Tinker Creek* (1974; repr., New York: Harper Perennial, 2013), 36.

44. Berry, *A Small Porch,* 10. Copyright 2012; reprinted by permission of Counterpoint.

45. Berry, *This Day,* 369. Copyright 2013; reprinted by permission of Counterpoint.

46. Berry, *New Collected Poems,* 261. Copyright 2012; reprinted by permission of Counterpoint.

47. Ibid. Copyright 2012; reprinted by permission of Counterpoint.

48. Genesis 1:2 (King James Version); John 5:4 (New King James Version). Berry has indicated his debt to the King James Version, so I generally quote from that one. In this case, however, I cite the New King James rendering of the passage from John because it uses the verb "stir" twice, as does Berry's poem. The KJV uses "troubled," so it is possible I am seeing an allusion here that Berry did not intend.

49. Berry, *New Collected Poems,* 261. Copyright 2012; reprinted by permission of Counterpoint.

50. Jayber Crow, describing the first time he saw Mattie Keith, uses this language of reversal: "The brief, laughing look that she had given me made me feel extraordinarily seen, as if after that I might be visible in the dark." Wendell Berry, *Jayber Crow: The Life Story of Jayber Crow, Barber, of the Port William Membership, as Written by Himself* (Washington, D.C.: Counterpoint, 2000), 10.

51. Berry's sense of the physicality of poetry and his use of stones as a metaphor for making sense may echo Gary Snyder's famous poem "Riprap," in *The Gary Snyder Reader: Prose, Poetry, and Translations* (1999; repr., Washington, D.C.: Counterpoint, 2012), 404.

52. In *Leavings* this line reads: "upon your walk, upon the stream." In the older version the language you speak changes your actions in the world (your walk) and your place (the stream), but in the revision Berry emphasizes that the flux of language changes the way we are able to make meaning.

53. Berry, *This Day,* 288–89. Copyright 2013; reprinted by permission of Counterpoint.

54. Ibid., 289.

55. Ibid., 80. Copyright 2013; reprinted by permission of Counterpoint.

56. Ibid. Copyright 2013; reprinted by permission of Counterpoint.

57. Ibid., 329. Copyright 2013; reprinted by permission of Counterpoint.

58. Berry, *New Collected Poems,* 354. Copyright 2012; reprinted by permission of Counterpoint.

59. Edward Mendelson, "In the Depths of the Digital Age," *New York Review of Books,* June 23, 2016, www.nybooks.com/articles/2016/06/23/depths-of-the-digital-age/. See also Carr, *The Shallows.*

60. J. R. R. Tolkien, *The Fellowship of the Ring: Being the First Part of The Lord of the Rings* (1965) (New York: Ballantine, 2001), 34.

61. Marion, "The Saturated Phenomenon," 121.

62. C. S. Lewis, *The Four Loves* (New York: Harcourt Brace, 1960), 61.

2. Gratitude

1. "Ice Bucket Challenge," *Wikipedia, the Free Encyclopedia,* August 1, 2016, https://en.wikipedia.org/w/index.php?title=Ice_Bucket_Challenge&oldid=732524020.

2. Charles Taylor makes a similar point about the buffered self in a spiritual key: "People go to movies about the uncanny in order to experience a frisson. Our peasant ancestors would have thought us insane. You can't get a frisson from what is really in fact terrifying you." Taylor, *A Secular Age,* 38.

3. Berry, *This Day,* 9. Copyright 2013; reprinted by permission of Counterpoint.

4. Ibid., 8. Copyright 2013. Reprinted by permission of Counterpoint. Thomas Gardner offers a helpful reading of this poem in the context of Jesus' ministry. Thomas Gardner, *John in the Company of Poets: The Gospel in Literary Imagination* (Waco: Baylor University Press, 2011), 73–76.

5. Berry, *This Day,* 71.

6. Marion, *Being Given,* 249.

7. Taylor, *A Secular Age,* 37–43.

8. Taylor opposes the buffered self with the "porous self," which shares some similarities with Marion's recipient. Taylor, however, uses this term in making a historical, descriptive argument, and Marion is making a phenomenological, normative argument, so these terms are not congruent.

9. In describing Berry's grateful self as similar to Marion's recipient, I am treading on highly contested philosophical grounds. Marion avoids the term *gratitude* (although, as quoted below, he does criticize the "ungrateful person"), apparently in deference to Derrida's critique of gratitude as part of an economy of exchange that erases the gift. Jacques Derrida, *Given Time: I. Counterfeit Money,* trans. Peggy Kamuf (Chicago: University of Chicago Press, 1992). Thus, Peter Leithart concludes that "gratitude does not fare particularly well" in Marion's thought. Peter Leithart, *Gratitude: An Intellectual History* (Waco: Baylor University Press, 2014), 213. Something like Marion's understanding of being's givenness is present in Berry's poetry, however, and for Berry, this perception leads to gratitude. Ragan Sutterfield reads Berry's entire body of work as predicated on this sense of givenness in *Wendell Berry and the Given Life.*

10. Marion, *Being Given,* 249.

11. Ibid., 289.

12. Berry articulates this sense of dependence when writing about the way in which his place has shaped him: "There is a startling reversal of our ordinary sense of things in the recognition that we are the belongings of the world, not its owners. The social convention of ownership must be qualified by this stern fact, and by the humility it implies, if we are not to be blinded altogether to where we are." Berry, "The Long-Legged House," 143.

13. Berry, *This Day,* 288–89. Hans-Georg Gadamer articulates this notion of the self in a hermeneutic key when he asserts that because of our status as contingent human beings, we can never interpret from some ahistorical point d'appui: "History does not belong to us; we belong to it. Long before we understand ourselves through the process of self-examination, we understand ourselves in a self-evident way in the family, society,

and state in which we live. . . . That is why the prejudices of the individual, far more than his judgments, constitute the historical reality of his being." Hans-Georg Gadamer, *Truth and Method,* trans. Joel Weinsheimer and Donald G. Marshall, 2nd ed. (London: Sheed and Ward, 1999), 276–77.

14. Berry, *This Day,* 9.

15. Jean-Luc Marion, *The Visible and the Revealed* (New York: Fordham University Press, 2008), 93–94.

16. Ibid., 83. For a more philosophical analysis of Derrida's famous critique of the gift and Marion's response, see Leithart, *Gratitude,* 195–216.

17. Marion, *The Visible and the Revealed,* 97.

18. Ibid., 88, 91.

19. Leithart explicitly points to Berry as a leading critic of this economic mode: "It is this sense that our economics is dominated by ingratitude, discontent, greed, sheer self-interest, and accumulation that accounts for the popularity of the works of Wendell Berry. His economics arise from wonder at the nature of things, and from grateful respect for the specific contours of the world as it comes to us." Leithart, *Gratitude,* 220. For a book-length exploration of a politics of gratitude, see Mark T. Mitchell, *The Politics of Gratitude: Scale, Place & Community in a Global Age* (Dulles, Va.: Potomac Books, 2012).

20. Luke 12:19.

21. Thomas Merton, *Conjectures of a Guilty Bystander* (Garden City, N.Y.: Doubleday, 1966), 81.

22. Walter Brueggemann, *Sabbath as Resistance: Saying No to the Culture of Now* (Louisville: Westminster John Knox Press, 2014), 67.

23. Taylor, *A Secular Age,* 473–75.

24. Wendell Berry, "Think Little," in *A Continuous Harmony: Essays Cultural and Agricultural* (New York: Harcourt Brace Jovanovich, 1972), 71.

25. Toyama describes this phenomenon in the context of purchasing a pair of Toms Shoes in *Geek Heresy,* 84–87. The scholarly study he cites provides further detail regarding when good actions permit selfish ones and when they reinforce further good habits. See Anna C. Merritt, Daniel A. Effron, and Benoît Monin, "Moral Self-Licensing: When Being Good Frees Us to Be Bad," *Social and Personality Psychology Compass* 4, no. 5 (2010): 344–57.

26. Brueggemann, *Sabbath as Resistance,* 87.

27. Berry, *This Day,* xxi.

28. Ibid., xxi–xxii.

29. Ibid., xxii.

30. Ibid., 8.

31. Exodus 20:2; Deuteronomy 5:15.

32. Berry, *Sabbaths 2013,* 12.

33. Berry, *This Day,* xxii.

34. Ibid., 25.

35. Berry, *New Collected Poems,* 174. Copyright 2012; reprinted by permission of Counterpoint.

36. Berry, *This Day,* 13. Copyright 2013; reprinted by permission of Counterpoint.

37. Berry and Snyder, *Distant Neighbors,* 55.

38. Berry, *This Day,* xxiii.

39. Ibid., 377–78. Copyright 2013; reprinted by permission of Counterpoint.

40. Luke 22:42.

41. The Garden of Gethsemane is a seminal biblical scene for Berry. In addition to *Jayber Crow,* which I draw on briefly at the end of this chapter, see his short story "Watch with Me," in *That Distant Land: The Collected Stories* (Washington, D.C.: Shoemaker & Hoard, 2004), 77–123. I consider why Gethsemane is such an important story for Berry in Bilbro, *Loving God's Wildness,* 138–140; 164–178.

42. Berry also considers this biblical story in other sabbath poems; see *This Day,* 38, 346.

43. Ibid., 242. Copyright 2013; reprinted by permission of Counterpoint.

44. Ibid., 241. Copyright 2013; reprinted by permission of Counterpoint.

45. John 4:10.

46. Berry, *New Collected Poems,* 173.

47. Fritz Oehlschlaeger, "Living Faithfully in the Debt of Love in Wendell Berry's Port William," in *Telling the Stories Right: Wendell Berry's Imagination of Port William,* ed. Jack R. Baker and Jeffrey Bilbro (Eugene, Ore.: Front Porch Republic Books, 2018), 108.

48. Berry, *This Day,* 3. Copyright 2013; reprinted by permission of Counterpoint

49. Berry's depiction of light in this poem recalls John's claim that "God is light" and James's promise that "every good gift and every perfect gift . . . cometh down from the Father of lights." 1 John 1:5; James 1:17.

50. Wendell Berry, *A Timbered Choir: The Sabbath Poems, 1979–1997* (Washington, D.C.: Counterpoint, 1998); Wendell Berry, *Leavings: Poems* (Berkeley, Calif.: Counterpoint, 2010).

51. Wendell Berry, *The Mad Farmer Poems* (Berkeley, Calif.: Counterpoint, 2008).

52. Berry, *This Day,* 44.

53. Ibid., 324.

54. Ibid., 71. Copyright 2013; reprinted by permission of Counterpoint.

55. Ibid.

56. Ibid., 280. Copyright 2013; reprinted by permission of Counterpoint.

57. Ibid., 288. Copyright 2013; reprinted by permission of Counterpoint.

58. Ibid.

59. Harold Bloom, *The Anxiety of Influence: A Theory of Poetry,* 2nd ed. (New York: Oxford University Press, 1997). Terence Ball links Bloom and Nietzsche in *Reappraising Political Theory: Revisionist Studies in the History of Political Thought* (Oxford: Oxford University Press, 1995), 292–93.

60. Berry, "Work of Local Culture," 165.

61. Berry, "In Defense of Literacy," 172. Berry develops this point in "Against the Nihil of the Age": "The proper concern of poetry is also to purify and vivify and renew the language, to enlarge the possibility of consciousness by enlarging the capability of speech. This poem, though technically imperfect, is nevertheless of vital importance because it revives the language needed to speak of the inherent sanctity of things." Wendell Berry, "Against the Nihil of the Age," in *Imagination in Place* (Berkeley, Calif.: Counterpoint, 2010), 129. For an analogous approach to enriching culture, see Marilyn McEntyre, *Caring for Words in a Culture of Lies* (Grand Rapids: Eerdmans, 2009), and Makoto Fujimura, *Culture Care: Reconnecting with Beauty for Our Common Life,* ed. Peter Edman, 2nd ed. (New York: International Arts Movement and the Fujimura Institute, 2014).

62. Leithart, *Gratitude,* 7; emphases in original.

63. Berry, "Gift of Good Land," 269. For an extended discussion of stewardship in the Christian tradition—and a response to Lynn White's famous essay critiquing Christian stewardship—see Wirzba, *The Paradise of God*, 123–48.

64. Berry, *This Day*, xxii.

65. I explore Berry's understanding of good work at greater length in Bilbro, *Loving God's Wildness*, 138–78.

66. One of his longer sabbath poems, "The Farm," imagines in some detail what a grateful farm economy might look like. *This Day*, 114–26.

67. Ibid., 160. Copyright 2013; reprinted by permission of Counterpoint.

68. Ibid., 280. Copyright 2013; reprinted by permission of Counterpoint.

69. Berry, *New Collected Poems*, 130. Copyright 2012; reprinted by permission of Counterpoint.

70. See also Berry's poem "The Peace of Wild Things," which concludes, "For a time / I rest in the grace of the world, and am free." Ibid., 79.

71. See, for example, Yi-Fu Tuan's critique of reciprocity in ancient, communal contexts in *Cosmos & Hearth: A Cosmopolite's Viewpoint* (Minneapolis: University of Minnesota Press, 1996), 147–48. Peter Leithart shows how Christianity and its Enlightenment heirs replaced this constricting gratitude with a "comprehensive gratitude toward an infinite God who was the source of all good gifts but who also relativized all those gifts by the self-gift of his Son." Leithart, *Gratitude*, 225–26. Jack Baker and I explore these dynamics at greater length in *Wendell Berry and Higher Education*, 116–39.

72. Anthony Kennedy, David Souter, and Sandra Day O'Connor, Planned Parenthood v. Casey, 505 U.S. 833, no. 91–744 (United States Supreme Court, June 29, 1992).

73. "Free, v.," *OED Online* (Oxford University Press). Berry notes this connection in an essay, drawing out its implications for how we understand identity: "We set our friends free by our love for them, with the implied restraints of faithfulness or loyalty. And this suggests that our 'identity' is located not in the impulse of selfhood but in deliberately maintained connections." "Faustian Economics," in *What Matters? Economics for a Renewed Commonwealth* (Washington, D.C.: Counterpoint, 2010), 45.

74. Marion, *Being Given*, 324.

75. Herman Melville, *Moby-Dick; or, The Whale* (1851), ed. Harrison Hayford, Hershel Parker, and G. Thomas Tanselle (Evanston: Northwestern University Press, 1988), 471–72.

76. Berry, *Jayber Crow*, 250–53.

3. Humility

1. Yale's costume guidelines are not unique among universities, many of which have various kinds of speech codes. See David Hudson, "Explainer: How Campus Policies Limit Free Speech," *Conversation*, May 31, 2016, http://theconversation.com/explainer -how-campus-policies-limit-free-speech-58974.

2. Liam Stack, "Yale's Halloween Advice Stokes a Racially Charged Debate," *New York Times*, November 8, 2015, www.nytimes.com/2015/11/09/nyregion/yale-culturally -insensitive-halloween-costumes-free-speech.html.

3. Conor Friedersdorf, "The New Intolerance of Student Activism," *Atlantic*, November 9, 2015, www.theatlantic.com/politics/archive/2015/11/the-new-intolerance-of -student-activism-at-yale/414810/.

4. "Sustainable Buildings," *Yale Sustainability,* 2016, http://sustainability.yale.edu /sustainable-slideshow/sustainable-buildings.

5. John H. Scofield, "Are U.S. 'Green Buildings' Really Saving Energy? The Facts May Surprise You," *Brink—The Edge of Risk,* June 10, 2015, www.brinknews.com/are-u-s -green-buildings-really-saving-energy-the-facts-may-surprise-you/; Carol Menassa et al., "Energy Consumption Evaluation of U.S. Navy LEED-Certified Buildings," *Journal of Performance of Constructed Facilities* 26, no. 1 (2012): 46–53, doi:10.1061/(ASCE)CF.1943 –5509.0000218; D. Oates and K. Sullivan, "Postoccupancy Energy Consumption Survey of Arizona's LEED New Construction Population," *Journal of Construction Engineering and Management* 138, no. 6 (2011): 742–50, doi:10.1061/(ASCE)C0.1943–7862.0000478; Arik Levinson, "California Energy Efficiency: Lessons for the Rest of the World, or Not?" *Journal of Economic Behavior & Organization* 107 (2014): 269–89.

6. Thomas Frank, "In U.S. Building Industry, Is It Too Easy to Be Green?," *USA Today,* June 13, 2013, www.usatoday.com/story/news/nation/2012/10/24/green-building-leed -certification/1650517/.

7. Berry, "The Burden of the Gospels," in *The Way of Ignorance: And Other Essays* (Berkeley, Calif.: Counterpoint, 2005), 132. See also Berry, *Life Is a Miracle,* 181.

8. Berry, "Preface," in *The Way of Ignorance: And Other Essays* (Berkeley, Calif.: Counterpoint, 2005), x; Wendell Berry, "Preface," in *Home Economics* (San Francisco: North Point Press, 1987), ix.

9. Berry, *Life Is a Miracle,* 10–11. Daniel Kahneman provides extensive analysis of "our apparent inability to acknowledge the full extent of our ignorance and the uncertainty of the world we live in." Daniel Kahneman, *Thinking, Fast and Slow* (New York: Farrar, Straus and Giroux, 2011), 14.

10. Berry, *Life Is a Miracle,* 10; emphases in original.

11. Berry, "Preface," in *The Way of Ignorance,* ix–x. For other perspectives on an "ignorance-based worldview," see William Vitek and Wes Jackson, eds., *The Virtues of Ignorance: Complexity, Sustainability, and the Limits of Knowledge* (Lexington: University Press of Kentucky, 2008). For a philosophical analysis of Berry's thoughts along these lines, see Robert Kirkman, "Beyond Doubt: Environmental Philosophy and the Human Predicament," in *Rethinking Nature: Essays in Environmental Philosophy,* ed. Bruce V. Foltz and Robert Frodeman (Bloomington: Indiana University Press, 2004), 165–79.

12. Berry, "Preface," in *The Way of Ignorance,* ix.

13. Berry, *Life Is a Miracle,* 12.

14. Berry, "The Way of Ignorance," in *The Way of Ignorance: And Other Essays* (Berkeley: Counterpoint, 2005), 53.

15. Berry critiques onerous sanitation requirements in "Sanitation and the Small Farm," in *The Gift of Good Land: Further Essays, Cultural and Agricultural* (Berkeley, Calif.: Counterpoint, 1981), 98–103, and Berry, *Unsettling of America,* 221. Vandana Shiva argues that packaging requirements are "tactic[s] used to displace cheaper and more efficient systems in which food is processed locally—in front of people's eyes— ensuring quality and freshness." Shiva, *Staying Alive,* xxii. The farmer and activist Joel Salatin offers a blistering indictment of such regulations in *Everything I Want to Do Is Illegal: War Stories from the Local Food Front* (Swoope, Va.: Polyface, 2007). He probably overstates his case—as I argue below, we can't just do away with rules—but he does expose the absurdities of many codes intended to promote sustainability and healthy food.

16. Berry's fiction provides several parallel critiques of code fixation. See "the man across the desk" in *Jayber Crow*, 289, and Detective Kyle Bode in "Fidelity," in *That Distant Land: The Collected Stories* (Washington, D.C.: Shoemaker & Hoard, 2004), 372–427.

17. Berry, *Life Is a Miracle*, 15.; emphasis in original.

18. Taylor, *A Secular Age*, 704.

19. Ibid.

20. Friedersdorf, "The New Intolerance of Student Activism."

21. Peter Arnett, "Major Describes Move," *New York Times*, March 15, 1968; Berry, "Way of Ignorance," 65.

22. Charles Taylor, "Foreword," in *The Rivers North of the Future: The Testament of Ivan Illich as Told to David Cayley*, by Ivan Illich, ed. David Cayley (Toronto: House of Anansi Press, 2005), xiii–xiv.

23. Berry, "Poetry and Place," 166.

24. Alan Jacobs, "Code Fetishists and Antinomians," *American Conservative*, July 29, 2015, www.theamericanconservative.com/articles/code-fetishists-and-normolaters/; emphases in original.

25. Alan Jacobs, "Renewing the University," *National Affairs*, Summer 2016, 8; emphasis in original.

26. Berry has apparently been an appreciative reader of Ivan Illich throughout his career. He cites Illich's *Energy and Equity* in *The Unsettling of America*, and he dedicates one of his 2012 sabbath poems to Illich. Berry, *This Day*, 385.

27. I have copied this passage exactly as it appears in Berry's *The Way of Ignorance*. The original passage appears in David Cayley, "Introduction," in *The Rivers North of the Future: The Testament of Ivan Illich as Told to David Cayley*, by Ivan Illich, ed. David Cayley (Toronto: House of Anansi Press, 2005), 25.

28. For a further discussion of Illich's reading of the parable of the Good Samaritan, one that also refers to Taylor, see Cavanaugh, *Field Hospital*, 117–20.

29. Illich, *The Rivers North of the Future*, 51.

30. Ibid., 52, 55. In an earlier essay, Berry likewise warns that "institutional neighborliness can function as the very opposite of neighborliness." Berry, "The Loss of the Future," 49. For a related example of how particular needy people—like the wounded man on the road—can inspire love where ethical codes fail to do so, see James Scott's consideration of the French residents of Le Chambon-sur-Lignon who aided fugitive Jews during the Vichy regime in *Two Cheers for Anarchism: Six Easy Pieces on Autonomy, Dignity, and Meaningful Work and Play* (Princeton: Princeton University Press, 2014), 129–33. Scott, perhaps wrongly, downplays their Huguenot, Christian convictions, but the point is that those who refused to help "Jews" in the abstract nevertheless responded to the call of a particular refugee.

31. The Orthodox church calls such participation theosis. Fritz Oehlschlaeger discusses the importance of theosis for both Taylor and Berry in *Achievement of Wendell Berry*, 93–94.

32. Robert Capon offers a similar reading of this parable, emphasizing its subtext of resurrection: "Neither the Samaritan nor, a fortiori, Jesus is an example of some broader, saving truth about the power of human niceness. Jesus is an example of nothing of the sort. He is the incarnation of the unique, saving mystery of death and resurrection." Robert Capon, *Parables of Grace* (Grand Rapids: Eerdmans, 1988), 63.

33. Taylor, *A Secular Age*, 769.

34. Berry, "Burden of the Gospels," 132–33.

35. Berry, "Preface," in *The Way of Ignorance*, ix. Berry reads the parable of the Good Samaritan as a rebuke of technologically efficient aid in "Leaving the Future Behind: A Letter to a Scientific Friend," in *The Art of Loading Brush: New Agrarian Writing* (Berkeley, Calif.: Counterpoint, 2017), 61–62.

36. Taylor, "Foreword," xii–xiii. For Taylor's understanding of Illich, see Taylor, *A Secular Age*, 737–44.

37. Taylor, "Foreword," xiii.

38. Taylor, *A Secular Age*, 707.

39. Berry calls his essays "occasional" in his interview with Harold Bush. Berry, "Hunting for Reasons to Hope: A Conversation with Wendell Berry," *Christianity and Literature* 56, no. 2 (2007): 221.

40. Berry, "Preface," in *Home Economics*, ix. Berry's understanding of the genre is akin to that of Scott Russell Sanders, who says that his essays begin in "puzzlement" and lead to answers that "are always partial and tentative." Sanders, *Earth Works: Selected Essays* (Bloomington: Indiana University Press, 2012), xiii.

41. Berry, "Christianity and the Survival of Creation," in *Sex, Economy, Freedom & Community: Eight Essays* (New York: Pantheon, 1993), 93.

42. T. S Eliot, *Collected Poems, 1909–1962* (1963; repr., New York: Harcourt Brace Jovanovich, 1991), 189. For one place where Berry critiques large solutions, see his "Way of Ignorance," 62.

43. Berry, "Preface," in *The Way of Ignorance*, x.

44. Berry, "Thoughts in the Presence of Fear," in *Citizenship Papers* (Washington, D.C.: Shoemaker & Hoard, 2003), 17.

45. Berry, "Out of Your Car, Off Your Horse: Twenty-Seven Propositions About Global Thinking and the Sustainability of Cities," in *Sex, Economy, Freedom & Community: Eight Essays* (New York: Pantheon, 1993), 19–26; Berry, "Peaceableness toward Enemies: Some Notes on the Gulf War," in *Sex, Economy, Freedom & Community*, 69–92; Berry, "Notes: Unspecializing Poetry"; Berry, "Twelve Paragraphs on Biotechnology," in *Citizenship Papers* (Washington, D.C.: Shoemaker & Hoard, 2003), 53–56; Berry, "Six Agricultural Fallacies," in *Home Economics* (San Francisco: North Point Press, 1987), 123–32; Berry, "Paragraphs from a Notebook," in *Our Only World: Ten Essays* (Berkeley, Calif.: Counterpoint, 2015), 3–14. For other essays composed entirely of numbered lists, see Berry, "Damage," in *What Are People For? Essays* (San Francisco: North Point Press, 1990), 5–8; Berry, "Healing," in *What Are People For?* 9–13; Berry, "Going to Work," in *Citizenship Papers*, 33–42; Berry, "For the 50-Year Farm Bill," in *Our Only World*, 159–65. In addition to these essays, a few are journal like and organized by date: Berry, "Notes from an Absence and a Return," in *A Continuous Harmony: Essays Cultural and Agricultural* (New York: Harcourt Brace Jovanovich, 1972), 36–55; Berry, "Irish Journal," in *Home Economics*, 21–48; Berry, "Three Ways of Farming in the Southwest," in *The Gift of Good Land: Further Essays, Cultural and Agricultural* (Berkeley, Calif.: Counterpoint, 1981), 47–76.

46. Berry, "The Total Economy," 70–71; Berry, "Conservation and Local Economy," in *Sex, Economy, Freedom & Community: Eight Essays* (New York: Pantheon, 1993), 3–4; Berry, "Solving for Pattern," 140–45; Berry, "Why I Am Not Going to Buy a Computer," in *What Are People For? Essays* (San Francisco: North Point Press, 1990), 171–72; Berry, "Our Deserted Country," 151–56; emphases in original.

47. For other examples of numbered lists within his essays, see Berry, *Life Is a Miracle,* 181; Berry, "We Have Begun," in *The Way of Ignorance: And Other Essays* (Berkeley, Calif.: Counterpoint, 2005), 13; Berry, "An Argument for Diversity," in *What Are People For? Essays* (San Francisco: North Point Press, 1990), 109–10; Berry, "Preface: The Joy of Sales Resistance," in *Sex, Economy, Freedom & Community: Eight Essays* (New York: Pantheon, 1993), xii–xviii; Berry, "Preserving Wildness," in *Home Economics* (San Francisco: North Point Press, 1987), 138–39; Berry, "A Defense of the Family Farm," in *Home Economics,* 177–78; Berry, "Standing by Words," 25; Berry, "Conserving Communities," in *Another Turn of the Crank* (Washington, D.C.: Counterpoint, 1995), 19–21; Berry, "Local Economies to Save the Land and the People," in *Our Only World: Ten Essays* (Berkeley, Calif.: Counterpoint, 2015), 63–66.

48. Berry, "Major in Homecoming: For Commencement, Northern Kentucky University," in *What Matters? Economics for a Renewed Commonwealth* (Berkeley, Calif.: Counterpoint, 2010), 34–35. For other places where Berry asks a series of questions, see Berry, *Life Is a Miracle,* 14; Berry, "The Purpose of a Coherent Community," in *The Way of Ignorance: And Other Essays* (Berkeley, Calif.: Counterpoint, 2005), 72; Berry, "Preserving Wildness," 146; Berry, "Agriculture from the Roots Up," 109; Berry, "Burden of the Gospels," 128–29; Berry, "On Receiving One of the Dayton Literary Peace Prizes," in *Our Only World: Ten Essay* (Berkeley, Calif.: Counterpoint, 2015), 100–101; Berry, "The Thought of Limits in a Prodigal Age," in *The Art of Loading Brush: New Agrarian Writings* (Berkeley, Calif.: Counterpoint, 2017), 33–34. Such an approach apparently characterized Berry's teaching. In describing a class he took from Berry, Morris Grubbs writes, "A set of critical and practical questions emerged from our conversations with the text and with each other. . . . These questions became our mantra." Morris Allen Grubbs, "A Practical Education: Wendell Berry the Professor," in *Wendell Berry: Life and Work,* ed. Jason Peters (Lexington: University Press of Kentucky, 2007), 137. Jack Baker and I explore some of the benefits that this approach might bring in *Wendell Berry and Higher Education,* 185–86.

49. Berry, "Imagination in Place," in *Imagination in Place* (Berkeley, Calif.: Counterpoint, 2010), 2.

50. Berry, "Preface," *Home Economics,* ix–x.

51. Berry, "People, Land, and Community," in *Standing by Words: Essays* (Washington, D.C.: Shoemaker & Hoard, 2005), 77.

52. Berry, "The Responsibility of the Poet," 90.

53. Berry, "The Purpose of a Coherent Community," 76.

54. Berry, "A Citizen's Response," in *Citizenship Papers* (Washington, D.C.: Shoemaker & Hoard, 2003), 9.

55. Berry, "Conservation of Nature," 84; emphasis in original. In a *Harper's Magazine* forum on abortion, Berry made a similar point: "A pregnancy is not an isolated event. Pregnancy is connected to sexuality, sexuality is connected to fertility, fertility is connected to nature. In choosing to take part in sexuality, one chooses, wittingly or not, to take part in an enterprise far greater than oneself. If one is to be human, one must manage to be generous toward the results." Berry, "She's Come for an Abortion. What Do You Say?" *Harper's Magazine,* November 1992, 50–51.

56. Berry, "The Problem of Tobacco," in *Sex, Economy, Freedom & Community: Eight Essays* (New York: Pantheon, 1993), 58–59.

57. Berry, *Hidden Wound,* 111.

58. Ibid., 104.

59. bell hooks, *Belonging: A Culture of Place* (New York: Routledge, 2008), 174–83.

60. Berry, "Standing by Words," 29–30; emphasis in original.

61. In an apt illustration of the gap between what we know and what we do, James Smith describes reading a collection of Berry's essays in the Costco food court. Smith, *Imagining the Kingdom*, 8–10.

62. Berry, "Two Economies"; Berry, "Two Minds," in *Citizenship Papers* (Washington, D.C.: Shoemaker & Hoard, 2003), 85–105; Berry, "Quantity vs. Form," in *The Way of Ignorance: And Other Essays* (Berkeley, Calif.: Counterpoint, 2005), 81–89.

63. Berry, "Standing by Words," 60; emphasis in original. See also Berry, "The Loss of the Future," 60.

64. Berry, *It All Turns on Affection*, 10–11.

65. Alan Jacobs, "On Stickers and Boomers," *American Conservative*, May 29, 2013, http://www.theamericanconservative.com/jacobs/on-stickers-and-boomers/.

66. Berry, "Conservation of Nature," 69.

67. I wrote a brief essay replying to Alan Jacobs's critique of Berry, and he was kind enough to respond in the comments. Bilbro, "Place Isn't Just Geographical," *Front Porch Republic*, May 2013, www.frontporchrepublic.com/2013/05/place-isnt-just-geographical/.

68. In this regard, Berry sees the reductive codes of boomerism or the industrial economy in the same way that Chesterton diagnoses the minds of the insane or of modern thinkers; their minds operate according to a tightly circumscribed logic, and the only possible remedy "is a desperate remedy. . . . Curing a madman is not arguing with a philosopher; it is casting out a devil." To be healed, according to Chesterton, they "must desire health." *Orthodoxy*, 26.

69. Berry, "Caught in the Middle," 94. To borrow terms from Cathleen Kaveny, Berry condemns without contemning. See Kaveny, *Prophecy without Contempt: Religious Discourse in the Public Square* (Cambridge: Harvard University Press, 2016), ix–x.

70. Deuteronomy 11:26–32; Matthew 7:17–20, 24–27, 25:31–46. See also J. Richard Middleton, *A New Heaven and a New Earth: Reclaiming Biblical Eschatology* (Grand Rapids: Baker Academic, 2014), 96–98.

71. Kaveny, *Prophecy without Contempt*, 288. Kaveny expands on this claim, arguing that "the rhetoric of prophetic indictment is best understood as a sort of *moral chemotherapy*, a reaction to a potentially life-threatening distortion in ordinary, day-to-day moral discussion. Deliberative discourse is, in fact, that ordinary form of moral discussion. . . . In some cases, however, our ordinary form of discussion can be gravely corrupted, perhaps by the incorporation of a false major premise, perhaps because of the dependence on a mistaken minor premise. Such mistakes are made all the time in matters small and large. In some few cases, however, the mistake is about such a fundamental matter that it threatens to undermine the very possibility of moral and political reasoning within the community. . . . Prophetic indictment relentlessly—and sometimes ruthlessly—targets the corruption that, left unchecked, would undermine the possibility of sound moral deliberation more generally" (287–88; see also 308–16). Berry's use of the prophetic mode parallels Walter Brueggemann's description in his seminal *Prophetic Imagination*, 2nd ed. (Minneapolis: Fortress Press, 2001). Other scholars have situated Berry in the context of Old Testament prophecy: see Davis, *Scripture, Culture, and Agriculture*, and Todd Edmondson, *Priest, Prophet, Pilgrim: Types and Distortions of Spiritual

Vocation in the Fiction of Wendell Berry and Cormac McCarthy (Eugene, Ore.: Wipf and Stock, 2014), 47–54.

72. Berry, "Two Economies," 54–55.

73. Berry, "Letter to Wes Jackson"; emphasis in original. Vandana Shiva offers a similar critique of a forest manager who described the diversity of a natural forest as "chaos." Shiva, *The Vandana Shiva Reader*, 82–83.

74. Berry, "Quantity vs. Form," 88–89.

75. Taylor, *A Secular Age*, 704.

76. Berry, "Notes: Unspecializing Poetry," 90.

77. In some respects, then, Berry's formal standards act on what Daniel Kahneman terms System 1, the fast, instinctual method we use to make most of our decisions; see Kahneman, *Thinking, Fast and Slow*.

78. Cayley, "Introduction," 25.

79. Taylor, "Foreword," xi.

80. Berry quotes Illich on attunement and reflects further on the role of art in tuning individuals to their communities in *The Poetry of William Carlos Williams of Rutherford* (Berkeley, Calif.: Counterpoint, 2011), 43.

81. For a robust theological and philosophical articulation of how affection and imagination are at the heart of persons and cultures, see the first two volumes of Jamie Smith's Cultural Liturgies series, *Desiring the Kingdom: Worship, Worldview, and Cultural Formation* (Grand Rapids: Baker Academic, 2009); and his *Imagining the Kingdom*.

82. Berry, "Quantity vs. Form," 83.

83. Ibid., 88.

84. Jayber's "ideal [of marriage] rides ahead of the real, renewing beyond it, perishing in it—unreachable, surely, but made new over and over again just by hope and by the passage of time; what has not yet failed remains possible. And the ideal, remaining undiminished and perfect, out of reach, makes possible a judgment of failure, and a just grief and sympathy." Berry, *A Place on Earth*, 72. I explore some of the ways that the form of marriage guides Berry's characters in Bilbro, "A Form for Living in the Midst of Loss: Faithful Marriage in the Revisions of Wendell Berry's *A Place on Earth*," *Southern Literary Journal* 42, no. 2 (2010): esp. 96–101.

85. Berry, "People, Land, and Community," 66–67; emphases in original.

86. Ibid., 77.

4. Hope

1. Jedidiah Purdy offers a critique of such political and technological solutions, even as he advocates for a more animated democratic process, in *After Nature: A Politics for the Anthropocene* (Cambridge: Harvard University Press, 2015), 256–88. He freely admits, though, that democracy is no silver bullet.

2. Cary Funk and Brian Kennedy, "The Politics of Climate," *Pew Research Center,* October 4, 2016, http://assets.pewresearch.org/wp-content/uploads/sites/14/2016/10 /14080900/PS_2016.10.04_Politics-of-Climate_FINAL.pdf. Commenting on this tendency, Clive Hamilton writes, "There is something increasingly desperate about placing more faith in technological cleverness when it is the unrelenting desire to command the natural world that has brought us to this point." Clive Hamilton, *Earthmasters: The Dawn of the Age of Climate Engineering* (New Haven: Yale University Press, 2013), 199.

3. Elon Musk, "Elon Musk: The Mind behind Tesla, SpaceX, SolarCity," interview by Chris Anderson, March 19, 2013, https://www.youtube.com/watch?v=IgKWPdJWuBQ.

4. David Keith, *A Case for Climate Engineering* (Cambridge: MIT Press, 2013); Oliver Morton, *The Planet Remade: How Geoengineering Could Change the World* (Princeton: Princeton University Press, 2015).

5. Paul J. Crutzen, "Albedo Enhancement by Stratospheric Sulfur Injections: A Contribution to Resolve a Policy Dilemma?" *Climatic Change* 77, no. 3–4 (2006): 212, doi:10.1007/s10584-006-9101-y.

6. The Ocean Cleanup, "The Largest Cleanup in History," 2018, www.theoceancleanup.com/.

7. As an article on Silicon Valley preppers notes, "Those impulses are not as contradictory as they seem. Technology rewards the ability to imagine wildly different futures, Roy Bahat, the head of Bloomberg Beta, a San Francisco–based venture-capital firm, told me. 'When you do that, it's pretty common that you take things ad infinitum, and that leads you to utopias and dystopias,' he said. It can inspire radical optimism—such as the cryonics movement, which calls for freezing bodies at death in the hope that science will one day revive them—or bleak scenarios. Tim Chang, the venture capitalist who keeps his bags packed, told me, 'My current state of mind is oscillating between optimism and sheer terror.'" Evan Osnos, "Doomsday Prep for the Super-Rich," *New Yorker,* January 30, 2017, www.newyorker.com/magazine/2017/01/30/doomsday-prep-for-the-super-rich. This essential kinship is why Berry groups together the "deterministic optimists and pessimists"; "Leaving the Future Behind," 58.

8. Wendell Berry, "On Being Asked for 'A Narrative for the Future,'" in *Our Only World: Ten Essays* (Berkeley, Calif.: Counterpoint, 2015), 173. Berry makes a similar argument in "Leaving the Future Behind," 69–72.

9. Loren Eiseley's well-known story about a man throwing starfish back into the ocean seems to have a similar point. Loren Eiseley, *The Unexpected Universe* (San Diego: Harcourt Brace Jovanovich, 1969). For a slightly different reading of this story, one I'll question later in this chapter, see Daniel Västfjäll, Paul Slovic, and Marcus Mayorga, "Pseudoinefficacy and the Arithmetic of Compassion," in *Numbers and Nerves: Information, Emotion, and Meaning in a World of Data,* ed. Scott Slovic and Paul Slovic (Corvallis: Oregon State University Press, 2015), 48–50.

10. It should be noted that not all eschatologies are equal. Some Christians hold a "pie in the sky when you die" eschatology, one that legitimates wanton environmental destruction, but Berry's theology is quite different. Though he doesn't cite these theologians, his vision would generally align with the views laid out by N. T. Wright and J. Richard Middleton: N. T. Wright, *Surprised by Hope: Rethinking Heaven, the Resurrection, and the Mission of the Church* (2008; repr., London: SPCK Publishing, 2011); Middleton, *A New Heaven and a New Earth.* In the words of Stanley Hauerwas, "The apocalyptic character of the Gospel paradoxically makes possible the everyday. Because time has been redeemed we have time to marry, have children, feed the hungry, enjoy singing, be friends, and worship God." Stanley Hauerwas, *Disrupting Time: Sermons, Prayers, and Sundries* (Eugene, Ore.: Wipf and Stock, 2004), 8. For more on Berry's eschatology, see Bonzo and Stevens, *Wendell Berry and the Cultivation of Life,* 74–86.

11. Berry, "The Purpose of a Coherent Community," 79.

12. Taylor, *A Secular Age,* 76–77.

13. Ibid., 63.

14. Ibid., 80.

15. Chris Jennings, *Paradise Now: The Story of American Utopianism* (New York: Random House, 2016).

16. Smith, *How (Not) to Be Secular*, 37.

17. Taylor, *A Secular Age*, 643. James Smith points out that Taylor's chapter on conversions fittingly proceeds by examples, and he sees this as a particularly Catholic method: "Would a Protestant proceed this way? Not likely. This celebration of exemplars bubbles up from a Catholic imaginary that accords an iconic role to the saints. Chapter 20 can be read as a sort of verbal stained glass constellation of Taylor's saints: Illich, Maritain, and Péguy." Smith, *How (Not) to Be Secular*, 133. Whether or not this is distinctively Catholic, it's very similar to Berry's method in his essays, as we will see.

18. Berry, "God, Science, and Imagination," 183.

19. Västfjäll, Slovic, and Mayorga, "Pseudoinefficacy and the Arithmetic of Compassion," 44.

20. Elsewhere Taylor offers a partial defense of efficacy and instrumental reason. If these values are enframed in an ethic of care, they can further efforts to love our neighbors. Charles Taylor, *The Ethics of Authenticity* (Cambridge: Harvard University Press, 1991), 104–8.

21. Berry, "Discipline and Hope," 131.

22. Yale University, "The Chubb Fellowship—Wendell Berry," *Chubb Fellowship*, December 7, 2013, http://chubbfellowship.org/speakers/current/wendell_berry. John Ehrenfeld and Andrew Hoffman make a similar contrast between hope and optimism in *Flourishing*, 119–36. See also Christopher Lasch, who in an interview distinguished the two and called himself "hopeful, not optimistic"; see Miller, *Hope in a Scattering Time*, 383. For a fuller explanation of Lasch's vision of hope, see Christopher Lasch, *The True and Only Heaven: Progress and Its Critics* (New York: W. W. Norton, 1991).

23. Berry, "On Being Asked for 'A Narrative for the Future,'" 176.

24. Elsewhere I draw on Certeau's notion of "making do" to elucidate the kind of hope found in Berry's fiction, particularly in his short story "Dismemberment," and to compare this hope to that practiced by marginalized communities. Bilbro, "Andy Catlett's Missing Hand: Making Do as Wounded Members," in *Telling the Stories Right: Wendell Berry's Imagination of Port William*, ed. Jack R. Baker and Jeffrey Bilbro (Eugene, Ore.: Front Porch Republic Books, 2018), 71–88.

25. Michel de Certeau, *The Practice of Everyday Life*, trans. Steven Rendall (Berkeley: University of California Press, 1984), 96.

26. Ibid., 26; emphasis in original.

27. Ibid., 18.

28. Ibid., 29; emphases in original.

29. Berry, *New Collected Poems*, 174. Copyright 2012; reprinted by permission of Counterpoint.

30. Berry, *Hidden Wound*, 115.

31. hooks, *Belonging*, 180, 194.

32. Wendell Berry, *Harlan Hubbard: Life and Work* (Lexington: University Press of Kentucky, 1990); Berry, *Poetry of William Carlos Williams*; Berry, *The Unforeseen Wilderness*; Berry, "A Forest Conversation," in *Our Only World: Ten Essays* (Berkeley, Calif.: Counterpoint, 2015), 21–52; Berry, "Seven Amish Farms," in *The Gift of Good Land: Further Essays, Cultural and Agricultural* (Berkeley, Calif.: Counterpoint, 1981), 249–63; Berry, *Hidden Wound*.

33. Berry, *Life Is a Miracle*, 3.

34. Berry, *Poetry of William Carlos Williams*, 47.

35. For a good analysis of how Williams shaped Berry's style of writing, see Joseph R. Wiebe, *The Place of Imagination: Wendell Berry and the Poetics of Community, Affection, and Identity* (Waco: Baylor University Press, 2017), 13–32.

36. Berry, *Poetry of William Carlos Williams*, 5–8.

37. Berry, *Harlan Hubbard*, 85–88.

38. Berry, *Poetry of William Carlos Williams*, 9.

39. Ibid., 11.

40. Berry, *Harlan Hubbard*, 96.

41. Berry, *Poetry of William Carlos Williams*, 56.

42. Ibid., 125–26.

43. Ibid., 27.

44. Ibid., 170–71.

45. Berry, *Harlan Hubbard*, 33.

46. Ibid., 56.

47. Ibid., 70.

48. Ibid., 32–33.

49. Ibid., 8.

50. Ibid., 24.

51. Berry, *Poetry of William Carlos Williams*, 23.

52. Ibid., 30.

53. Ibid., 49.

54. Linda Moss, "Calling All Babies Delivered by the Poet Who Gave 'Paterson' Life," *Bergen Count (N.J.) Record*, July 7, 2015, article excerpt at https://www.questia.com /newspaper/1P2-38491373/calling-all-babies-delivered-by-the-poet-who-gave.

55. Berry, *Poetry of William Carlos Williams*, 63.

56. Ibid., 64.

57. Ibid., 142.

58. Berry, *Harlan Hubbard*, 16.

59. Ibid., 48–49.

60. Ibid., 39.

61. Ibid., 48–49. Berry later chose this painting for the cover of *Jayber Crow*.

62. Ibid., 16.

63. Ibid., 97.

64. Ibid., 101.

65. Berry, *Poetry of William Carlos Williams*, 177.

66. Berry, "Imagination in Place," 11; Berry, *Harlan Hubbard*, 88; Berry, "Tuscany," in *Citizenship Papers* (Washington, D.C.: Shoemaker & Hoard, 2003), 175–80; Berry, "Irish Journal"; Berry, "An Agricultural Journey in Peru," in *The Gift of Good Land: Further Essays, Cultural and Agricultural* (Berkeley, Calif.: Counterpoint, 1981), 3–46.

67. Wendell Berry, "Maury Telleen, 1928–2011," in *It All Turns on Affection: The Jefferson Lecture and Other Essays* (Berkeley, Calif.: Counterpoint, 2012), 113.

68. Berry, "A Defense of the Family Farm," 177. For other places where Berry acknowledges Amish shortcomings or limitations, see Berry, *Conversations with Wendell Berry*, ed. Morris Allen Grubbs (Jackson: University Press of Mississippi, 2007), 159; Berry, "The Purpose of a Coherent Community," 78.

69. Berry and Snyder, *Distant Neighbors*, 48.

70. Berry, *Unsettling of America,* 210–12.

71. Berry, "Out of Your Car," 20.

72. Berry, *Unsettling of America,* 216–17. See also Berry, "Foreword," in *The Gift of Good Land: Further Essays, Cultural and Agricultural* (Berkeley, Calif.: Counterpoint, 1981), xiii–xiv; Berry, "Seven Amish Farms," 258–61.

73. Berry, *This Day,* 160. Copyright 2013; reprinted by permission of Counterpoint. Berry writes more about David Kline in "Foreword," in *Great Possessions: An Amish Farmer's Journal,* by David Kline (1990; repr., Wooster, Ohio: Wooster Book Co., 2001). Later in this poem he also cites Maury Telleen's equation for "price," which he discusses at greater length in "Maury Telleen, 1928–2011."

74. Matthew 10:39.

75. Berry, "Does Community Have a Value?," in *Home Economics* (San Francisco: North Point Press, 1987), 189.

76. For another account of Berry's extensive debt to *King Lear,* see Nancy A. Barta-Smith, "On the Edge between Hope and Despair: *Lear* as Guide and Consolation in the Life and Work of Wendell Berry," in *Inhabited by Stories: Critical Essays on Tales Retold,* ed. Nancy A. Barta-Smith and Danette DiMarco (Newcastle upon Tyne: Cambridge Scholars Publishing, 2012), 337–66.

77. Berry, *Life Is a Miracle,* 3–4. In an interview Berry also emphasizes the important influence this play has had on his thinking: "I've been a reader of *King Lear* since I was a freshman in college, which was a fairly long time ago. It seems to me there's immense teaching in that play." He notes particularly that it teaches "what it is to be a servant, what it means to be a servant." Berry, "Hunting for Reasons to Hope," 219. In what follows, I draw on essays that he published over a span of thirty years, and his basic reading of the play appears to have remained consistent throughout.

78. Berry, *Conversations with Wendell Berry,* 189.

79. Berry, "The Uses of Adversity," in *Imagination in Place* (Berkeley, Calif.: Counterpoint, 2010), 169.

80. Berry, *Conversations with Wendell Berry,* 189.

81. Berry, *Life Is a Miracle,* 4.

82. Ibid., 5–6.

83. Ibid., 7.

84. Ibid., 8. Elsewhere Berry expands on the theological meaning of living fully in terms of what Jesus called a more abundant life; Berry, "Burden of the Gospels."

85. Berry, *Life Is a Miracle,* 9.

86. Berry, "The Uses of Adversity," 167–68.

87. Ibid., 168.

88. William Shakespeare, *King Lear* (1608), ed. Alfred Harbage (Baltimore: Penguin Books, 1958), 1.4.

89. Berry, "The Uses of Adversity," 169.

90. Shakespeare, *King Lear,* 4.6.50, 55.

91. Ibid., 213–15.

92. Berry, *Unsettling of America,* 99, 107.

93. Berry, *Life Is a Miracle,* 10.

94. Shakespeare, *King Lear,* 5.3.199.

95. Berry, "The Uses of Adversity," 175. Berry acknowledges that many critics disagree with his reading. One theologian whose interpretation of the play concurs with

Berry's is David Bentley Hart, who contrasts *King Lear*'s portrayal of death with that of Attic tragedy and emphasizes its "imagery of resurrection and talk of forgiveness." Hart, *The Beauty of the Infinite*, 393.

96. Berry, "The Uses of Adversity," 177–78.

97. Berry, "Hunting for Reasons to Hope," 222–23.

98. Berry makes this point in one essay by reference to the Shakers, who believed in the imminent end of the world and yet did beautiful work. Berry, "Leaving the Future Behind," 99.

5. Memory

1. Garson O'Toole, "Life Is Just One Damn Thing after Another," *Quote Investigator*, September 2, 2015, http://quoteinvestigator.com/2015/09/02/life-one/.

2. Taylor, *A Secular Age*, 59.

3. Illich, *Energy and Equity*.

4. My distinction between chronos and kairos parallels Paul Griffiths's contrast between metronomic time and systolic time in *Decreation*, 89–108.

5. Taylor, *A Secular Age*, 55.

6. In his early sabbath poems, Berry gestures to this cyclical understanding of time by repeatedly rhyming *time* and *rhyme*. Berry, *This Day*, 12, 16, 22, 57, 59, 77, 102. Hannah Coulter offers an explicit interpretation of this metaphor: "It is hard to say what it means to be at work and thinking of a person you loved and love still who did that same work before you and who taught you to do it. It is a comfort ever and always, like hearing the rhyme come when you are singing a song." Berry, *Hannah Coulter* (2004; repr., Berkeley, Calif.: Counterpoint, 2005), 107. Understood in this way, rhyme is a form of patterned memory, shaping us to stitch together different sounds or events.

7. On the way both left and right collaborate in creating such a "liberated" self, see Patrick J. Deneen, "Unsustainable Liberalism," *First Things*, August 2012, https://www.firstthings.com/article/2012/08/unsustainable-liberalism.

8. Crawford, *The World beyond Your Head*, 41.

9. William Cavanaugh gestures to the incredible power of nationalist narratives when he asks, "How does a provincial farm boy become persuaded that he must travel as a soldier to another part of the world and kill people he knows nothing about?" Through the many embodied narratives that constitute a self as a citizen, nations (along with industrial capitalism) assert a view of time that is "without termination or telos." William Cavanaugh, *Theopolitical Imagination* (London: T & T Clark, 2002), 1, 5.

10. Berry, *Unsettling of America*, 103.

11. Ellen Davis makes a similar claim in the context of her reading of the Genesis creation story: "*Metanoia*, like poetry, is largely a work of the insightful memory." Davis, *Scripture, Culture, and Agriculture*, 47.

12. Augustine, *The Trinity* (ca. 417), trans. Stephen McKenna (Washington, D.C.: Catholic University of America Press, 2002), 14.15.

13. Ibid., 14.22.

14. Augustine, *Confessions* (ca. 398), trans. Henry Chadwick (Oxford: Oxford University Press, 1998), 10.12.

15. Ibid., 10.40.

16. Dominic Manganiello provides a helpful summary of Augustine's view of memory in *T. S. Eliot and Dante* (New York: St. Martin's, 1989), 101.

17. Alasdair MacIntyre critiques Descartes in similar terms for being insufficiently aware of his embeddedness in narrative and tradition. MacIntyre, "Epistemological Crises, Dramatic Narrative, and the Philosophy of Science," in *Why Narrative? Readings in Narrative Theology,* ed. Stanley Hauerwas and L. Gregory Jones (Grand Rapids: Eerdmans, 1990), 143–45. Stratford Caldecott, citing Arthur Lovejoy's *The Revolt against Dualism,* likewise points out the flawed assumptions behind Descartes's *cogito ergo sum:* "As Arthur Lovejoy explains, the road to philosophical idealism and subjectivism started when Descartes confined his reflection to the present moment, without observing that the self transcends the moment. *Memini ergo fui:* I remember, therefore I was. We cannot be conscious of the self if we are conscious *only* of the present moment." Stratford Caldecott, *Beauty in the Word: Rethinking the Foundations of Education* (Tacoma, Wash.: Angelico Press, 2012), 75.

18. Davis, *Scripture, Culture, and Agriculture,* 153; see also 79.

19. David L. Jeffrey, ed., *The King James Bible and the World It Made* (Waco: Baylor University Press, 2011), 6. This understanding of memory is also akin to what Eric Auerbach calls "figural" interpretation in *Mimesis: The Representation of Reality in Western Literature,* trans. Willard R. Trask (1953; repr., Princeton: Princeton University Press, 2013).

20. Alan Jacobs, "What Narrative Theology Forgot," *First Things,* August 2003, https://www.firstthings.com/article/2003/08/what-narrative-theology-forgot. I am indebted to John Leax's essay on memory and Wendell Berry for drawing my attention to this essay by Alan Jacobs. Leax examines *A World Lost,* a short novel narrated by Andy, and concludes, "Memory for Andy is functioning much as it did for Saint Augustine." It does this by constructing a whole out of disparate events: "By his act of memory he discerns and creates a story that gives shape to the discrete, unplotted events of Uncle Andrew's life." John Leax, "Memory and Hope in the World of Port William," in *Wendell Berry: Life and Work,* ed. Jason Peters (Lexington: University Press of Kentucky, 2009), 71.

21. For a very different kind of narrative form that likewise explores the consequences of kairos time from a Christian perspective, see George Mackay Brown's stunning *Magnus* (London: Hogarth Press, 1973).

22. Leax, "Memory and Hope," 70.

23. Donnelly, "Biblical Convocation in Wendell Berry's *Remembering.*"

24. Berry, "Acceptance Speech," *Chesterton Review* 24, no. 1/2 (1998): 238–41. For a recent acknowledgment of Eliot's influence, see the introduction to *This Day,* xxiii, where Berry quotes lines from "The Rock" and one of Eliot's essays. For a good consideration of some further parallels between Eliot and Berry, see Gracy Olmstead, "'The End of All Our Exploring': Homecoming and Membership in *Remembering,*" in *Telling the Stories Right: Wendell Berry's Imagination of Port William,* ed. Jack R. Baker and Jeffrey Bilbro (Eugene, Ore.: Front Porch Republic Books, 2018), 153–71.

25. Eliot, *Collected Poems, 1909–1962,* 208.

26. Ibid., 194, 187–88.

27. Ibid., 188.

28. Ibid., 205.

29. Seamus Heaney, "For Liberation: Brian Friel and the Use of Memory," in *The Achievement of Brian Friel,* ed. Alan J. Peacock (Gerrards Cross, U.K.: Colin Smythe, 1993), 229.

30. T. S. Eliot, "Introduction," in *The Collected Works of Paul Valéry,* vol. 7, *The Art of Poetry,* by Paul Valéry, trans. Denise Folliot (Princeton: Princeton University Press, 1989), xiv.

31. Manganiello, *T. S. Eliot and Dante,* 118.

32. Eliot, *Collected Poems, 1909-1962,* 208.

33. Berry acknowledges that "with some significant differences, Andy Catlett's life is *like* my own." Berry, "Introduction," in *The Art of Loading Brush: New Agrarian Writing* (Berkeley, Calif.: Counterpoint, 2017), 15. For more on Andy as an autobiographical character, see Bilbro, "Andy Catlett's Missing Hand," 71–72.

34. Berry, "Pray without Ceasing," in *That Distant Land: The Collected Stories* (Washington, D.C.: Shoemaker & Hoard, 2004), 38.

35. Ibid. Andy's emphasis on the present as the portal through which memory connects us to the eternally present Creator may also be influenced by Dante: in the *Inferno,* the damned souls can see the past and future but not the present, and at the end of time, when there is no more future, they will be locked in an endless repetition of their sinful pasts.

36. Ibid. Berry returns to this theme repeatedly. For one example, see his essay "The Work of Local Culture," 157, 160, where he describes the "vast amnesia" that infects local American communities and contrasts this with the biblical norm where generational succession in one place "is seen as one of the rewards of righteousness."

37. David L. Jeffrey and Gregory Maillet, *Christianity and Literature: Philosophical Foundations and Critical Practice* (Downers Grove, Ill.: IVP Academic, 2011), 113–14.

38. Phillip Donnelly also points out how Andy's personal story of restoration, both here and in *Remembering,* is told through the context of the biblical, covenantal narrative. Donnelly, "Biblical Convocation in Wendell Berry's *Remembering,*" 287.

39. Berry, "Pray without Ceasing," 39.

40. Ibid.

41. Ibid., 42.

42. Ibid., 41.

43. Ibid., 43.

44. Ibid., 43–44.

45. Ibid., 44.

46. Ibid., 60–61.

47. Ibid., 59.

48. Ibid., 62.

49. Ibid., 48, 50.

50. Ibid., 68.

51. Ibid., 69–70. Interestingly, Andy claims that "my hand still bears [Margaret's] touch, invisible and yet indelible as a tattoo," but by the time he narrates this story, his right hand has been cut off by a piece of farm machinery, the event that lies behind his troubles in *Remembering.* I'm not entirely sure what to make of this, but perhaps the "invisible" here modifies not only "touch," but also "my hand"; even though his hand has been lost, his body still carries its remembered sensation, indelible as a tattoo.

52. Ibid., 64.

53. Ibid., 70.

54. Ibid., 74–75.

55. Eliot, *Collected Poems, 1909-1962,* 205.

56. Berry, "Pray without Ceasing," 72.

57. Ibid., 73.

58. Berry, *A Place on Earth,* 109–12.

59. Berry practices such memory in many essays. For one example, see "Foreword," in Abernathy et al., *Kentucky's Natural Heritage,* xiv–xvii.

60. Berry, *Hannah Coulter,* 113.

6. Fidelity

1. Berry, "Pray without Ceasing," 62.

2. Berry, *A Place on Earth* (2001), 262.

3. Taylor, *The Ethics of Authenticity,* 62.

4. While Taylor doesn't distinguish between "original" and "new," his critique of the Romantic obsession with novelty parallels George Steiner's famous claim that "originality is antithetical to novelty. The etymology of the word alerts us. It tells of 'inception' and of 'instauration,' of a return, in substance and in form, to beginnings. In exact relation to their originality, to their spiritual-formal force of innovation, aesthetic inventions are 'archaic.' They carry in them the pulse of the distant source." George Steiner, *Real Presences* (Chicago: University of Chicago Press, 1989), 27–28.

5. In literary studies, of course, Harold Bloom is the foremost proponent of such creativity. As Bloom claims, "The essential condition for poetic strength is that the new song, one's own, must always be a song of one's self." He calls this "the poetic will to immortality," and it represents a rejection of death rather than a redemptive response to it. Harold Bloom, *Ruin the Sacred Truths: Poetry and Belief from the Bible to the Present* (Cambridge: Harvard University Press, 1989), 125–26.

6. Elsewhere, Jack Baker and I offer a Berry-ian critique of Yi-Fu Tuan's cosmopolitanism, which has many parallels to Florida's notion of creativity. Baker and Bilbro, *Wendell Berry and Higher Education,* 147–52.

7. In fairness to Florida, his 2017 book seems to mark a shift in his thinking as he acknowledges that the cities built around the Creative Class continue to struggle with segregation and inequality. He doesn't fundamentally revise his understanding of creativity, however. Richard Florida, *The New Urban Crisis: How Our Cities Are Increasing Inequality, Deepening Segregation, and Failing the Middle Class—and What We Can Do about It* (New York: Basic Books, 2017).

8. Richard Florida, *The Rise of the Creative Class—Revisited,* 2nd ed. (New York: Basic Books, 2012), 8–9; Richard Florida, *Who's Your City? How the Creative Economy Is Making Where to Live the Most Important Decision of Your Life* (New York: Basic Books, 2008), 76.

9. Florida, *Who's Your City?* 87.

10. Florida, *The Rise of the Creative Class—Revisited,* 249.

11. Florida's own biases against those who are less mobile come out in his dismissive tone toward people like his own "parents [who] may have been happy, but . . . were rooted." These biases lead him to denigrate those who don't leave their homes as uneducated and unambitious: "Many of the rooted have relatively little education or money and relatively low professional aspirations or personal expectations." Florida, *Who's Your City?* 85–86.

12. Ibid., 89.

13. Jamie Peck, "Struggling with the Creative Class," *International Journal of Urban and Regional Research* 29, no. 4 (2005): 746, doi:10.1111/j.1468-2427.2005.00620.x.

14. Jennings, *The Christian Imagination;* hooks, *Belonging.*

15. Jennings, *The Christian Imagination,* 24–29, 62–64.

16. Florida, *The Rise of the Creative Class—Revisited,* 38.

17. Charles Taylor, "The Dialogical Self," in *The Interpretive Turn: Philosophy, Science, Culture,* ed. David R. Hiley, James F. Bohman, and Richard Shusterman (Ithaca: Cornell University Press, 1992), 304–14.

18. Florida, *The Rise of the Creative Class—Revisited,* xiv.

19. In his essay "Writer and Region," Berry provides an extended reading of *The Adventures of Huckleberry Finn,* arguing that Twain succumbs to the false dichotomy between civilization and freedom that runs through the American character. Such a dichotomy prevents us from imagining a middle ground of healthy community life. Berry, "Writer and Region," in *What Are People For? Essays* (San Francisco: North Point Press, 1990), 71–87.

20. Taylor, *The Ethics of Authenticity,* 40–41; emphasis in original.

21. David Bentley Hart makes this point from a theological perspective, drawing on the Trinity as a model of relational personhood. Hart, *The Beauty of the Infinite,* 170–75.

22. Berry, "Pray without Ceasing," 62.

23. Taylor, *The Ethics of Authenticity,* 53.

24. Berry, "Poetry and Marriage," 100.

25. John 12:24–25; Berry, *Unsettling of America,* 193.

26. Matthew B. Crawford, *Shop Class as Soulcraft: An Inquiry into the Value of Work* (New York: Penguin Books, 2009), 51.

27. Crawford, *The World beyond Your Head,* 129.

28. Berry, "Poetry and Marriage," 97.

29. Ibid.

30. Ibid., 98.

31. Berry, "Work of Local Culture," 153.

32. Berry, *Life Is a Miracle,* 139; emphasis in original.

33. Ibid., 72.

34. Goodrich also links Berry's revision process with resurrection and renewal, but her focus on Berry as an autobiographical writer leads to a narrow critical frame that tends to warp her readings. Janet Goodrich, *The Unforeseen Self in the Works of Wendell Berry* (Columbia: University of Missouri Press, 2001), 50.

35. Berry, *Life Is a Miracle,* 83–84; emphasis in original.

36. Berry's next novel underwent a more minor revision: *The Memory of Old Jack* was published in 1974, and an updated edition came out in 1999. Berry also revises his essays and poems, although his revisions in these genres are not as drastic and have received less attention than have his revisions to his fiction. For earlier considerations of Berry's revisions to his novels and stories, see Goodrich, *The Unforeseen Self in the Works of Wendell Berry,* 16–21, 42–52; Matthew R. Horton, "'Remembering' the Wayward: Wendell Berry's 'The Wild Birds,' the Possibilities of Membership, and the Short-Story Cycle Genre," *South Atlantic Review* 69, no. 2 (2004): 42–43; Bilbro, "A Form for Living"; Oehlschlaeger, *Achievement of Wendell Berry,* 292–93; Ethan Mannon, "The Gift of Good Death: Revising *Nathan Coulter,*" in *Telling the Stories Right: Wendell Berry's Imagination of Port William,* ed. Jack R. Baker and Jeffrey Bilbro (Eugene, Ore.: Front Porch Republic Books,

2018), 89–103. I made a line-by-line comparison between the editions of *A Place on Earth*, and I am indebted to the meticulous work of my research assistants Katlyne Heath and Kerry Wade for comprehensive comparisons between the editions of *Nathan Coulter* and *The Memory of Old Jack*. Katlyne Heath also wrote an excellent honors thesis on *Nathan Coulter*, from which I learned much, titled "'From Revision to Revision': The Sticker's Role in Imagining Port William."

37. Berry, *Three Short Novels: Nathan Coulter, Remembering, A World Lost* (Washington, D.C.: Counterpoint, 2002), 7.

38. Ibid., 7–8.

39. Oehlschlaeger, *Achievement of Wendell Berry*, 2011, 159; Berry, *Three Short Novels*, 17–18.

40. Berry, "The Brothers," 6.

41. Berry, *Nathan Coulter* (Boston: Houghton Mifflin, 1960), 29; Berry, *Three Short Novels*, 19.

42. Though the novel never specifies the boys' ages, Danny Branch is born the year after their mother dies. According to the Port William family tree printed with Berry's later novels, Danny is born in 1932 and Tom and Nathan are born in 1922 and 1924, respectively. Berry, *Three Short Novels*, 35. Elsewhere, however, Burley says the boys were only seven and five when their mother dies. Berry, "Stand by Me," in *A Place in Time: Twenty Stories of the Port William Membership* (Berkeley, Calif.: Counterpoint, 2012), 99. Hannah Coulter dates Dave's death, which marks the end of the revised novel, to 1940. Berry, *Hannah Coulter*, 3.

43. Berry, "The Brothers," 9–10. Nathan's father in this version of the story is named Ralph, but he is clearly an earlier rendering of the same character.

44. Oehlschlaeger is right, then, to read Jarrat's grief sympathetically: "We might read this as a refusal of comfort on his part, but I believe a more charitable reading would stress the failure of the available religious language—with its prettified images of heaven—to reach into Jarrat's soul." Oehlschlaeger, *Achievement of Wendell Berry*, 159.

45. Berry, *Nathan Coulter*, 100.

46. Berry, *Three Short Novels*, 66.

47. Berry, *Nathan Coulter*, 101.

48. See Andrew Harvey's analysis for a fuller treatment of why Berry's vision is not ultimately stoic in "Curriculum and Culture according to Wendell Berry," 155–57.

49. Berry, *Three Short Novels*, 66–67.

50. Ibid., 117.

51. Berry, *Hannah Coulter*, 4.

52. For Hannah Coulter's meditation on what it means to "tell the stories right" see ibid., 113.

53. Berry, *A Place on Earth: A Novel* (San Francisco: North Point Press, 1983), preface.

54. The reading that follows is partially drawn from my essay "A Form for Living."

55. Berry, *A Place on Earth* (1983), preface.

56. Berry, *A Place on Earth: A Novel* (New York: Avon Books, 1969). Gideon Crop, 177, 197; Burly Coulter, 367–68, 465–68, 471–72, 479–80, 482–87; Ernest Finley, 46, 48–52, 252–59, 307–8, 418. I am citing the Avon 1969 printing only because it is much cheaper and more readily available than the 1967 Harcourt, Brace, and World edition. As far as I can tell, these texts are exactly the same, although the pagination is different. Two

excerpts from the novel were published in 1966, and both were condensed for the 1967 edition. Berry, "A Day in the History of Old Jack's Place," contains a portion of Jack's autobiography that was cut from the novel but forms the germ of *The Memory of Old Jack,* so the changes between these two stories and the novel exhibit the same trajectory as the changes between the novel's first two editions. Berry, "From *A Place on Earth,*" *Mad River Review* 2, no. 1 (1966): 71–76; Berry, "A Day in the History of Old Jack's Place," *Texas Quarterly* 9, no. 4 (1966): 107–27.

57. Berry, *A Place on Earth* (1969), 137–65.

58. Ibid., 369–71, 378–81, 391–94, 403–6, 472–74, 478–83, 487, 498.

59. Berry, *A Place on Earth* (2001), 9.

60. Berry, "Style and Grace," in *What Are People For? Essays* (San Francisco: North Point Press, 1990), 66.

61. Berry, *A Place on Earth* (2001), 9.

62. Berry, *A Place on Earth* (1969), 177.

63. Ibid., 370, 487, 498.

64. Berry, *A Place on Earth* (2001), 321.

65. For a complementary reading of *A Place on Earth,* one that also emphasizes the novel's redemptive trajectory, see John E. McEntyre, "Practicing Resurrection: Community and Continuity in Wendell Berry's *A Place on Earth,*" *Theology Today* 52, no. 3 (1995): 374–81.

66. Berry, "Poetry and Marriage," 97.

7. Convocation

1. Berry, *New Collected Poems,* 279. Copyright 2012; reprinted by permission of Counterpoint.

2. Wendell Berry, "The Wild Birds," in *That Distant Land: The Collected Stories* (Washington, D.C.: Shoemaker & Hoard, 2004), 356.

3. "Be Who You Wanna Be," *Disney Junior Pirate and Princess Summer,* 2015, https://www.youtube.com/watch?v=x6kN9BaCBFs. This is apparently a riff on a quotation attributed to Abraham Lincoln; see Cavanaugh, *Field Hospital,* 74.

4. Luke Epplin, "You Can Do *Anything:* Must Every Kids' Movie Reinforce the Cult of Self-Esteem?" *Atlantic,* August 13, 2013, https://www.theatlantic.com/entertainment/archive/2013/08/you-can-do-em-anything-em-must-every-kids-movie-reinforce-the-cult-of-self-esteem/278596/.

5. Christopher Lasch, "Conservatism against Itself," *First Things,* April 1990, https://www.firstthings.com/article/1990/04/conservatism-against-itself. MacIntyre makes a similar point: "Only in fantasy do we live what story we please. . . . We enter upon a stage which we did not design and find ourselves part of an action that was not of our making." MacIntyre, *After Virtue,* 213. See also Wilfred McClay, who summarizes our culture's "appetite for fables of personal liberation" and concludes: "Yet autonomy, like the 'self' that purports to exercise it, turns out to be an elusive and unreliable god, which never delivers what it promises. Even the most energetically 'unencumbered self' is always already a 'person' enmeshed in social, intellectual, and institutional frameworks that are not neutral, but instead structure and enable the ideal of autonomy." Wilfred McClay, "Introduction: From Self to Person—Some Preliminary Thoughts," in *Figures in the*

Carpet: Finding the Human Person in the American Past, ed. Wilfred M. McClay (Grand Rapids: Eerdmans, 2007), 7.

6. Several Pixar films, perhaps most notably *Finding Dory,* are proof that other animated movies find better ways to narrate identity development. Andrew Stanton, dir., *Finding Dory* (Walt Disney Studios, 2016). For a reading of *Moana* that argues it avoids the "generic 'follow your heart' children's movie [plot] in which the spunky princess heroine defies unreasonable authorities to achieve her dream," see Geoffrey Reiter, "'We Were Voyagers!' Disney's *Moana* Revels in the Quickening Power of Tradition," *Christ and Pop Culture,* May 9, 2017, https://christandpopculture.com/disney-moana-revels-quickening -power-tradition/.

7. Cavanaugh, *Field Hospital,* 74–75.

8. Ibid., 93.

9. Taylor, "The Dialogical Self," 314, 312. This basic insight that our deepest desires and our understanding of the world are formed through conversation with others forms the basis of both René Girard's theory of mimetic desire and Hans-Georg Gadamer's hermeneutics; René Girard, *Deceit, Desire, and the Novel: Self and Other in Literary Structure* (Baltimore: Johns Hopkins University Press, 1976); Gadamer, *Truth and Method.*

10. Berry, *Unsettling of America,* 111.

11. Berry makes a related point regarding his Christian tradition: "There are an enormous number of people—and I am one of them—whose native religion, for better or worse, is Christianity. We were born to it; we began to learn about it before we became conscious; it is, whatever we think of it, an intimate belonging of our being; it informs our consciousness, our language, and our dreams. We can turn away from it or against it, but that will only bind us tightly to a reduced version of it. A better possibility is that this, our native religion, should survive and renew itself so that it may become as largely and truly instructive as we need it to be." Berry, "Christianity and the Survival of Creation," in *Sex, Economy, Freedom & Community: Eight Essays* (New York: Pantheon, 1993), 95–96.

12. Cited in Rodney Clapp, ed., *The Consuming Passion: Christianity and the Consumer Culture* (Downers Grove, Ill.: InterVarsity Press, 1997), 185.

13. Berry, *New Collected Poems,* 360–62. Copyright 2012; reprinted by permission of Counterpoint. Berry refers to the "convocation of ghosts" that inhabit Andy Catlett's mind in his story "The Order of Loving Care," in *The Art of Loading Brush: New Agrarian Writings* (Berkeley, Calif.: Counterpoint, 2017), 188.

14. Berry, "Health Is Membership," 89.

15. See Romans 12 and 1 Corinthians 12–13. Travis Kroeker provides an excellent summary of how Berry inherits Paul's understanding of love and membership. Kroeker, "Sexuality and the Sacramental Imagination," 131–32. For more on the Christian roots of Berry's notion of membership, see D. Brent Laytham, "'The Membership Includes the Dead': Wendell Berry's Port William Membership as *Communio Sanctorum,*" in *Wendell Berry and Religion: Heaven's Earthly Life,* ed. Joel James Shuman and L. Roger Owens (Lexington: University Press of Kentucky, 2009), 173–89; Thomas W. Stanford III, "Membership and Its Privileges: The Vision of Family and Community in the Fiction of Wendell Berry," *Logos* 14, no. 2 (2011): 118–30; Sutterfield, *Wendell Berry and the Given Life,* 89–100. For an incisive cultural reading of Paul's metaphor that overlaps significantly with Berry's understanding, see C. S. Lewis, "Membership," in *The Weight of Glory and Other Addresses* (New York: Macmillan, 1949), 30–42.

16. Berry, *Conversations with Wendell Berry,* 23. In this interview Berry contrasts his reading of Saint Paul's inclusive *we* with Christian institutions, but elsewhere he suggests that Saint Paul himself imagined membership in a too-narrow sense and that Burley was "improving on St. Paul" by extending the metaphor of membership beyond the church. Ibid., 206–7.

17. Colossians 1:18.

18. Berry, *This Day,* 329.

19. Berry, *A Small Porch,* 104.

20. Berry, *Life Is a Miracle,* 25; emphasis in original.

21. Donnelly, "Biblical Convocation in Wendell Berry's *Remembering.*" See also Stephen Barnes's essay tracing further literary convocations in *Remembering,* "Pagan Mythology in Wendell Berry's *Remembering,*" *Explicator* 73, no. 4 (2015): 312–15.

22. Berry, *Remembering,* 19.

23. Berry, "The Responsibility of the Poet," 89. Berry's articulation of poetic tradition in this essay, and elsewhere, parallels T. S. Eliot's argument in "Tradition and the Individual Talent," in *Selected Prose of T. S. Eliot,* ed. Frank Kermode (New York: Harcourt Brace Jovanovich, 1975), 37–44.

24. Jack Baker and I briefly address Berry's critique of racism through literary convocation in *Wendell Berry and Higher Education,* 102–4. For Berry's further writings on racism, see Berry, *Hidden Wound;* Berry, "Think Little"; Berry, "The Regional Motive," in *A Continuous Harmony: Essays Cultural and Agricultural* (New York: Harcourt Brace Jovanovich, 1972), 63–70.

25. Jennings, *The Christian Imagination.*

26. Wiebe, *The Place of Imagination,* 47.

27. hooks, *Belonging.* Berry's understanding of membership may be informed also by the work of Ernest Gaines, who was a fellow student of Berry's at Stanford. Berry has pointed out how Gaines's novels beautifully imagine communal identity. See Wendell Berry, "American Imagination and the Civil War," in *Imagination in Place: Essays* (Berkeley, Calif.: Counterpoint, 2010), 36–38. See also hooks, *Belonging,* 186–87.

28. Wendell Berry, *Andy Catlett: Early Travels* (Emeryville, Calif.: Shoemaker & Hoard, 2006), 77, cf. 19–28, 72–77. See also the short story "Drouth," in which Andy reflects further on Dick Watson. Berry, "Drouth," in *A Place in Time: Twenty Stories of the Port William Membership* (Berkeley, Calif.: Counterpoint, 2012), 88–97.

29. On Berry's fictional attention to the marginalized, see Michael R. Stevens, "Hiding in the Hedgrows: Wendell Berry's Treatment of Marginal Characters in His Fiction," in *Telling the Stories Right: Wendell Berry's Imagination of Port William,* ed. Jack R. Baker and Jeffrey Bilbro (Eugene, Ore.: Front Porch Republic Books, 2018), 121–38.

30. Berry, *Jayber Crow,* 205.

31. Berry, *Unsettling of America,* 111.

32. Milton, *Paradise Lost,* in *The Riverside Milton,* 4.51–57.

33. Berry, *Andy Catlett,* 105.

34. Ibid., 119–20. Fritz Oehlschlaeger offers a similar reading of this passage in *Achievement of Wendell Berry,* 152. Elsewhere, Oehschlaeger describes Berry's gratitude for our dependence on others in Kierkegaardian terms: "By something like a Kierkegaardian movement of the infinite, we change within, coming to rest in the debt of love and willing to remain so. We still gladly do what we feel required to do, knowing full well we can never discharge our debts but only 'strive to accomplish the duty of being in love's

debt to each other,' as Kierkegaard puts it." Oehschlaeger, "Living Faithfully in the Debt of Love in Wendell Berry's Port William," 105. For more on Berry's contrast between monetary debt and the unpayable debt of membership, see Horton, "'Remembering' the Wayward."

35. Berry, "A Desirable Woman," in *A Place in Time: Twenty Stories of the Port William Membership* (Berkeley, Calif.: Counterpoint, 2012), 62.

36. "Down in the Valley Where the Green Grass Grows," "Burley Coulter's Fortunate Fall," "Stand by Me," and "The Requirement," all collected in *A Place in Time.*

37. Berry, "The Wild Birds," 351.

38. Ibid., 357.

39. Berry, "Stand by Me," 104; Berry, "The Wild Birds," 345.

40. Berry, "Burley Coulter's Fortunate Fall," in *A Place in Time: Twenty Stories of the Port William Membership* (Berkeley, Calif.: Counterpoint, 2012), 36.

41. Berry, "A Desirable Woman," 50.

42. Ibid., 52.

43. Ibid., 50.

44. Berry, *Jayber Crow*, 216.

45. Horton, "'Remembering' the Wayward," 28–29.

46. Ibid., 50.

47. Berry, "Burley Coulter's Fortunate Fall," 29.

48. Ibid., 30.

49. Ibid., 35.

50. Ibid., 35–36.

51. Oehschlaeger, "Living Faithfully in the Debt of Love in Wendell Berry's Port William," 115–16.

52. Berry, "Burley Coulter's Fortunate Fall," 36, 34.

53. Berry, "Stand by Me," 98.

54. Berry, "The Wild Birds," 357.

55. Berry, *Three Short Novels*, 6.

56. Berry, "Fidelity," 424.

57. Berry, "Stand by Me," 99.

58. For more on Berry's rich understanding of vocation, see Kiara Jorgenson, "Called to Affection: Exploring the Ecology of Christian Vocation in Port William," in *Telling the Stories Right: Wendell Berry's Imagination of Port William*, ed. Jack R. Baker and Jeffrey Bilbro (Eugene, Ore.: Front Porch Republic Books, 2018), 37–49.

59. Berry, "Stand by Me," 104.

60. Berry, "The Wild Birds," 350.

61. Ibid., 356.

62. Berry, "The Uses of Adversity," 169.

63. Berry, "Stand by Me," 100–101.

64. Ibid., 107.

65. Ibid., 105.

66. Ibid., 107. A similar conflict occurs between Hannah Steadman (later Hannah Coulter) and her stepmother, but Hannah's grandmother protects her from the brunt of this conflict and gives her space to develop. Berry, *Hannah Coulter*, 7–15.

67. Though I don't have space to explore it in depth here, Burley's disagreement with Wheeler in "The Wild Birds" is a good example of how convocation entails correcting

those voices that are wrong or at least incomplete. As Berry comments in an interview, he thinks both Wheeler and Burley are right in this story, and that they need each other: "I think that Wheeler's argument is valid: you have to try for order. Burley's argument is valid: as far as human order is concerned, it's a failure." Berry, *Conversations with Wendell Berry,* 45. As Horton concludes about this story, "What results from their conflict is an increased awareness of obligation to each other." Horton, "'Remembering' the Wayward," 44. For one analysis of how this story fits into Burley's growth, see Baker and Bilbro, *Wendell Berry and Higher Education,* 140–47.

68. Berry, *Jayber Crow,* 214–15. Jayber learns from Athey's example to practice this defense of the marginalized. Later, during the Vietnam War, Troy makes a comment that he wishes all the war protestors and communists would kill each other, and Jayber "thought of Athey's reply" before saying himself, "Love your enemies, bless them that curse you, do good to them that hate you." Jayber admits that this exchange "would have been a great moment in the history of Christianity, except that I did not love Troy." Ibid., 287.

69. Berry, "Stand by Me," 109–10.

70. Burley continues his care for Jarrat even when Jarrat moves to a rest home. Though Jarrat can no longer speak, Burley regularly visits to narrate the ongoing conversation of their place for his brother. Berry, *Remembering,* 96–97.

71. Berry, "Stand by Me," 110.

72. Ibid., 111–12.

73. Berry, "Pray without Ceasing," 62.

74. Berry, "Fidelity" (2004), 425.

75. Ibid., 372, 375; Revelation 1:15.

76. Berry, "Fidelity" (2004), 376.

77. Ibid., 387.

78. Ibid., 397–99.

79. Berry, *Hannah Coulter,* 109–10.

80. Berry, "Fidelity" (2004), 383.

81. Ibid., 386.

82. Berry, *This Day,* 329.

83. Berry, "Fidelity" (2004), 392.

84. Berry, "Fidelity," *Orion,* Summer 1992, 106; Berry, "Fidelity," in *Fidelity: Five Stories* (New York: Pantheon, 1993), 136.

85. Berry, "Watch with Me," 111; Berry, "A Friend of Mine," in *That Distant Land: The Collected Stories* (Washington, D.C.: Shoemaker & Hoard, 2004), 331; Berry, "The Wild Birds," 347. It comes up in at least two other stories as well: Berry, *Jayber Crow,* 115; Berry, "The Dark Country," in *A Place in Time: Twenty Stories of the Port William Membership* (Berkeley, Calif.: Counterpoint, 2012), 126.

86. Berry, "Burley Coulter's Fortunate Fall," 34. For more on the eschatological visions that several of Berry's characters have of Port William redeemed and made whole, see Ingrid Pierce, "Dreaming in Port William: Foreknowledge, Consolation, and Medieval Dream Vision Literature," in *Telling the Stories Right: Wendell Berry's Imagination of Port William,* ed. Jack R. Baker and Jeffrey Bilbro (Eugene, Ore.: Front Porch Republic Books, 2018), 21–36.

87. Berry, "Fidelity" (2004), 413–14.

88. Ibid., 418.

89. Ibid., 412.

90. Ibid., 420.

91. Ibid., 424–25.

92. Ibid., 426.

93. Berry, *New Collected Poems,* 130.

94. For more on how Berry defines a "good death" and how palliative care might facilitate such deaths, see Mannon, "The Gift of Good Death." For more on how Berry's insights might apply to medical care, see Joel James Shuman and Brian Volck, *Reclaiming the Body: Christians and the Faithful Use of Modern Medicine* (Grand Rapids: Brazos Press, 2006).

95. Berry, "The Wild Birds," 356.

96. Berry, *This Day,* 241.

Epilogue

1. John 12:24.

2. Berry, "The Branch Way of Doing," in *The Art of Loading Brush: New Agrarian Writings* (Berkeley, Calif.: Counterpoint, 2017), 233–34.

3. Milton, *Paradise Lost,* in *The Riverside Milton,* 12.571.

Bibliography

Angyal, Andrew J. *Wendell Berry*. New York: Twayne Publishers, 1995.

Arnett, Peter. "Major Describes Move." *New York Times,* March 15, 1968.

Auden, W. H. *Collected Poems*. 1976. Reprint. New York: Vintage, 1991.

Auerbach, Erich. *Mimesis: The Representation of Reality in Western Literature*. Translated by Willard R. Trask. 1953. Reprint. Princeton: Princeton University Press, 2013.

Augustine. *Confessions* (ca. 398). Translated by Henry Chadwick. Oxford: Oxford University Press, 1998.

———. *The Trinity* (ca. 417). Translated by Stephen McKenna. Washington, D.C.: Catholic University of America Press, 2002.

Baker, Jack R., and Jeffrey Bilbro. "Introduction." In *Telling the Stories Right: Wendell Berry's Imagination of Port William,* edited by Jack R. Baker and Jeffrey Bilbro, xiii–xxii. Eugene, Ore.: Front Porch Republic Books, 2018.

———. *Wendell Berry and Higher Education: Cultivating Virtues of Place*. Lexington: University Press of Kentucky, 2017.

Balko, Radley. "And Now: The Criminalization of Parenthood." *Washington Post,* July 14, 2014. https://www.washingtonpost.com/news/the-watch/wp/2014/07/14/and-now-the-criminalization-of-parenthood/.

Ball, Terence. *Reappraising Political Theory: Revisionist Studies in the History of Political Thought*. Oxford: Oxford University Press, 1995.

Balthasar, Hans Urs von. *Epilogue*. Translated by Edward T. Oakes. San Francisco: Ignatius Press, 2004.

———. *Love Alone Is Credible*. Translated by D. C. Schindler. San Francisco: Ignatius Press, 2005.

Barnes, Stephen D. "Pagan Mythology in Wendell Berry's *Remembering*." *Explicator* 73, no. 4 (2015): 312–15. doi:10.1080/00144940.2015.1090385.

Barta-Smith, Nancy A. "On the Edge between Hope and Despair: *Lear* as Guide and Consolation in the Life and Work of Wendell Berry." In *Inhabited by Stories: Critical Essays on Tales Retold,* edited by Nancy A. Barta-Smith and Danette DiMarco, 337–66. Newcastle upon Tyne: Cambridge Scholars Publishing, 2012.

Bercovici, Jeff. "Peter Thiel Is Very, Very Interested in Young People's Blood." *Inc.,* August 1, 2016. www.inc.com/jeff-bercovici/peter-thiel-young-blood.html.

Berger, Peter L., ed. *The Desecularization of the World: Resurgent Religion and World Politics*. Grand Rapids: Eerdmans, 1999.

Berry, Wendell. "Acceptance Speech." *Chesterton Review* 24, no. 1/2 (1998): 238–41.

————. "Against the Nihil of the Age." In *Imagination in Place,* 115–40. Berkeley, Calif.: Counterpoint, 2010.

————. "An Agricultural Journey in Peru." In *The Gift of Good Land: Further Essays, Cultural and Agricultural,* 3–46. Berkeley, Calif.: Counterpoint, 1981.

————. "Agriculture from the Roots Up." In *The Way of Ignorance: And Other Essays,* 105–12. Berkeley, Calif.: Counterpoint, 2005.

————. "American Imagination and the Civil War." In *Imagination in Place: Essays,* 17–38. Berkeley, Calif.: Counterpoint, 2010.

————. *Andy Catlett: Early Travels.* Emeryville, Calif.: Shoemaker & Hoard, 2006.

————. "An Argument for Diversity." In *What Are People For? Essays,* 109–22. San Francisco: North Point Press, 1990.

————. "Bellarmine Commencement Address," 2007. http://christianstudycenter.org/wp-content/uploads/2009/10/WendellBerry-BellarmineCommencement.pdf.

————. "The Branch Way of Doing." In *The Art of Loading Brush: New Agrarian Writings,* 227–35. Berkeley, Calif.: Counterpoint, 2017.

————. "The Brothers." *Carolina Quarterly* 8, no. 3 (1956): 5–11.

————. "The Burden of the Gospels." In *The Way of Ignorance: And Other Essays,* 127–37. Berkeley, Calif.: Counterpoint, 2005.

————. "Burley Coulter's Fortunate Fall." In *A Place in Time: Twenty Stories of the Port William Membership,* 27–36. Berkeley, Calif.: Counterpoint, 2012.

————. "Caught in the Middle." In *Our Only World: Ten Essays,* 73–96. Berkeley, Calif.: Counterpoint, 2015.

————. "Christianity and the Survival of Creation." In *Sex, Economy, Freedom & Community: Eight Essays,* 93–116. New York: Pantheon, 1993.

————. "A Citizen's Response." In *Citizenship Papers,* 1–16. Washington, D.C.: Shoemaker & Hoard, 2003.

————. "Conservation and Local Economy." In *Sex, Economy, Freedom & Community: Eight Essays,* 3–18. New York: Pantheon, 1993.

————. "The Conservation of Nature and the Preservation of Humanity." In *Another Turn of the Crank: Essays,* 64–85. Washington, D.C.: Counterpoint, 1995.

————. "Conserving Communities." In *Another Turn of the Crank: Essays,* 8–24. Washington, D.C.: Counterpoint, 1995.

————. *Conversations with Wendell Berry.* Edited by Morris Allen Grubbs. Jackson: University Press of Mississippi, 2007.

————. "Damage." In *What Are People For? Essays,* 5–8. San Francisco: North Point Press, 1990.

————. "The Dark Country." In *A Place in Time: Twenty Stories of the Port William Membership,* 116–32. Berkeley, Calif.: Counterpoint, 2012.

————. "A Day in the History of Old Jack's Place." *Texas Quarterly* 9, no. 4 (1966): 107–27.

————. "A Defense of the Family Farm." In *Home Economics: Fourteen Essays,* 162–78. San Francisco: North Point Press, 1987.

————. "A Desirable Woman." In *A Place in Time: Twenty Stories of the Port William Membership,* 48–68. Berkeley, Calif.: Counterpoint, 2012.

————. "Discipline and Hope." In *A Continuous Harmony: Essays Cultural and Agricultural,* 86–168. New York: Harcourt Brace Jovanovich, 1972.

————. "Does Community Have a Value?" In *Home Economics: Fourteen Essays,* 179–92. San Francisco: North Point Press, 1987.

———. "Drouth." In *A Place in Time: Twenty Stories of the Port William Membership,* 88–97. Berkeley, Calif.: Counterpoint, 2012.

———. "Energy and Agriculture." In *The Gift of Good Land: Further Essays, Cultural and Agricultural,* 125–33. Berkeley: Counterpoint, 1981.

———. "Faustian Economics." In *What Matters? Economics for a Renewed Commonwealth,* 41–53. Washington, D.C.: Counterpoint, 2010.

———. "Fidelity." *Orion,* Summer 1992, 97–123.

———. "Fidelity." In *Fidelity: Five Stories,* 107–90. New York: Pantheon, 1993.

———. "Fidelity." In *That Distant Land: The Collected Stories,* 372–427. Washington, D.C.: Shoemaker & Hoard, 2004.

———. "A Forest Conversation." In *Our Only World: Ten Essays,* 21–52. Berkeley, Calif.: Counterpoint, 2015.

———. "Foreword." In *The Gift of Good Land: Further Essays Cultural and Agricultural,* ix–xviii. Berkeley, Calif.: Counterpoint, 1981.

———. "Foreword." In *Great Possessions: An Amish Farmer's Journal,* by David Kline. 1990. Reprint. Wooster, Ohio: Wooster Book Co., 2001.

———. "Foreword." In *The Holy Earth* (1915), by Liberty Hyde Bailey, vii–xvii, edited by John Linstrom. Berkeley, Calif.: Counterpoint, 2015.

———. "Foreword." In *Kentucky's Natural Heritage: An Illustrated Guide to Biodiversity,* edited by Greg Abernathy, Deborah White, Ellis L. Laudermilk, and Marc Evans, ix–xvii. Lexington: University Press of Kentucky, 2010.

———. "Foreword." In *The Vandana Shiva Reader,* by Vandana Shiva, vii–viii. Lexington: University Press of Kentucky, 2014.

———. "Foreword." In *Wendell Berry and Higher Education: Cultivating Virtues of Place,* edited by Jack R. Baker and Jeffrey Bilbro. Lexington: University Press of Kentucky, 2017.

———. "For the 50-Year Farm Bill." In *Our Only World: Ten Essays,* 159–65. Berkeley, Calif.: Counterpoint, 2015.

———. "A Friend of Mine." In *That Distant Land: The Collected Stories,* 319–36. Washington, D.C.: Shoemaker & Hoard, 2004.

———. "From *A Place on Earth.*" *Mad River Review* 2, no. 1 (1966): 71–76.

———. "The Gift of Good Land." In *The Gift of Good Land: Further Essays, Cultural and Agricultural,* 267–81. Berkeley, Calif.: Counterpoint, 1981.

———. "God, Science, and Imagination." In *Imagination in Place: Essays,* 179–91. Berkeley, Calif.: Counterpoint, 2010.

———. "Going to Work." In *Citizenship Papers: Essays,* 33–42. Washington, D.C.: Shoemaker & Hoard, 2003.

———. *Hannah Coulter.* 2004. Reprint. Berkeley: Counterpoint, 2005.

———. *Harlan Hubbard: Life and Work.* Lexington: University Press of Kentucky, 1990.

———. "Healing." In *What Are People For? Essays,* 9–13. San Francisco: North Point Press, 1990.

———. "Health Is Membership." In *Another Turn of the Crank: Essays,* 86–109. Washington, D.C.: Counterpoint, 1995.

———. *The Hidden Wound.* 1970; repr., Berkeley, Calif.: Counterpoint, 2010.

———. "Hunting for Reasons to Hope: A Conversation with Wendell Berry." *Christianity and Literature* 56, no. 2 (2007): 215–34.

———. "Imagination in Place." In *Imagination in Place,* 1–16. Berkeley, Calif.: Counterpoint, 2010.

———. "In Defense of Literacy." In *A Continuous Harmony: Essays Cultural and Agricultural,* 169–73. New York: Harcourt Brace Jovanovich, 1972.

———. "Introduction." In *The Art of Loading Brush: New Agrarian Writings,* 5–18. Berkeley, Calif.: Counterpoint, 2017.

———. "Irish Journal." In *Home Economics: Fourteen Essays,* 21–48. San Francisco: North Point Press, 1987.

———. "It All Turns on Affection." In *It All Turns on Affection: The Jefferson Lecture and Other Essays,* 9–40. Berkeley, Calif.: Counterpoint, 2012.

———. *It All Turns on Affection: The Jefferson Lecture and Other Essays.* Berkeley, Calif.: Counterpoint, 2012.

———. *Jayber Crow: The Life Story of Jayber Crow, Barber, of the Port William Membership, as Written by Himself.* Washington, D.C.: Counterpoint, 2000.

———. *Leavings: Poems.* Berkeley, Calif.: Counterpoint, 2010.

———. "Leaving the Future Behind: A Letter to a Scientific Friend." In *The Art of Loading Brush: New Agrarian Writings,* 57–102. Berkeley, Calif.: Counterpoint, 2017.

———. "Letter to Wes Jackson." In *What Are People For? Essays,* 3–5. San Francisco: North Point Press, 1990.

———. *Life Is a Miracle: An Essay against Modern Superstition.* Washington, D.C.: Counterpoint, 2000.

———. "Local Economies to Save the Land and the People." In *Our Only World: Ten Essays,* 53–67. Berkeley, Calif.: Counterpoint, 2015.

———. "Local Knowledge in the Age of Information." In *The Way of Ignorance: And Other Essays,* 113–25. Berkeley, Calif.: Counterpoint, 2005.

———. "The Long-Legged House." In *The Long-Legged House,* 108–69. Washington, D.C.: Shoemaker & Hoard, 2004.

———. "The Loss of the Future." In *The Long-Legged House,* 45–63. Washington, D.C.: Shoemaker & Hoard, 2004.

———. *The Mad Farmer Poems.* Berkeley, Calif.: Counterpoint, 2008.

———. "Major in Homecoming: For Commencement, Northern Kentucky University." In *What Matters? Economics for a Renewed Commonwealth,* 31–36. Berkeley, Calif.: Counterpoint, 2010.

———. "The Making of a Marginal Farm." In *Recollected Essays: 1965–1980,* 329–40. San Francisco: North Point Press, 1981.

———. "Maury Telleen, 1928–2011." In *It All Turns on Affection: The Jefferson Lecture and Other Essays,* 111–25. Berkeley, Calif.: Counterpoint, 2012.

———. *Nathan Coulter.* Boston: Houghton Mifflin, 1960.

———. "A Native Hill." In *The Long-Legged House,* 170–213. Washington, D.C.: Shoemaker & Hoard, 2004.

———. *New Collected Poems.* Berkeley, Calif.: Counterpoint, 2012.

———. "New Introduction." In *The Soil and Health: A Study of Organic Agriculture,* by Albert Howard, xiii–xxiv. Lexington: University Press of Kentucky, 2006.

———. "Notes: Unspecializing Poetry." In *Standing by Words: Essays,* 80–91. 1983. Reprint. Washington, D.C.: Shoemaker & Hoard, 2005.

———. "Notes from an Absence and a Return." In *A Continuous Harmony: Essays Cultural and Agricultural,* 36–55. New York: Harcourt Brace Jovanovich, 1972.

————. "On Being Asked for 'A Narrative for the Future.'" In *Our Only World: Ten Essays,* 167–76. Berkeley, Calif.: Counterpoint, 2015.

————. "On Receiving One of the Dayton Literary Peace Prizes." In *Our Only World: Ten Essays,* 97–103. Berkeley, Calif.: Counterpoint, 2015.

————. "The Order of Loving Care." In *The Art of Loading Brush: New Agrarian Writings,* 179–216. Berkeley, Calif.: Counterpoint, 2017.

————. "Our Deserted Country." In *Our Only World: Ten Essays,* 105–57. Berkeley, Calif.: Counterpoint, 2015.

————. "Out of Your Car, Off Your Horse: Twenty-seven Propositions about Global Thinking and the Sustainability of Cities." In *Sex, Economy, Freedom & Community: Eight Essays,* 19–26. New York: Pantheon, 1993.

————. "Paragraphs from a Notebook." In *Our Only World: Ten Essays,* 3–14. Berkeley, Calif.: Counterpoint, 2015.

————. "Peaceableness toward Enemies: Some Notes on the Gulf War." In *Sex, Economy, Freedom & Community: Eight Essays,* 69–92. New York: Pantheon, 1993.

————. "People, Land, and Community." In *Standing by Words: Essays,* 64–79. 1983. Reprint. Washington, D.C.: Shoemaker & Hoard, 2005.

————. *A Place on Earth: A Novel.* New York: Harcourt, Brace, and World, 1967.

————. *A Place on Earth: a Novel.* New York: Avon Books, 1969.

————. *A Place on Earth: A Novel.* San Francisco: North Point Press, 1983.

————. *A Place on Earth: A Novel.* Washington, D.C.: Counterpoint, 2001.

————. "The Pleasures of Eating." In *What Are People For? Essays,* 145–52. San Francisco: North Point Press, 1990.

————. "Poetry and Marriage." In *Standing by Words: Essays,* 92–105. 1983. Reprint. Washington, D.C.: Shoemaker & Hoard, 2005.

————. "Poetry and Place." In *Standing by Words: Essays,* 106–213. 1983. Reprint. Washington, D.C.: Shoemaker & Hoard, 2005.

————. *The Poetry of William Carlos Williams of Rutherford.* Berkeley, Calif.: Counterpoint, 2011.

————. "Pray without Ceasing." In *That Distant Land: The Collected Stories.* Washington, D.C.: Shoemaker & Hoard, 2004.

————. "Preface." In *Home Economics: Fourteen Essays,* ix–xi. San Francisco: North Point Press, 1987.

————. "Preface." In *The Way of Ignorance: And Other Essays,* ix–xi. Berkeley, Calif.: Counterpoint, 2005.

————. "Preface: The Joy of Sales Resistance." In *Sex, Economy, Freedom & Community: Eight Essays,* xi–xxii. New York: Pantheon, 1993.

————. "Preserving Wildness." In *Home Economics: Fourteen Essays,* 137–51. San Francisco: North Point Press, 1987.

————. "The Problem of Tobacco." In *Sex, Economy, Freedom & Community: Eight Essays,* 53–68. New York: Pantheon, 1993.

————. "The Purpose of a Coherent Community." In *The Way of Ignorance: And Other Essays,* 69–79. Berkeley, Calif.: Counterpoint, 2005.

————. "Quantity vs. Form." In *The Way of Ignorance: And Other Essays,* 81–89. Berkeley, Calif.: Counterpoint, 2005.

————. "The Regional Motive." In *A Continuous Harmony: Essays Cultural and Agricultural,* 63–70. New York: Harcourt Brace Jovanovich, 1972.

————. *Remembering: A Novel.* Berkeley, Calif.: Counterpoint, 2008.

————. "Renewing Husbandry." In *The Way of Ignorance: And Other Essays,* 91–104. Berkeley, Calif.: Counterpoint, 2005.

————. "The Responsibility of the Poet." In *What Are People For? Essays,* 88–92. San Francisco: North Point Press, 1990.

————. *Sabbaths 2013.* Monterey, Ky.: Larkspur Press, 2014.

————. "Sanitation and the Small Farm." In *The Gift of Good Land: Further Essays, Cultural and Agricultural,* 98–103. Berkeley, Calif.: Counterpoint, 1981.

————. "Seven Amish Farms." In *The Gift of Good Land: Further Essays, Cultural and Agricultural,* 249–63. Berkeley, Calif.: Counterpoint, 1981.

————. "Sex, Economy, Freedom, and Community." In *Sex, Economy, Freedom and Community: Eight Essays,* 117–73. New York: Pantheon Books, 1993.

————. "She's Come for an Abortion. What Do You Say?" *Harper's Magazine,* November 1992, 50–51.

————. "Six Agricultural Fallacies." In *Home Economics: Fourteen Essays,* 123–32. San Francisco: North Point Press, 1987.

————. *A Small Porch: Sabbath Poems 2014 and 2015, Together with "The Presence of Nature in the Natural World: A Long Conversation."* Berkeley, Calif.: Counterpoint, 2016.

————. "Solving for Pattern." In *The Gift of Good Land: Further Essays, Cultural and Agricultural,* 134–47. Berkeley, Calif.: Counterpoint, 1981.

————. "The Specialization of Poetry." In *Standing by Words: Essays,* 3–23. 1983. Reprint. Washington, D.C.: Shoemaker & Hoard, 2005.

————. "Stand by Me." In *A Place in Time: Twenty Stories of the Port William Membership,* 98–112. Berkeley, Calif.: Counterpoint, 2012.

————. "Standing by Words." In *Standing by Words: Essays,* 24–63. 1983. Reprint. Washington, D.C.: Shoemaker & Hoard, 2005.

————. "Style and Grace." In *What Are People For? Essays,* 64–70. San Francisco: North Point Press, 1990.

————. "Think Little." In *A Continuous Harmony: Essays Cultural and Agricultural,* 71–85. New York: Harcourt Brace Jovanovich, 1972.

————. *This Day: Collected and New Sabbath Poems.* Berkeley, Calif.: Counterpoint, 2013.

————. "The Thought of Limits in a Prodigal Age." In *The Art of Loading Brush: New Agrarian Writings,* 19–56. Berkeley, Calif.: Counterpoint, 2017.

————. "Thoughts in the Presence of Fear." In *Citizenship Papers,* 17–22. Washington, D.C.: Shoemaker & Hoard, 2003.

————. *Three Short Novels: Nathan Coulter, Remembering, A World Lost.* Washington, D.C.: Counterpoint, 2002.

————. "Three Ways of Farming in the Southwest." In *The Gift of Good Land: Further Essays, Cultural and Agricultural,* 47–76. Berkeley, Calif.: Counterpoint, 1981.

————. *A Timbered Choir: The Sabbath Poems, 1979–1997.* Washington, D.C.: Counterpoint, 1998.

————. "The Total Economy." In *Citizenship Papers: Essays,* 63–76. Washington, D.C.: Shoemaker & Hoard, 2003.

————. "Tuscany." In *Citizenship Papers,* 175–80. Washington, D.C.: Shoemaker & Hoard, 2003.

————. "Twelve Paragraphs on Biotechnology." In *Citizenship Papers*, 53–56. Washington, D.C.: Shoemaker & Hoard, 2003.

————. "Two Economies." In *Home Economics: Fourteen Essays*, 54–75. San Francisco: North Point Press, 1987.

————. "Two Minds." In *Citizenship Papers*, 85–105. Washington, D.C.: Shoemaker & Hoard, 2003.

————. *The Unforeseen Wilderness: Kentucky's Red River Gorge.* Photographs by Ralph Eugene Meatyard. Revised edition. San Francisco: North Point Press, 1991.

————. *The Unsettling of America: Culture & Agriculture.* 3rd edition. San Francisco: Sierra Club Books, 1996.

————. "The Uses of Adversity." In *Imagination in Place*, 141–78. Berkeley, Calif.: Counterpoint, 2010.

————. "Watch with Me." In *That Distant Land: The Collected Stories*, 77–123. Washington, D.C.: Shoemaker & Hoard, 2004.

————. "The Way of Ignorance." In *The Way of Ignorance: And Other Essays*, 53–67. Berkeley, Calif.: Counterpoint, 2005.

————. "We Have Begun." In *The Way of Ignorance: And Other Essays*, 13–16. Berkeley, Calif.: Counterpoint, 2005.

————. "The Whole Horse." In *Citizenship Papers*, 113–26. Washington, D.C.: Shoemaker & Hoard, 2003.

————. "Why I Am Not Going to Buy a Computer." In *What Are People For? Essays*, 170–77. San Francisco: North Point Press, 1990.

————. "The Wild Birds." In *That Distant Land: The Collected Stories*, 337–64. Washington, D.C.: Shoemaker & Hoard, 2004.

————. "The Work of Local Culture." In *What Are People For? Essays*, 153–69. San Francisco: North Point Press, 1990.

————. "Writer and Region." In *What Are People For? Essays*, 71–87. San Francisco: North Point Press, 1990.

Berry, Wendell, and Gary Snyder. *Distant Neighbors: The Selected Letters of Wendell Berry & Gary Snyder.* Edited by Chad Wriglesworth. Berkeley, Calif.: Counterpoint, 2014.

"Be Who You Wanna Be." *Disney Junior Pirate and Princess Summer*, 2015. https://www.youtube.com/watch?v=x6kN9BaCBFs.

Bible: Authorized King James Version, The. Edited by Robert Carroll and Stephen Prickett. New York: Oxford University Press, 2008.

Bilbro, Jeffrey. "Andy Catlett's Missing Hand: Making Do as Wounded Members." In *Telling the Stories Right: Wendell Berry's Imagination of Port William*, edited by Jack R. Baker and Jeffrey Bilbro, 71–88. Eugene, Ore.: Front Porch Republic Books, 2018.

————. "The Ecology of Memory: Augustine, Eliot, and the Form of Wendell Berry's Fiction." *Christianity & Literature* 65, no. 3 (2016): 327–42.

————. "A Form for Living in the Midst of Loss: Faithful Marriage in the Revisions of Wendell Berry's *A Place on Earth*." *Southern Literary Journal* 42, no. 2 (2010): 89–105.

————. *Loving God's Wildness: The Christian Roots of Ecological Ethics in American Literature.* Tuscaloosa: University of Alabama Press, 2015.

————. "Place Isn't Just Geographical." *Front Porch Republic*, May 2013. www.frontporchrepublic.com/2013/05/place-isnt-just-geographical/.

————. "Review of *This Day: New and Collected Sabbath Poems*." *Christianity and Literature* 65, no. 4 (2016): 524–28.

———. "Sublime Failure: Why We'd Better Start Seeing Our World as Beautiful." *South Atlantic Review* 80, no. 1–2 (2015): 133–58.

———. "A Way of Happening." *Curator,* December 14, 2015. www.curatormagazine .com/jeffrey-bilbro/a-way-of-happening/.

———. "Wendell Berry Opts Out of the 'Culture of Violence.'" *Front Porch Republic,* April 6, 2015. www.frontporchrepublic.com/2015/04/wendell-berry-opts-out-of-the -culture-of-violence/.

Bloom, Harold. *The Anxiety of Influence: A Theory of Poetry.* 2nd edition. New York: Oxford University Press, 1997.

———. *Ruin the Sacred Truths: Poetry and Belief from the Bible to the Present.* Cambridge: Harvard University Press, 1989.

Bonzo, J. Matthew, and Michael R. Stevens. *Wendell Berry and the Cultivation of Life: A Reader's Guide.* Grand Rapids: Brazos Press, 2008.

Brown, George Mackay. *Magnus.* London: Hogarth Press, 1973.

Brueggemann, Walter. *The Prophetic Imagination.* 2nd edition. Minneapolis: Fortress Press, 2001.

———. *Sabbath as Resistance: Saying No to the Culture of Now.* Louisville: Westminster John Knox Press, 2014.

Burleigh, Anne Husted. "Marriage in the Membership." In *The Humane Vision of Wendell Berry,* edited by Mark Mitchell and Nathan Schlueter, 7–18. Wilmington, Del.: ISI Books, 2011.

Caldecott, Stratford. *Beauty in the Word: Rethinking the Foundations of Education.* Tacoma, Wash.: Angelico Press, 2012.

Capon, Robert Farrar. *Food for Thought: Resurrecting the Art of Eating.* New York: Harcourt Brace Jovanovich, 1978.

———. *Parables of Grace.* Grand Rapids: Eerdmans, 1988.

Carr, Nicholas. *The Glass Cage: Automation and Us.* New York: W. W. Norton, 2014.

———. *The Shallows: What the Internet Is Doing to Our Brains.* New York: W. W. Norton, 2011.

Cavanaugh, William T. *Being Consumed: Economics and Christian Desire.* Grand Rapids: Eerdmans, 2008.

———. *Field Hospital: The Church's Engagement with a Wounded World.* Grand Rapids: Eerdmans, 2016.

———. *Theopolitical Imagination.* London: T & T Clark, 2002.

Cayley, David. "Introduction." In *The Rivers North of the Future: The Testament of Ivan Illich as Told to David Cayley,* by Ivan Illich, 1–46. Toronto: House of Anansi Press, 2005.

Certeau, Michel de. *The Practice of Everyday Life.* Translated by Steven Rendall. Berkeley: University of California Press, 1984.

Chesterton, G. K. *Orthodoxy.* 1908. Reprint. San Francisco: Ignatius Press, 1995.

Clapp, Rodney, ed. *The Consuming Passion: Christianity and the Consumer Culture.* Downers Grove, Ill.: InterVarsity Press, 1997.

Cohen, Rich. "They Taught America How to Watch Football." *Atlantic,* October 2012. www.theatlantic.com/magazine/archive/2012/10/they-taught-america-to-watch -football/309083/.

Community Environmental Legal Defense Fund. "Rights of Nature." 2016. http://celdf .org/rights/rights-of-nature/.

Conly, Sarah. *One Child: Do We Have a Right to More?* New York: Oxford University Press, 2015.

Cornell, Daniel. "'The Country of Marriage': Wendell Berry's Personal Political Vision." *Southern Literary Journal* 16, no. 1 (1983): 59–70.

Crawford, Matthew B. *Shop Class as Soulcraft: An Inquiry into the Value of Work.* New York: Penguin Books, 2009.

———. *The World beyond Your Head: On Becoming an Individual in an Age of Distraction.* New York: Farrar, Straus and Giroux, 2015.

Crutzen, Paul J. "Albedo Enhancement by Stratospheric Sulfur Injections: A Contribution to Resolve a Policy Dilemma?" *Climatic Change* 77, no. 3–4 (2006): 211–19. doi:10.1007/s10584-006-9101-y.

"Cryonics Institute." www.cryonics.org/.

Darwin, Charles. *The Autobiography of Charles Darwin and Selected Letters* (1887). Edited by Francis Darwin. New York: Dover, 1958.

———. *The Origin of Species by Means of Natural Selection; or, The Preservation of Favoured Races in the Struggle for Life* (1859). London: John Murray, 1873.

Davis, Ellen F. *Scripture, Culture, and Agriculture: An Agrarian Reading of the Bible.* New York: Cambridge University Press, 2008.

Deneen, Patrick J. "Unsustainable Liberalism." *First Things,* August 2012. https://www .firstthings.com/article/2012/08/unsustainable-liberalism.

———"Wendell Berry and the Alternative Tradition in American Political Thought." In *Wendell Berry: Life and Work,* edited by Jason Peters, 300–315. Lexington: University Press of Kentucky, 2007.

———. *Why Liberalism Failed.* New Haven: Yale University Press, 2018.

Derrida, Jacques. *Given Time: I. Counterfeit Money.* Translated by Peggy Kamuf. Chicago: University of Chicago Press, 1992.

Desmond, Matthew. *Evicted: Poverty and Profit in the American City.* New York: Crown, 2016.

Diamond, Jared. "What's Your Consumption Factor?" *New York Times,* January 2, 2008. www.nytimes.com/2008/01/02/opinion/02diamond.html.

Dillard, Annie. *Pilgrim at Tinker Creek.* 1974. Reprint. New York: Harper Perennial, 2013.

Doctorow, Cory. "Writing in the Age of Distraction." *Locus Magazine,* January 2009. www.locusmag.com/Features/2009/01/cory-doctorow-writing-in-age-of.html.

Donnelly, Phillip. "Biblical Convocation in Wendell Berry's *Remembering.*" *Christianity and Literature* 56, no. 2 (2007): 275–96.

———. *Milton's Scriptural Reasoning: Narrative and Protestant Toleration.* Cambridge: Cambridge University Press, 2009.

Dugatkin, Lee Alan. *Cooperation among Animals: An Evolutionary Perspective.* Oxford: Oxford University Press, 1997.

Edmondson, Todd. *Priest, Prophet, Pilgrim: Types and Distortions of Spiritual Vocation in the Fiction of Wendell Berry and Cormac McCarthy.* Eugene, Ore.: Wipf and Stock, 2014.

Ehrenfeld, John R., and Andrew J. Hoffman. *Flourishing: A Frank Conversation about Sustainability.* Stanford: Stanford University Press, 2013.

Eiseley, Loren C. *The Unexpected Universe.* San Diego: Harcourt Brace Jovanovich, 1969.

Eisnitz, Gail A. *Slaughterhouse: The Shocking Story of Greed, Neglect, and Inhumane Treatment inside the U.S. Meat Industry.* 2nd edition. Amherst, N.Y.: Prometheus Books, 2006.

Eliot, T. S. *Collected Poems, 1909–1962.* 1963. Reprint. New York: Harcourt Brace Jovanovich, 1991.

———. "Introduction." In *The Collected Works of Paul Valéry,* vol. 7, *The Art of Poetry,* by Paul Valéry, vii–xxiv. Translated by Denise Folliot. Princeton: Princeton University Press, 1989.

———. "Tradition and the Individual Talent." In *Selected Prose of T. S. Eliot,* edited by Frank Kermode, 37–44. New York: Harcourt Brace Jovanovich, 1975.

Epplin, Luke. "You Can Do *Anything*: Must Every Kids' Movie Reinforce the Cult of Self-Esteem?" *Atlantic,* August 13, 2013. https://www.theatlantic.com/entertainment /archive/2013/08/you-can-do-em-anything-em-must-every-kids-movie-reinforce -the-cult-of-self-esteem/278596/.

Florida, Richard. *The New Urban Crisis: How Our Cities Are Increasing Inequality, Deepening Segregation, and Failing the Middle Class—and What We Can Do about It.* New York: Basic Books, 2017.

———. *The Rise of the Creative Class—Revisited.* 2nd edition. New York: Basic Books, 2012.

———. *Who's Your City? How the Creative Economy Is Making Where to Live the Most Important Decision of Your Life.* New York: Basic Books, 2008.

Frank, Thomas. "In U.S. Building Industry, Is It Too Easy to Be Green?" *USA Today,* revised June 13, 2013. www.usatoday.com/story/news/nation/2012/10/24/green -building-leed-certification/1650517/.

Franklin, Benjamin. *The Autobiography of Benjamin Franklin.* Boston: Houghton, Mifflin, 1886.

Friedersdorf, Conor. "The New Intolerance of Student Activism." *Atlantic,* November 9, 2015. www.theatlantic.com/politics/archive/2015/11/the-new-intolerance-of-student -activism-at-yale/414810/.

Fujimura, Makoto. *Culture Care: Reconnecting with Beauty for Our Common Life.* Edited by Peter Edman. 2nd edition. New York: International Arts Movement and the Fujimura Institute, 2014.

Funk, Cary, and Brian Kennedy. "The Politics of Climate." *Pew Research Center,* October 4, 2016. http://assets.pewresearch.org/wp-content/uploads/sites/14/2016/10 /14080900/PS_2016.10.04_Politics-of-Climate_FINAL.pdf.

Gadamer, Hans Georg. *Truth and Method.* Translated by Joel Weinsheimer and Donald G. Marshall. 2nd edition. London: Sheed and Ward, 1999.

Gardner, Thomas. *John in the Company of Poets: The Gospel in Literary Imagination.* Waco: Baylor University Press, 2011.

Girard, René. *Deceit, Desire, and the Novel: Self and Other in Literary Structure.* Baltimore: Johns Hopkins University Press, 1976.

Glendon, Mary Ann. *Rights Talk: The Impoverishment of Political Discourse.* 1991. Reprint. New York: Free Press, 1993.

Godfrey-Smith, Peter, and Kim Sterelny. "Biological Information" (revised edition). In *Stanford Encyclopedia of Philosophy Archives,* edited by Edward N. Zalta, Summer 2016. http://plato.stanford.edu/archives/sum2016/entries/information-biological/.

Goodrich, Janet. *The Unforeseen Self in the Works of Wendell Berry.* Columbia: University of Missouri Press, 2001.

Gorski, Philip, David Kyuman Kim, John Torpey, and Jonathan VanAntwerpen, eds. *The Post-Secular in Question: Religion in Contemporary Society*. New York: New York University Press, 2012.

Gottlieb, Roger S., ed. *The Oxford Handbook of Religion and Ecology*. Oxford: Oxford University Press, 2006.

Graham, David A. "'Alternative Facts': The Needless Lies of the Trump Administration." *Atlantic*, January 22, 2017. https://www.theatlantic.com/politics/archive/2017/01/the-pointless-needless-lies-of-the-trump-administration/514061/.

Grant, George. *Collected Works of George Grant*, vol. 3, *1960–1969*. Edited by Arthur Davis and Henry Roper Roper. Toronto: University of Toronto Press, 2005.

Griffiths, Paul J. *Decreation: The Last Things of All Creatures*. Waco: Baylor University Press, 2014.

Grubbs, Morris Allen. "A Practical Education: Wendell Berry the Professor." In *Wendell Berry: Life and Work*, edited by Jason Peters, 137–41. Lexington: University Press of Kentucky, 2007.

Hamilton, Clive. *Earthmasters: The Dawn of the Age of Climate Engineering*. New Haven: Yale University Press, 2013.

Harcourt, Bernard E. *Exposed: Desire and Disobedience in the Digital Age*. Cambridge: Harvard University Press, 2015.

Hart, David Bentley. *The Beauty of the Infinite: The Aesthetics of Christian Truth*. Grand Rapids: Eerdmans, 2004.

Harvey, Andrew J. "Curriculum and Culture according to Wendell Berry." In *Faith, Freedom, and Higher Education: Historical Analysis and Contemporary Reflections*, edited by P. C. Kemeny, 149–64. Eugene, Ore.: Wipf and Stock, 2013.

Hauerwas, Stanley. *Disrupting Time: Sermons, Prayers, and Sundries*. Eugene, Ore: Wipf and Stock, 2004.

Heaney, Seamus. "For Liberation: Brian Friel and the Use of Memory." In *The Achievement of Brian Friel*, edited by Alan J. Peacock, 229–40. Gerrards Cross, U.K.: Colin Smythe, 1993.

Hill, Wesley. "Jigs for Marriage and Celibacy." *Comment*, Winter 2016. www.cardus.ca/comment/article/4987/jigs-for-marriage-and-celibacy/.

Hölldobler, Bert, and Edward O. Wilson. *The Ants*. Cambridge: Harvard University Press, 1990.

hooks, bell. *Belonging: A Culture of Place*. New York: Routledge, 2008.

Horton, Matthew R. "'Remembering' the Wayward: Wendell Berry's 'The Wild Birds,' the Possibilities of Membership, and the Short-Story Cycle Genre." *South Atlantic Review* 69, no. 2 (2004): 25–53.

Howard, Sir Albert, and Yeshwant D. Wad. *The Waste Products of Agriculture: Their Utilization as Humus*. Oxford: Oxford University Press, 1931.

Hudson, David. "Explainer: How Campus Policies Limit Free Speech." *Conversation*, May 31, 2016. http://theconversation.com/explainer-how-campus-policies-limit-free-speech-58974.

"Ice Bucket Challenge." *Wikipedia, the Free Encyclopedia*, August 1, 2016. https://en.wikipedia.org/w/index.php?title=Ice_Bucket_Challenge&oldid=732524020.

Illich, Ivan. *Energy and Equity*. New York: Harper & Row, 1974.

———. *The Rivers North of the Future: The Testament of Ivan Illich as Told to David Cayley*. Edited by David Cayley. Toronto: House of Anansi Press, 2005.

Jacobs, Alan. "Attending to Technology: Theses for Disputation." *New Atlantis,* Winter 2016, 16–45.

———. "Code Fetishists and Antinomians." *American Conservative,* July 29, 2015. www.theamericanconservative.com/articles/code-fetishists-and-normolaters/.

———. "Habits of Mind in an Age of Distraction." *Comment,* Summer 2016, 38–46.

———. "On Stickers and Boomers." *American Conservative,* May 29, 2013. www .theamericanconservative.com/jacobs/on-stickers-and-boomers/.

———. "Renewing the University." *National Affairs,* Summer 2016. https://www .nationalaffairs.com/publications/detail/renewing-the-university.

———. "What Narrative Theology Forgot." *First Things,* August 2003. https://www .firstthings.com/article/2003/08/what-narrative-theology-forgot.

Jakicic, John M., Kelliann K. Davis, Renee J. Rogers, Wendy C. King, Marsha D. Marcus, Diane Helsel, Amy D. Rickman, Abdus S. Wahed, and Steven H. Belle. "Effect of Wearable Technology Combined with a Lifestyle Intervention on Long-Term Weight Loss: The IDEA Randomized Clinical Trial." *JAMA* 316, no. 11 (2016): 1161–71.

Jeffrey, David L., ed. *The King James Bible and the World It Made.* Waco: Baylor University Press, 2011.

Jeffrey, David L, and Gregory Maillet. *Christianity and Literature: Philosophical Foundations and Critical Practice.* Downers Grove, Ill.: IVP Academic, 2011.

Jennings, Chris. *Paradise Now: The Story of American Utopianism.* New York: Random House, 2016.

Jennings, Willie James. *The Christian Imagination: Theology and the Origins of Race.* New Haven: Yale University Press, 2010.

Jorgenson, Kiara. "Called to Affection: Exploring the Ecology of Christian Vocation in Port William." In *Telling the Stories Right: Wendell Berry's Imagination of Port William,* edited by Jack R. Baker and Jeffrey Bilbro, 37–49. Eugene, Ore.: Front Porch Republic Books, 2018.

Kahneman, Daniel. *Thinking, Fast and Slow.* New York: Farrar, Straus and Giroux, 2011.

Kaveny, Cathleen. *Prophecy without Contempt: Religious Discourse in the Public Square.* Cambridge: Harvard University Press, 2016.

Keith, David. *A Case for Climate Engineering.* Cambridge: MIT Press, 2013.

Kennedy, Anthony, David Souter, and Sandra Day O'Connor. Planned Parenthood v. Casey, 505 U.S. 833, no. 91–744. United States Supreme Court, June 29, 1992.

King, Franklin Hiram. *Farmers of Forty Centuries; or, Permanent Agriculture in China, Korea and Japan.* Madison, Wisc.: Mrs. F. H. King, 1911.

Kirkman, Robert. "Beyond Doubt: Environmental Philosophy and the Human Predicament." In *Rethinking Nature: Essays in Environmental Philosophy,* edited by Bruce V. Foltz and Robert Frodeman, 165–79. Bloomington: Indiana University Press, 2004.

Kroeker, P. Travis. "Sexuality and the Sacramental Imagination: It All Turns on Affection." In *Wendell Berry: Life and Work,* edited by Jason Peters, 119–36. Lexington: University Press of Kentucky, 2007.

Kummer, Corby. "Last Word with Farmer-Author Wendell Berry." *Modern Farmer,* October 20, 2015. http://modernfarmer.com/2015/10/last-word-with-farmer-author -wendell-berry/.

Lang, John. "'Close Mystery': Wendell Berry's Poetry of Incarnation." *Renascence* 35, no. 4 (1983): 258–68.

Lasch, Christopher. "Conservatism against Itself." *First Things,* April 1990. https://www
.firstthings.com/article/1990/04/conservatism-against-itself.

———. *The Culture of Narcissism: American Life in an Age of Diminishing Expectations.*
New York: W. W. Norton, 1991.

———. *The True and Only Heaven: Progress and Its Critics.* New York: W. W. Norton,
1991.

Laytham, D. Brent. "'The Membership Includes the Dead': Wendell Berry's Port William
Membership as *Communio Sanctorum.*" In *Wendell Berry and Religion: Heaven's
Earthly Life,* edited by Joel James Shuman and L. Roger Owens, 173–89. Lexington:
University Press of Kentucky, 2009.

Leax, John. "Memory and Hope in the World of Port William." In *Wendell Berry: Life
and Work,* edited by Jason Peters, 66–75. Lexington: University Press of Kentucky,
2007.

Leithart, Peter J. *Gratitude: An Intellectual History.* Waco: Baylor University Press, 2014.

Leonard, Sarah. "Nature as an Ally: An Interview with Wendell Berry." *Dissent,* Spring
2012. www.dissentmagazine.org/article/nature-as-an-ally-an-interview-with-wendell
-berry.

Levinson, Arik. "California Energy Efficiency: Lessons for the Rest of the World, or Not?"
Journal of Economic Behavior & Organization 107 (2014): 269–89.

Lewis, C. S. *The Abolition of Man; or, Reflections on Education with Special Reference to
the Teaching of English in the Upper Forms of Schools.* 1943. Reprint. San Francisco:
Harper, 2001.

———. *An Experiment in Criticism.* Cambridge: Cambridge University Press, 1961.

———. *The Four Loves.* New York: Harcourt Brace, 1960.

———. "Membership." In *The Weight of Glory and Other Addresses,* 30–42. New York:
Macmillan, 1949.

Lowe, Kevin M. *Baptized with the Soil: Christian Agrarians and the Crusade for Rural
America.* Oxford: Oxford University Press, 2015.

Lundin, Roger. "Wendell Berry and the Poetics of Marriage and Embodiment." *Christianity and Literature* 56, no. 2 (2007): 333–42.

Macfarlane, Robert. *Landmarks.* London: Penguin, 2015.

———. "Rereading: Robert Macfarlane on The Monkey Wrench Gang." *Guardian,*
September 25, 2009, https://www.theguardian.com/books/2009/sep/26/robert
-macfarlane-monkey-wrench-gang.

MacIntyre, Alasdair. *After Virtue: A Study in Moral Theory.* 2nd edition. Notre Dame,
Ind.: University of Notre Dame Press, 1984.

———. "Epistemological Crises, Dramatic Narrative, and the Philosophy of Science." In
Why Narrative? Readings in Narrative Theology, edited by Stanley Hauerwas and
L. Gregory Jones, 138–57. Grand Rapids: Eerdmans, 1990.

———. *The MacIntyre Reader.* Edited by Kelvin Knight. Notre Dame, Ind.: University
of Notre Dame Press, 1998.

Major, William H. *Grounded Vision: New Agrarianism and the Academy.* Tuscaloosa:
University of Alabama Press, 2011.

Manganiello, Dominic. *T. S. Eliot and Dante.* New York: St. Martin's, 1989.

Mannon, Ethan. "The Gift of Good Death: Revising *Nathan Coulter.*" In *Telling the Stories
Right: Wendell Berry's Imagination of Port William,* edited by Jack R. Baker and
Jeffrey Bilbro, 89–103. Eugene, Ore.: Front Porch Republic Books, 2018.

————. "Leisure and Technology in Port William: Wendell Berry's Revelatory Fiction." *Mississippi Quarterly* 67, no. 2 (2014): 171–92.

Marion, Jean-Luc. *Being Given: Toward a Phenomenology of Givenness*. Stanford: Stanford University Press, 2002.

————. *God without Being: Hors-Texte*. Translated by Thomas A Carlson. Chicago: University of Chicago Press, 1995.

————. *The Idol and Distance: Five Studies*. Translated by Thomas A. Carlson. New York: Fordham University Press, 2001.

————. "The Saturated Phenomenon." *Philosophy Today* 40, no. 1 (1996): 103–24.

————. *The Visible and the Revealed*. New York: Fordham University Press, 2008.

McClay, Wilfred M. "Introduction: From Self to Person—Some Preliminary Thoughts." In *Figures in the Carpet: Finding the Human Person in the American Past,* edited by Wilfred M. McClay, 1–12. Grand Rapids: Eerdmans, 2007.

McEntyre, John E. "Practicing Resurrection: Community and Continuity in Wendell Berry's *A Place on Earth*." *Theology Today* 52, no. 3 (1995): 374–81.

McEntyre, Marilyn. *Caring for Words in a Culture of Lies*. Grand Rapids: Eerdmans, 2009.

McLuhan, Marshall. *Understanding Media: The Extensions of Man [1964]: Critical Edition*. Edited by W. Terrence Gordon. Corte Madera, Calif.: Gingko Press, 2003.

Melville, Herman. *Moby-Dick; or, The Whale* (1851). Edited by Harrison Hayford, Hershel Parker, and G. Thomas Tanselle. Evanston, Ill.: Northwestern University Press, 1988.

Menassa, Carol, Seth Mangasarian, Mounir El Asmar, and Carl Kirar. "Energy Consumption Evaluation of U.S. Navy LEED-Certified Buildings." *Journal of Performance of Constructed Facilities* 26, no. 1 (2012): 46–53. doi:10.1061/(ASCE) CF.1943-5509.0000218.

Mendelson, Edward. "In the Depths of the Digital Age." *New York Review of Books,* June 23, 2016. www.nybooks.com/articles/2016/06/23/depths-of-the-digital-age/.

Merritt, Anna C., Daniel A. Effron, and Benoît Monin. "Moral Self-Licensing: When Being Good Frees Us to Be Bad." *Social and Personality Psychology Compass* 4, no. 5 (2010): 344–57.

Merton, Thomas. *Conjectures of a Guilty Bystander*. Garden City, N.Y.: Doubleday, 1966.

Middleton, J. Richard. *A New Heaven and a New Earth: Reclaiming Biblical Eschatology*. Grand Rapids: Baker Academic, 2014.

Milbank, John. *Theology and Social Theory: Beyond Secular Reason*. 2nd edition. Oxford: Wiley-Blackwell, 2006.

Miller, Eric. *Hope in a Scattering Time: A Life of Christopher Lasch*. Grand Rapids: Eerdmans, 2010.

Milton, John. *The Riverside Milton*. Edited by Roy Flannagan. Boston: Houghton Mifflin, 1998.

Mitchell, Mark T. *The Politics of Gratitude: Scale, Place & Community in a Global Age*. Dulles, Va.: Potomac Books, 2012.

Montgomery, David R. *Dirt: The Erosion of Civilizations*. Berkeley: University of California Press, 2008.

Morton, Oliver. *The Planet Remade: How Geoengineering Could Change the World*. Princeton: Princeton University Press, 2015.

Morton, Timothy. *The Ecological Thought*. Cambridge: Harvard University Press, 2010.

Moss, Linda. "Calling All Babies Delivered by the Poet Who Gave 'Paterson' Life." *Bergen County (N.J.) Record,* July 7, 2015. Article excerpt at https://www.questia.com/newspaper/1P2-38491373/calling-all-babies-delivered-by-the-poet-who-gave.

Musk, Elon. "Elon Musk: The Mind behind Tesla, SpaceX, SolarCity." Interview by Chris Anderson, March 19, 2013. https://www.youtube.com/watch?v=IgKWPdJWuBQ.

Nash, Roderick Frazier. *The Rights of Nature: A History of Environmental Ethics.* Madison: University of Wisconsin Press, 1989.

Niccol, Andrew, writer and dir. *In Time.* Film. 2011.

Nietzsche, Friedrich Wilhelm. *The Birth of Tragedy* (1872). Translated by Douglas Smith. Oxford: Oxford University Press, 2000.

Nisbet, Robert A. *The Quest for Community: A Study in the Ethics of Order and Freedom.* New York: Oxford University Press, 1953.

Nixon, Rob. *Slow Violence and the Environmentalism of the Poor.* Cambridge: Harvard University Press, 2011.

Northcott, Michael S. *Place, Ecology and the Sacred: The Moral Geography of Sustainable Communities.* London: Bloomsbury Academic, 2015.

Nossaman, Lucas. "The Wisdom of 'The Farm': Sabbath Theology and Wendell Berry's Pastoralism." *Renascence* 70, no 1 (2018): 3–22.

Nye, David E. *American Technological Sublime.* Cambridge: MIT Press, 1996.

Oates, D., and K. Sullivan. "Postoccupancy Energy Consumption Survey of Arizona's LEED New Construction Population." *Journal of Construction Engineering and Management* 138, no. 6 (2011): 742–50. doi:10.1061/(ASCE)C0.1943-7862.0000478.

Ocean Cleanup, The. "The Largest Cleanup in History." 2018. www.theoceancleanup.com/.

Oehlschlaeger, Fritz. *The Achievement of Wendell Berry: The Hard History of Love.* Lexington: University Press of Kentucky, 2011.

———. "Living Faithfully in the Debt of Love in Wendell Berry's Port William." In *Telling the Stories Right: Wendell Berry's Imagination of Port William,* edited by Jack R. Baker and Jeffrey Bilbro, 104–20. Eugene, Ore.: Front Porch Republic Books, 2018.

O'Grady, John P. "How Sustainable Is the Idea of Sustainability?" *Interdisciplinary Studies in Literature and Environment* 10, no. 1 (2003): 1–10.

Olmstead, Gracy. "'The End of All Our Exploring': Homecoming and Membership in *Remembering.*" In *Telling the Stories Right: Wendell Berry's Imagination of Port William,* edited by Jack R. Baker and Jeffrey Bilbro, 153–71. Eugene, Ore.: Front Porch Republic Books, 2018.

———. "Is 'Free-Range Parenting' Bad?" *American Conservative,* March 4, 2015. www.theamericanconservative.com/olmstead/is-free-range-parenting-bad/.

Osnos, Evan. "Doomsday Prep for the Super-Rich." *New Yorker,* January 30, 2017. www.newyorker.com/magazine/2017/01/30/doomsday-prep-for-the-super-rich.

O'Toole, Garson. "Life Is Just One Damn Thing after Another." *Quote Investigator,* September 2, 2015. http://quoteinvestigator.com/2015/09/02/life-one/.

Peck, Jamie. "Struggling with the Creative Class." *International Journal of Urban and Regional Research* 29, no. 4 (2005): 740–70. doi:10.1111/j.1468-2427.2005.00620.x.

Pevear, Richard. "On the Prose of Wendell Berry." *Hudson Review* 35, no. 2 (1982): 341–47.

Pierce, Ingrid. "Dreaming in Port William: Foreknowledge, Consolation, and Medieval Dream Vision Literature." In *Telling the Stories Right: Wendell Berry's Imagination of*

Port William, edited by Jack R. Baker and Jeffrey Bilbro, 21–36. Eugene, Ore.: Front Porch Republic Books, 2018.

Pierotti, Raymond John. *Indigenous Knowledge, Ecology, and Evolutionary Biology*. New York: Routledge, 2011.

Pollan, Michael. *The Omnivore's Dilemma: A Natural History of Four Meals*. New York: Penguin, 2006.

Purdy, Jedediah. *After Nature: A Politics for the Anthropocene*. Cambridge: Harvard University Press, 2015.

Putnam, Robert D. *Bowling Alone: The Collapse and Revival of American Community*. New York: Simon & Schuster, 2000.

Ransom, John Crowe. *Land! The Case for an Agrarian Economy*. Edited by Jason Peters. Notre Dame, Ind.: University of Notre Dame Press, 2017.

Reiter, Geoffrey. " 'We Were Voyagers!' Disney's *Moana* Revels in the Quickening Power of Tradition." *Christ and Pop Culture*, May 9, 2017. https://christandpopculture.com /disney-moana-revels-quickening-power-tradition/.

Reitter, Paul, and Chad Wellmon. "Better Living through Bibliotherapy." *Hedgehog Review* 18, no. 2 (2016). www.iasc-culture.org/THR/THR_article_2016_Summer _ReitterWellmon.php.

Roberts, Alexander, James Donaldson, A. Cleveland Coxe, and Allan Menzies, eds. *Ante-Nicene Fathers: The Writings of the Fathers down to A.D. 325* (1867–73). Peabody, Mass.: Hendrickson Publishers, 2004.

Salatin, Joel. *Everything I Want to Do Is Illegal: War Stories from the Local Food Front*. Swoope, Va.: Polyface, 2007.

Salvucci, Emiliano. "Selfishness, Warfare, and Economics; or Integration, Cooperation, and Biology." *Frontiers in Cellular and Infection Microbiology* 2, no. 54 (2012): 1–12. doi:10.3389/fcimb.2012.00054.

Sanders, Scott Russell. *Earth Works: Selected Essays*. Bloomington: Indiana University Press, 2012.

Scheer, Roddy, and Doug Moss. "Use It and Lose It: The Outsize Effect of U.S. Consumption on the Environment." *Scientific American*, September 14, 2012. www.scientificamerican.com/article/american-consumption-habits/.

Schmidt, Eric, and Jared Cohen. *The New Digital Age: Reshaping the Future of People, Nations and Business*. New York: Knopf, 2013.

Scigaj, Leonard M. *Sustainable Poetry: Four American Ecopoets*. Lexington: University Press of Kentucky, 1999.

Scofield, John H. "Are U.S. 'Green Buildings' Really Saving Energy? The Facts May Surprise You." *Brink—The Edge of Risk*, June 10, 2015. www.brinknews.com/are-u-s -green-buildings-really-saving-energy-the-facts-may-surprise-you/.

Scott, James C. *Two Cheers for Anarchism: Six Easy Pieces on Autonomy, Dignity, and Meaningful Work and Play*. Princeton: Princeton University Press, 2014.

Shakespeare, William. *King Lear* (1608). Edited by Alfred Harbage. Baltimore: Penguin Books, 1958.

Shiva, Vandana. *Staying Alive: Women, Ecology, and Development*. Berkeley, Calif.: North Atlantic Books, 2016.

———. *The Vandana Shiva Reader*. Lexington: University Press of Kentucky, 2014.

Shuman, Joel James, and L. Roger Owens, eds. *Wendell Berry and Religion: Heaven's Earthly Life*. Lexington: University Press of Kentucky, 2009.

Shuman, Joel James, and Brian Volck. *Reclaiming the Body: Christians and the Faithful Use of Modern Medicine.* Grand Rapids: Brazos Press, 2006.

Slovic, Scott. *Seeking Awareness in American Nature Writing: Henry Thoreau, Annie Dillard, Edward Abbey, Wendell Berry, Barry Lopez.* Salt Lake City: University of Utah Press, 1992.

Smith, James K. A. *Desiring the Kingdom: Worship, Worldview, and Cultural Formation.* Grand Rapids: Baker Academic, 2009.

———. *How (Not) to Be Secular: Reading Charles Taylor.* Grand Rapids: Eerdmans, 2014.

———. *Imagining the Kingdom: How Worship Works.* Grand Rapids: Baker Books, 2013.

Smith, Kimberly K. *Wendell Berry and the Agrarian Tradition: A Common Grace.* Lawrence: University Press of Kansas, 2003.

Snyder, Gary. *The Gary Snyder Reader: Prose, Poetry, and Translations.* 1999. Reprint. Washington, D.C.: Counterpoint, 2012.

Spenser, Edmund. *The Works of Edmund Spenser.* Edited by R. Morris. London: Macmillan, 1899.

Stack, Liam. "Yale's Halloween Advice Stokes a Racially Charged Debate." *New York Times,* November 8, 2015. www.nytimes.com/2015/11/09/nyregion/yale-culturally-insensitive-halloween-costumes-free-speech.html.

Stanford, Thomas W., III. "Membership and Its Privileges: The Vision of Family and Community in the Fiction of Wendell Berry." *Logos* 14, no. 2 (2011): 118–30.

Stanton, Andrew, dir. *Finding Dory.* Film. Walt Disney Studios, 2016.

Steiner, George. *Real Presences.* Chicago: University of Chicago Press, 1989.

Stevens, Michael R. "Hiding in the Hedgrows: Wendell Berry's Treatment of Marginal Characters in His Fiction." In *Telling the Stories Right: Wendell Berry's Imagination of Port William,* edited by Jack R. Baker and Jeffrey Bilbro, 121–38. Eugene, Ore.: Front Porch Republic Books, 2018.

St. George, Donna. "'Unsubstantiated' Child Neglect Finding for Free-Range Parents." *Washington Post,* March 2, 2015. https://www.washingtonpost.com/local/education/decision-in-free-range-case-does-not-end-debate-about-parenting-and-safety/2015/03/02/5a919454-c04d-11e4-ad5c-3b8ce89f1b89_story.html.

Stone, Linda. "Continuous Partial Attention." November 29, 2009. https://lindastone.net/qa/continuous-partial-attention/.

Sunstein, Cass R. *#Republic: Divided Democracy in the Age of Social Media.* Princeton: Princeton University Press, 2017.

Sussman, Robert W., Paul A. Garber, and Jim M. Cheverud. "Importance of Cooperation and Affiliation in the Evolution of Primate Sociality." *American Journal of Physical Anthropology* 128, no. 1 (2005): 84–97.

"Sustainable Buildings." *Yale Sustainability,* 2016. http://sustainability.yale.edu/sustainable-slideshow/sustainable-buildings.

Sutterfield, Ragan. *Wendell Berry and the Given Life.* Cincinnati: Franciscan Media, 2017.

Taylor, Charles. "The Dialogical Self." In *The Interpretive Turn: Philosophy, Science, Culture,* edited by David R. Hiley, James F. Bohman, and Richard Shusterman, 304–14. Ithaca: Cornell University Press, 1992.

———. *The Ethics of Authenticity.* Cambridge: Harvard University Press, 1991.

———. "Foreword." In *The Rivers North of the Future: The Testament of Ivan Illich as Told to David Cayley,* by Ivan Illich, ix–xiv. Edited by David Cayley. Toronto: House of Anansi Press, 2005.

————. *A Secular Age.* Cambridge: Belknap Press of Harvard University Press, 2007.

Tennyson, Alfred, Baron. *In Memoriam A.H.H.* (1850). London: Bankside Press, 1900.

Tolkien, J. R. R. *The Fellowship of the Ring: Being the First Part of The Lord of the Rings* (1954). New York: Ballantine, 2001.

————. *The Two Towers: Being the Second Part of The Lord of the Rings* (1954). New York: Ballantine, 2001.

Toyama, Kentaro. *Geek Heresy: Rescuing Social Change from the Cult of Technology.* New York: Public Affairs, 2015.

Tuan, Yi-Fu. *Cosmos & Hearth: A Cosmopolite's Viewpoint.* Minneapolis: University of Minnesota Press, 1996.

Turkle, Sherry. *Alone Together: Why We Expect More from Technology and Less from Each Other.* New York: Basic Books, 2011.

Van Alstyne, Marshall, and Erik Brynjolfsson. "Global Village or Cyber-Balkans? Modeling and Measuring the Integration of Electronic Communities." *Management Science* 51, no. 6 (2005): 851–68.

Vance, J. D. *Hillbilly Elegy: A Memoir of a Family and Culture in Crisis.* New York: Harper, 2016.

Västfjäll, Daniel, Paul Slovic, and Marcus Mayorga. "Pseudoinefficacy and the Arithmetic of Compassion." In *Numbers and Nerves: Information, Emotion, and Meaning in a World of Data,* edited by Scott Slovic and Paul Slovic, 42–52. Corvallis: Oregon State University Press, 2015.

Vitek, William, and Wes Jackson, eds. *The Virtues of Ignorance: Complexity, Sustainability, and the Limits of Knowledge.* Lexington: University Press of Kentucky, 2008.

Wallis, Bryan. "More Real Than Real: The Weird Localism of Ralph Eugene Meatyard and Wendell Berry." *Australasian Journal of Ecocriticism and Cultural Ecology (AJE)* 2 (2012): 75–95.

Wendell Berry Speaks at Georgetown College, 2013. https://www.youtube.com/watch?v=MnfZOLEb7p4.

White, Lynn, Jr. "The Historical Roots of Our Ecologic Crisis." *Science* 155, no. 3767 (1967): 1203–7. doi:10.1126/science.155.3767.1203.

White House, Office of the Press Secretary. "President Obama to Award 2010 National Medal of Arts and National Humanities Medal." March 1, 2011. https://obamawhitehouse.archives.gov/the-press-office/2011/03/01/president-obama-award-2010-national-medal-arts-and-national-humanities-m.

————. "Remarks by the President on Opportunity for All and Skills for America's Workers." January 30, 2014. https://www.whitehouse.gov/the-press-office/2014/01/30/remarks-president-opportunity-all-and-skills-americas-workers.

Wiebe, Joseph R. *The Place of Imagination: Wendell Berry and the Poetics of Community, Affection, and Identity.* Waco: Baylor University Press, 2017.

Wirzba, Norman. *Food and Faith: A Theology of Eating.* Cambridge: Cambridge University Press, 2011.

————. *From Nature to Creation: A Christian Vision for Understanding and Loving Our World.* Grand Rapids: Baker Academic, 2015.

————. "On Learning to See a Fallen and Flourishing Creation: Alternate Ways of Looking at the World." In *Evolution and the Fall,* edited by William T. Cavanaugh and James K. A. Smith, 156–77. Grand Rapids: Eerdmans, 2017.

———. *The Paradise of God: Renewing Religion in an Ecological Age*. Oxford: Oxford University Press, 2007.

Wohlleben, Peter. *The Hidden Life of Trees: What They Feel, How They Communicate— Discoveries from a Secret World*. Vancouver: Greystone, 2016.

Wolterstorff, Nicholas. *Justice: Rights and Wrongs*. Princeton: Princeton University Press, 2008.

Wright, N. T. *Surprised by Hope: Rethinking Heaven, the Resurrection, and the Mission of the Church*. 2008. Reprint. London: SPCK Publishing, 2011.

Yale University. "The Chubb Fellowship—Wendell Berry." *Chubb Fellowship,* December 7, 2013. http://chubbfellowship.org/speakers/current/wendell_berry.

Yates, Joshua. "A Conversation with Wendell Berry and Wes Jackson." *Hedgehog Review* 14, no. 2 (2012). http://www.iasc-culture.org/THR/THR_article_2012_Summer _Interview_Berry_Jackson.php.

Yeats, William Butler. *Per Amica Silentia Lunae*. New York: Macmillan, 1918.

Zapf, Hubert. *Literature as Cultural Ecology: Sustainable Texts*. London: Bloomsbury, 2016.

Index

Culture of the Land: A Series in the New Agrarianism

This series is devoted to the exploration and articulation of a new agrarianism that considers the health of habitats and human communities together. It demonstrates how agrarian insights and responsibilities can be worked out in diverse fields of learning and living: history, science, art, politics, economics, literature, philosophy, religion, urban planning, education, and public policy. Agrarianism is a comprehensive worldview that appreciates the intimate and practical connections that exist between humans and the earth. It stands as our most promising alternative to the unsustainable and destructive ways of current global, industrial, and consumer culture.

Series Editor
Norman Wirzba, Duke University, North Carolina

Advisory Board
Wendell Berry, Port Royal, Kentucky
Ellen Davis, Duke University, North Carolina
Patrick Holden, Soil Association, United Kingdom
Wes Jackson, Land Institute, Kansas
Gene Logsdon, Upper Sandusky, Ohio
Bill McKibben, Middlebury College, Vermont
David Orr, Oberlin College, Ohio
Michael Pollan, University of California at Berkeley, California
Jennifer Sahn, *Orion* magazine, Massachusetts
Vandana Shiva, Research Foundation for Science, Technology & Ecology, India
Bill Vitek, Clarkson University, New York

CPSIA information can be obtained
at www.ICGtesting.com
Printed in the USA
LVHW111200120922
728158LV00003B/157